MANAGEMENT IN ACTION

Guidelines for New Managers

MANAGEMENT IN ACTION

Guidelines for New Managers

William D. Hitt

 **BATTELLE PRESS**

Columbus • Richland

Printed in the United States of America.

Library of Congress Cataloging in Publication Data

Hitt, William D.
  Management in action.

  Bibliography: p.
  1. Management. I. Title.
  HD31.H534   1984   658.4   84–18430
  ISBN 0-935470-20-4

Battelle Press
505 King Avenue
Columbus, Ohio 43201
Phone 614-424-6393

For Diane

Contents

Acknowledgements

I am greatly indebted to a large number of people for making this book possible. First, I want to express my gratitude to the management theorists whose ideas are quoted throughout the ten chapters. Second, I want to acknowledge the many managers who have participated in my Principles of Management Workshop — the men and women who truly "sharpened my thinking" about the real world of management. Finally, I want to express my appreciation to Cindy Bisciotti for typing the manuscript and to Richard Webster for reviewing it.

Preface

The purpose of this book is to help new and developing managers understand the basics of management within a practical framework that is both meaningful and useful.

Management In Action is designed for professionals who find themselves in management positions without the benefit of formal training in management. The book may be used either as the basic text in a continuing education course dealing with the fundamentals of management or as a resource for the manager who is pursuing his or her own self-development program.

There already are a number of excellent books on theory of management, and an equal number on the basics of management. But there is a lack of material that effectively unites theory and practice. The principal contribution of *Management In Action* is that it integrates the basics of management within an understandable framework of theory. And throughout, it offers helpful guidelines for putting theory into practice.

The text is intended to give the reader a holistic view of management—in the form of a management model that can be adapted to his or her particular situation. While not covering any one topic in great depth, the text does cover all major aspects of management. In addition, the framework provided is relevant to the manager's job at any level: first-level, middle-level, or upper-level (although, of course, the application of the model would vary according to the level of management). Thus, the intent is that the reader will fully grasp the management model that is presented and then refine and embellish it over the years ahead as he or she advances in management responsibilities.

In addition to being a holistic approach, the proposed management model is prescriptive rather than descriptive. There are no small number of current management texts of a descriptive nature—describing in considerable detail what excellent companies and excellent managers actually do. There is much useful information in these books, but, after reading such a book, the new manager may very well ask, "But how can I actually use this information in my present job?" By building on much of this descriptive material and by integrating it within a meaningful theoretical framework, *Management In Action* attempts to provide practical answers to the question raised by the new manager—in the form of a prescriptive model of management.

The name given to this prescriptive model of management is "Theory Z," since it derives logically from Douglas McGregor's Theory X and Theory Y. And it is consistent with the work of other theorists, notably, Rensis Likert (System 4 Managment), Robert Blake and Jane Mouton (9,9 Orientation), Abraham Maslow (Eupsychian Management), and William Ouchi (Theory Z).

The ten chapters in *Management In Action* are presented in a logical sequence:

I. Philosophy of Management: an integration of values, goals, and strategies that serves as the basic foundation and cornerstone of a mangement model.

II. The Manager as an Effective Human Being: a description of the personal characteristics of the effective manager, the human being who carries out the functions of management.

III. Leadership Styles: a discussion of four different styles and their relative effectiveness.

IV. Participative Management: a presentation of a broad strategy of management that involves all team members in key decisions that influence their work.

V. Management by Objectives: a presentation of a second broad strategy of management that applies to all of the major management functions.

VI. Planning: a discussion of basic principles of planning and their application to three types of planning—strategic, tactical, and project.

VII. Organizing: a discussion of basic principles of organizing, three fundamental types of organizational structure, and the importance of delegation.

VIII. Staffing and Staff Development: guidelines for obtaining the staff, developing the staff, and evaluating their performance.

IX. Motivating: a discussion of Abraham Maslow's theory of motivation and how it applies to the manager's job of motivating employees.

X. Controlling: a discussion of basic principles of controlling — making sure that plans succeed; ending with some guidelines on controlling your time.

Sequencing of Chapters

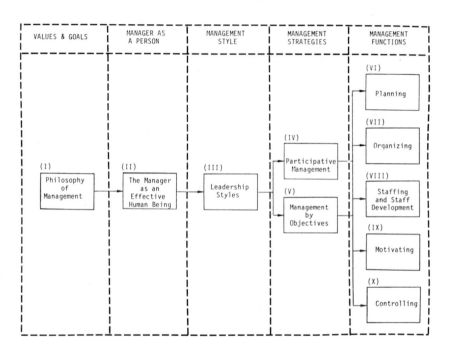

Notably, there is no chapter on Communicating. Because of the importance of this function of management (and its pervasiveness across all other functions), communicating is treated as an essential part of every chapter rather than highlighted in a separate chapter. In essence, the entire book is about communicating.

At the end of each chapter are exercises for the reader. The intent of these exercises is to help the reader achieve a better grasp of the proposed management model and to identify ways in which the model can be applied to his or her management job.

As an Appendix to the text, the reader will find an assessment inventory that serves as a summary of the entire management model as well as a practical instrument that could be used in assessing the management system in a given organization.

A comprehensive Bibliography also is appended.

I

A Philosophy of Management

> The bedrock of any Z company is its philosophy. The thought of mixing practical business matters with pie-in-the-sky concerns may seem strange, but popular belief aside, philosophy and business are the most compatible of bed-fellows. To the extent that practical, no-nonsense business decisions come from a consistent, integrated set of ideals, they are more likely to prove successful in the long run.
>
> William Ouchi
> *Theory Z* [96, p. 131]

Introduction • Theoretical Framework • Requirements for an Effective Philosophy of Management • Values Underlying Theory Z Management • Goals of Theory Z Management • Strategies of Theory Z Management • Summing Up

---

INTRODUCTION

A philosophy of management provides direction and consistency for managerial actions. Without the guidance of a well articulated philosophy of management, the manager's actions will appear to be random and haphazard. But managers who are guided by a well-thought-out philosophy will demonstrate consistency in their actions. It will be evident to others that these managers have a rationale for their actions.

There are a number of existing philosophies of management from which a manager might choose. The question then becomes: What

1

criteria should be used in guiding this selection? Or, similarly, if a manager decides to develop his or her own philosophy of management rather than select an existing philosophy, what criteria should be used in guiding this development? Two criteria appear to be of utmost importance: (1) the philosophy is consistent with one's own values and (2) it gets results. With regard to being consistent with one's values, this means that the manager "feels comfortable" with a particular philosophy of management: there is a match between the values implicit in the philosophy and the manager's own personal values. With regard to getting results, the philosophy helps the manager operate a productive enterprise in terms of both effectiveness and efficiency. It is important that a management philosophy satisfy both of these criteria.

The purpose of this chapter is to present a philosophy of management that satisfies the above criteria. First, through surveys conducted by the author, the philosophy has been found to be compatible with the values of most (not all, most) managers in the U.S. as well as in several other cultures. Second, through empirical research by a number of investigators, it has been found to produce better results (in terms of long-term productivity) than other management philosophies.

The name given to the proposed philosophy of management is "Theory Z." This is not a new theory but rather an integration of the ideas of a number of theorists. Included are Douglas McGregor (Theory X and Theory Y), Rensis Likert (System 4 Management), Robert Blake and Jane Mouton (9,9 Orientation), Abraham Maslow (Eupsychian Management), and William Ouchi (Theory Z).

To elaborate on the meaning of Theory Z management, it will be useful to: (1) present the theoretical framework; (2) describe the requirements for an effective philosophy of management; (3) articulate the values underlying Theory Z management; (4) communicate the goals of Theory Z management; and (5) elucidate the strategies of Theory Z management.

THEORETICAL FRAMEWORK

The importance of the management function has been stressed by Peter Drucker:[23, p. x]

For management is the organ, the lifegiving, acting,

2

> dynamic organ of the institution it manages. Without the
> institution there would be no management. But without
> management there would also be only a mob rather than
> an institution.

Indeed, management is the dynamic organ of the institution it manages. Management is not merely administration — ministering the paperwork that is required in any organization. Management is not merely controlling — regulating the work of others. Nor is management merely leadership — motivating and inspiring others to achieve organizational objectives. It is all of these and more than these.

A perspective of the role of the management function is shown in Figure 1, which depicts a systems view of an enterprise. At the top of the diagram is a clear statement of the enterprise's mission, goals, and objectives — the ends toward which the enterprise directs its efforts. In the center is a description of the enterprise's delivery system — the products or services that it provides to consumers. At the left is a listing of the enterprise's resources — in the form of people, equipment, facilities, and money. At the right is a statement of the constraints imposed on the enterprise — the restrictions that delimit the activities of the organization. At the bottom of the diagram is a delineation of the management system. It is this last element that makes certain that all the other elements are working in harmony and are directed toward the enterprise's goals.

In the light of this systems view of the management function, we propose the following general definition of management: *Management is the art and science of working with and through people to achieve organizational objectives.*

This definition includes three important elements. First, it seems clear that management is both an art and a science. There is a substantial body of scientifically derived knowledge that is applicable to management. The application of this knowledge to a particular situation, however, requires considerable judgment on the part of the manager, and the use of this judgment is an art in the best sense of the term. Second, the definition suggests that management involves both working *through* people and working *with* people. In the former, the manager is transmitting instructions that are to be carried out by others, but in the latter the manager is serving as a partner in dialogue. Third, "to achieve organizational objectives" denotes the essential purpose of the management function. It is assumed that every organization is in existence to achieve certain objectives, and it is clear

3

that this achievement of objectives will not come about automatically. Something must take place to make certain that it happens; this "something" is the management function.

The functions of the manager are fairly well agreed upon by the management theorists. There are slight variations from one writer to the next, but most find their roots in the universal classification scheme proposed by Henri Fayol, the father of modern management theory.[28a] The functions are considered "universal" because they apply to any type of undertaking (business, military, educational, etc.) and to any level of management (first-level, middle-level, or upper-level).

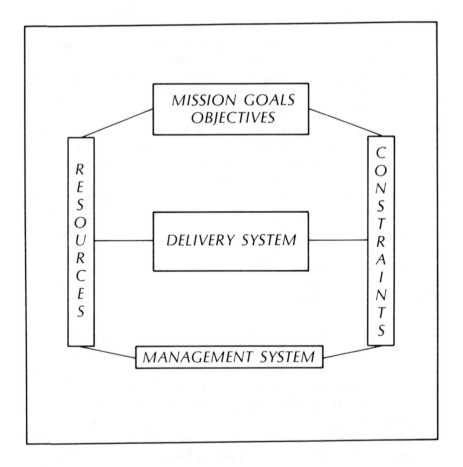

Figure 1.   A systems view of an organization

For purposes of this book, the universal functions of management are planning, organizing, staffing and staff development, motivating, and controlling. These five functions are defined as follows:

- **Planning**: Determining the objectives of the enterprise (or any part of the enterprise) and deciding how best to achieve the objectives.
- **Organizing**: Establishing a structure of roles, responsibilities, and authority that will be needed to accomplish the objectives of the enterprise.
- **Staffing and Staff Development**: Obtaining and building the staff that will be needed to accomplish the objectives of the enterprise.
- **Motivating**: Leading and inspiring employees so that they will strive willingly toward the achievement of the objectives of the enterprise.
- **Controlling**: Measuring performance against the objectives of the enterprise and taking corrective action as appropriate.

It should be noted that the authors of some management texts include communicating as one managerial function alongside the others. The author of the present text believes that communicating is too pervasive to be placed in the same category with these other functions. Communicating cuts across all five of the basic managerial functions, no one of which can be carried out — or even initiated — without communicating. Thus, it would be more appropriate to view communicating as a "metafunction" rather than simply as a function. (That is, it transcends the other functions.) For this reason, communicating will be treated as a vital part of each of the 10 chapters included in the text.

With this definition of management and the delineation of managerial functions as a starting point, we look next at the roots of Theory Z management.

Two Schools of Management

The roots of Theory Z management are found in scientific management and human relations management. These are the two major schools of management that have emerged over the past century, and most management texts present one or the other of the two schools. In briefly considering these two schools, we will start with the one that has the earlier beginning — scientific management.

Scientific management began with the pioneering work of Frederick Taylor in the early part of this century. Taylor believed that a rational and systematic approach to the design of the work situation — essentially a scientific approach — could lead to increased productivity. He was correct! Some of his projects involving time-and-motion analysis demonstrated increases in productivity in the range of 100–200 percent. Taylor's tomb at Germantown, Pennsylvania, bears the simple phrase "The Father of Scientific Management."

The many developments in scientific management since the time of Taylor's early work have several common features. First, considerable stress is placed on objectivity, which is based on observable phenomena and disregard of emotion or personal prejudice. Second, emphasis is placed on measurement and precision, on quantitative rather than qualitative indicators. Third, all of these methods and techniques are directed toward improving productivity.

Unfortunately, the strength of scientific management — found in objectivity, measurement, and precision — is also its primary shortcoming. Because such great stress is placed on the objective dimension of management, the subjective, or the more human dimension, is often ignored. As a result, employees who are subjected to scientific management in its extreme form often complain that they are being treated as objects or numbers rather than as human beings. Who can blame them for making such charges?

The human relations school of management emerged partly as a rebellion against the dehumanizing aspects of scientific management. This school was founded in the 1930s by Elton Mayo, who conducted the classic experiments at the Hawthorne plant of Western Electric. As most readers will recall, Mayo and his associates had embarked on an experiment to investigate the effects of different levels of illumination on the performance of female machine operators. The investigators were indeed puzzled when they discovered that performance continued to improve regardless of whether the level of illumination was increased or decreased. Subsequent interviews with the workers disclosed that their performance had improved because someone had *shown an interest* in what they were doing. And so the human relations school was launched.

A number of significant developments in support of the human relations school have emerged over the past 50 or so years. The focus of these developments is on the worker as a total human being, not merely as an object or "a pair of hands." It should not be surprising

6

that, when employees are treated as persons of worth, the results are positive — both for the good of the employee and the good of the organization.

Thus, it seems clear that we have available two distinct approaches to management, each characterized by obvious strengths and obvious limitations. Scientific management offers us rigor and precision but is found lacking when it comes to dealing with employees as living human beings.* Human relations management, on the other hand, fully supports the notion of concern for employees as living human beings but is found lacking when it comes to rigor and precision.

If forced into an either-or decision between scientific management and human relations management, many managers would be hard pressed to respond. Fortunately, there is an obvious "out": We can build on the strengths of both schools to form an integrated approach to management. The uniting of scientific management and human relations management is called "Theory Z."

Theories X, Y, and Z

The publication of Douglas McGregor's classic book *The Human Side of Enterprise* [88] was a major landmark in the evolution of Theory Z management. Most readers are familiar with his now-famous Theory X and Theory Y. In this present discussion of the roots of Theory Z management, it will be worthwhile to review briefly his basic ideas and then describe how management theory has progressed from Theory X and Theory Y to Theory Z.

McGregor was convinced that there is a close connection between a manager's assumptions about people and how the manager manages people. If the manager believes, for example, that people are basically lazy and simply want to take advantage of the company, this assumption obviously will influence how the manager deals with — and relates to — employees. On the other hand, if the manager believes that people are basically responsible persons who will excel under proper environmental conditions, then this assumption obviously will influence how the manager manages. It seems clear that there is a close connection between one's assumptions and one's actions.

---

*It should be noted that Taylor did in fact give due consideration to the human dimension in his model of management but that many of his followers focused almost exclusively on the scientific dimension.

McGregor made a study of the assumptions that seemed to underlie managerial practice in the U.S. during the 1950s. These assumptions — labeled "Theory X"— are listed in Table 1. In essence, these assumptions view the average employee as an irresponsible individual with little ambition, who must be coerced and threatened with punishment. Supervising such employees calls for an appropriate management style.

Table 1. Theory X Assumptions

1. The average human being has an inherent dislike of work and will avoid it if he can.

2. Because of this human characteristic of dislike of work, most people must be coerced, controlled, directed, threatened with punishment to get them to put forth adequate effort toward the achievement of organizational objectives.

3. The average human being prefers to be directed, wishes to avoid responsibility, has relatively little ambition, wants security above all.

Douglas McGregor — *The Human Side of Enterprise*, 1960, McGraw-Hill Book Company, Reprinted, by permission of the publisher.

McGregor made a qualitative leap in formulating an alternative set of assumptions about people. This new set of assumptions — labeled "Theory Y"— is presented in Table 2. It can be seen that these assumptions stand in sharp contrast to those embedded in Theory X. Here we have a view of the average employee as a responsible person desirous of making significant contributions, and who indeed will make these contributions if given the opportunity and provided with the proper environment. Certainly the presence of this type of employee will call for an appropriate management style — and one quite different from that which is associated with Theory X.

Which is closer to truth — Theory X or Theory Y? Over the past several years, the author has posed this question to several hundred managers. The variations in the responses have been considerable. A typical response from a Theory X advocate is: "Of course, Theory X is correct. This is the way people are in our company. If you would

Table 2.   Theory Y Assumptions

1. The expenditure of physical and mental effort in work is as natural as play or rest.

2. Humans will exercise self-direction and self-control in the service of objectives to which they are committed.

3. Commitment to objectives is a function of the rewards associated with their achievement.

4. The average human being learns, under proper conditions, not only to accept but to seek responsibility.

5. The capacity to exercise a relatively high degree of imagination, ingenuity, and creativity in the solution of organizational problems is widely, not narrowly, distributed in the population.

6. Within most organizations, the intellectual potentialities of the average human being are only partially utilized.

Douglas McGregor—*The Human Side of Enterprise*, 1960, McGraw-Hill Book Company, Reprinted, by permission of the publisher.

just spend one day in my factory, you would agree that Theory X is absolutely correct. It's a jungle out there!" Then, at the other end of the continuum, here is a typical response from a Theory Y supporter: "Of course, Theory Y is correct. This is the way people are in our organization. We have mature, responsible employees who are self-motivated. Many of our people truly look forward to coming to work each day!" It is both interesting and informative to note the sharp differences between these two points of view.

Rather than concurring with either of these two extreme views, a still larger number of managers state that they see some degree of truth in both Theory X and Theory Y. And this is essentially the position taken by Abraham Maslow in his *Eupsychian Management*, [82] in which he establishes a rationale for Theory Z. Maslow stresses the importance of recognizing individual differences among employees. As indicated in the assumptions listed in Table 3, Maslow suggests that Theory Y might be appropriate with mature, responsible employees who are psychologically healthy persons. But this same

Table 3. Theory Z Assumptions

1. *The best approach to management is that which best fits the objective requirements of the objective situation.*

2. *Where we have fairly evolved human beings able to grow, then Theory Y management principles seem to be fine. They will work, but only at the top of the hierarchy of human development.*

3. *A certain proportion of the population cannot take responsibility well and are frightened by freedom, which tends to throw them into anxiety, etc.*

4. *People are not perfectible, but they are improvable.*

5. *The good manager in most situations must have as a psychological prerequisite the ability to take pleasure in the growth and self-actualization of other people.*

Abraham Maslow— *Eupsychian Management: A Journal*, Homewood, Illinois: Richard D. Irwin, Inc., 1965, Reprinted, by permission of the publisher.

theory might be inappropriate for employees at a lower rung on the developmental ladder. Nevertheless, even though people are not perfectible, they are improvable. Thus, the real challenge for the manager is, first, to understand where each of his or her employees is with respect to the hierarchy of human development and, then, to do everything that is reasonably possible to help the employees move up the hierarchy. To the extent that employees move toward the top of the hierarchy, Theory Y will work with them. On the other hand, to the extent that employees remain at or near the bottom of the hierarchy, it will not work. Thus, in summary, Maslow is saying that Theory Y is an ideal toward which managers should strive, but, as an ideal — it does not represent the real world of the workplace.

Maslow emphasizes that the best approach to management is one that best fits the objective requirements of the objective situation. It is inappropriate to enter a situation with an *a priori* set of assumptions about people and a management style that is based solely on these *a priori* assumptions. A more fruitful approach is to ascertain first where the individual employees are with respect to the hierarchy of human development and then to deal with the situation accordingly.

The dialectic method helps us place Theories X, Y, and Z in perspective. According to this method, with any pair of competing ideas, we may find a thesis, an antithesis, and then a synthesis. Thus:

1. **The thesis (Theory X):** The average human being has an inherent dislike for work and must be coerced, controlled, and threatened with punishment.
2. **The antithesis (Theory Y):** The average human being enjoys work as much as play and simply must be provided the proper environment.
3. **The synthesis (Theory Z):** Human beings are at different positions in the developmental hierarchy and must be dealt with in terms of where they are. The ultimate goal is to help each of them move up the hierarchy.

A Two-Factor Theory of Management

Up to this point, we have reviewed two major developments: (1) the emergence of scientific management and human relations management as two distinct schools of management, with the conclusion being that we should build on the strengths of both schools; and (2) the elucidation of McGregor's Theory X and Theory Y as two opposing views of employees, with Theory Z offered as a more realistic view of the diversity of employees. These two developments provide the foundation for formulating a Theory Z philosophy of management.

The key elements of the proposed Theory Z philosophy of management are shown in Figure 2. Represented by the two axes are scientific management and human relations management, with the numbers from 1 to 10 reflecting the extent to which a particular approach to management is actually put into practice. The resulting diagram produces four types of management: (1) laissez-faire management (Theory L), which is low on both scientific management and human relations management; (2) production-oriented management (Theory X), which is high on scientific management but low on human relations management; (3) people-oriented management

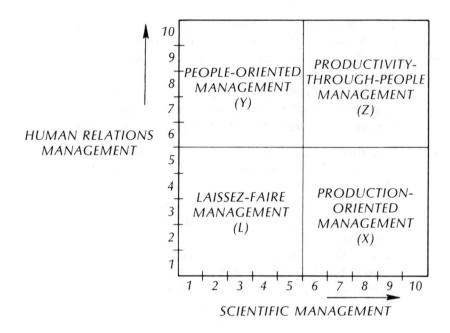

Figure 2. Two dimensions of management

(Theory Y), which is high on human relations management but low on scientific management; and (4) productivity-through-people management (Theory Z), which is high on both scientific management and human relations management.

The reader should now imagine a third dimension of Figure 2. This added dimension represents a collective set of productivity measures. Included here might be: absenteeism, voluntary turnover, profits, return on investment, return on equity, customer satisfaction, and other measures of productivity. The question then becomes: What is the relative effect of the four types of management on overall productivity? On the basis of numerous empirical studies reported in the literature, we can affirm the following:

1. **Laissez-faire management (Theory L)** will prove to be a disaster in any organization that has a mission and requires a coordination of efforts to achieve the mission.

2. **Production-oriented management (Theory X)** may achieve considerable success in organizations in the short run, but will lose out in the long run because of the undesirable side ef-

12

fects (such as low morale, high absenteeism, and high voluntary turnover).

3. **People-oriented management (Theory Y)** may be moderately successful in agencies that do not have to compete for funds but will be a failure in organizations that must function in a competitive environment.

4. **Productivity-through-people management (Theory Z) will surpass all other types of management in both public and private organizations** *in the long run,* but may not appear to be successful in the short run.

A key issue here concerns short-term success versus long-term success. Production-oriented management typically focuses on financial performance for this fiscal year, or even worse, this quarter or this month. Every effort is made to "cut corners," to "run a tight ship," which obviously precludes investments in staff development, R&D, or equipment and facilities. Thus, while the bottom line may indeed appear favorable in the short run, the undesirable long-run implications are obvious. Standing in sharp contrast to this short-term view is Theory Z management, which holds a long-term view of its responsibility — say, three, five, or even ten years into the future. This long-term view leads managers to make the appropriate investments in people, R&D, and equipment and facilities in order to realize a return-on-investment at a later date. This orientation also persuades managers that it may be necessary to operate "in the red" for a short period of time in order to achieve a long-term goal. Jack Kirker, President of GTE Communication Systems, puts the point in perspective when he says, "The effective manager wears bifocal glasses — with the upper lens directed toward the long term and the lower lens directed toward the short term."

REQUIREMENTS FOR AN EFFECTIVE PHILOSOPHY OF MANAGEMENT

The establishment of a philosophy of management in an enterprise is no small undertaking. To appreciate the magnitude of the task, the requirements for the establishment of a truly effective philosophy of management should be reviewed. The following are the basic requirements:

1. **The philosophy of management should be the foundation**

13

stone for the entire enterprise. A philosophy of management is like the center of a circle with the radii of the circle representing the functions of management. The center serves as the foundation stone — or "guiding light"— for the entire enterprise. To make certain that all members of the enterprise are headed in the same direction, it is of utmost importance that the circle be clear and illuminating.

2. **The philosophy of management should include a clear statement of values.** Values are preferences, fundamental principles of good and evil, right and wrong, success and failure, etc. While science and empiricism provide us with the "is," values provide us with the "ought." Values play a vital role in guiding decision making and action.

3. **The philosophy of management should contain a clear statement of goals.** Goals are statements of purpose, the aims toward which one's actions are directed. Why is the enterprise in existence? What is it intended to accomplish? These questions should be answered in the statement of organizational goals.

4. **The philosophy of management should contain a clear statement of strategies.** Strategies are the means for achieving the goals and satisfying the values. What methods or approaches will we use in achieving our goals? This is the *how* question of the philosophy of management.

5. **The philosophy of management should be internally consistent.** Each of the above elements — goals, values, and strategies — is an essential part of a philosophy of management. It is important that these elements be consistent with one another. They should be mutually reinforcing, not contradictory.

6. **The philosophy of management should demonstrate an awareness of the larger environment.** Every enterprise is a part of a larger environment. In this larger environment are found the marketplace, the economy, the labor supply, changing technology, governmental regulations, and a host of other factors. An effective philosophy of management will reflect a cognizance of these factors.

7. **The philosophy of management should be operational.** A philosophy of management is not something to be written and then placed in a file drawer. It must be capable of being put

14

into practice on a daily basis by all members of the management team. Then, and only then, will it become a reality. Otherwise, it will lie on the drawing board and gather dust.

8. **The philosophy of management should be internalized by all members of the management team.** If all members of the management team are operating according to the same general philosophy of management, they will be more effective and the enterprise will be more productive. To this end, all members must "internalize" the philosophy, make it a vital part of their thinking and feeling about management.

9. **The philosophy of management should be communicated to all employees.** To be truly effective, an enterprise needs members who share common values, common goals, and common strategies. All members of the enterprise must work as a team in directing their efforts toward common goals. To achieve this desirable state of affairs, it is essential that the philosophy of management be clearly and continually communicated to all members of the enterprise.

10. **The philosophy of management should be self-renewing.** An enterprise functions in an ever-changing environment. To reflect an awareness of this changing environment, members of management should redraw the philosophy of management as appropriate. No philosophy of management should be viewed as cast in concrete.

With these basic requirements serving as a foundation for the establishment of an effective philosophy of management, we look next at the three key elements of a philosophy of management: values, goals, and strategies. Specifically, we will look at the values, goals, and strategies of a Theory Z philosophy of management.

VALUES UNDERLYING THEORY Z MANAGEMENT

In considering the nature of Theory Z values, an excellent starting point is found in Warren Bennis' paper, "Changing Organizations."[4, p. 573] Bennis lists some recent changes in the basic philosophy that underlies managerial behavior:

1. A new concept of *human beings*, based on increased knowledge of their complex and shifting needs, which replaces the

15

oversimplified, innocent push-button idea of humans.

2. A new concept of *power,* based on collaboration and reason, which replaces the model of power based on coercion and fear.
3. A new concept of *organizational values,* based on humanistic-democratic ideals, which replaces the depersonalized mechanistic value system of bureaucracy.

A more extensive list of Theory Z values is provided by Robert Tannenbaum and Sheldon Davis in a classic paper, "Values, Man, and Organizations."[114] These values are listed below in the words of the present author:

1. **People are basically good.** Many are those who seem to believe that people are basically evil, that human beings are born with evil tendencies and society must take appropriate measures to control these impulses. In sharp contrast, a Theory Z view is that people are born into this world with great potential for good, but environmental conditions often thwart this potential.
2. **Treating people as persons rather than as objects.** A human being may be viewed as an "I" or an "It," as a self or a thing, as an end in himself or herself or simply as a means to some higher end. How individuals are viewed will influence greatly their perceptions of their work and their level of motivation.
3. **Viewing individuals as being in process.** It is a great injustice to view a given individual as being fixed or frozen in his or her particular stage of development. As an illustration, Charlie is rude in meetings and the supervisor is heard to remark, "Well, that's the way Charlie is." A Theory Z approach is one which views each person as being in process — meaning that persons are perceived in terms of both what they now are and what they might become.
4. **Accepting and utilizing individual differences.** Every person born into this world is a unique entity different from every other human being. Rather than decry this fact, the manager should accept it and utilize it by building on the unique strengths of each member of the work group.
5. **Viewing the individual as a whole person.** In employing personnel for work assignments, organizations in the Western world have been oriented toward "partial inclusion," which considers relevant only that part of the employee that con-

16

tributes directly to job performance (the technician's hands, the phone receptionist's voice, etc.). Standing in sharp contrast to partial inclusion is "complete inclusion," which considers the worker as a whole person, as a person with skills, knowledge, and feelings.

6. **Prizing authentic behavior.** Over the years, game playing and insincerity have been manifest in many — perhaps most — organizations. This type of behavior was recommended to the Prince by Machiavelli several centuries ago and described more recently by William Whyte in his book, *The Organization Man.*[126] In contrast to game playing and insincerity, the environment in a Theory Z organization is characterized by openness and honesty. Accurate communication pervades the organization and genuine dialogue becomes the norm. In the language of Abraham Maslow: "Phoniness is reduced toward the zero point."

7. **Fostering of trust.** Management at all levels must have credibility in the eyes of others, including employees, other managers, and customers. Without this credibility, all is lost. Establishing credibility is not a goal but an outcome that emerges when trust has been fostered throughout the organization. Perhaps the best way to achieve this trust is to make certain that managerial actions are consistent with managerial words.

8. **Confronting others with differences.** There are several ways of dealing with interpersonal and intergroup conflict: ignoring, suppressing, smoothing, or confronting. A characteristic of a healthy organization is that differences are dealt with honestly and openly through confrontation problem solving. It is accepted as a *sine qua non* that the creative, productive organization will generate differences of opinion and viewpoints among its members. These differences are viewed as a "plus" rather than a "minus."

9. **Willingness to risk.** The individual or organization obsessed with fear of failure is unlikely to achieve anything of significance. The healthy organization is willing to risk — not capriciously, but on the basis of well-thought-out plans. A batting-average concept prevails throughout the organization, meaning that no one is expected to bat 1.000 all the time. It is assumed, of course, that individuals will indeed learn

17

from their mistakes and, in turn, improve their batting averages.

10. **Viewing process work as essential to productivity.** Many are the managers who devote their full attention to the *content*, or purely technical aspects, of their jobs — getting orders out on schedule, completing projects within the budget, completing the designs according to specifications, etc. Underlying all of these activities, however, is a group of people guided by a manager. Along with the purely technical aspects of the services or products that the team is producing, due attention should be given to the way in which the group functions as a team.

11. **Emphasis on cooperation.** Many are the managers who promote "healthy competition" between individuals and between groups in their organizations. The managers assume that a certain amount of competition will spur employees on to higher levels of productivity. They may find, however, that this competitive spirit proves to be dysfunctional rather than functional. If two individuals or two groups need the assistance of each other to accomplish their own objectives, competition may be found to be a detriment to both parties. The problem with an environment that fosters competition rather than cooperation is that the participants often view the situation in terms of a "zero-sum" encounter, which will lead to a win-lose attitude rather than a win-win attitude. Thus, when choosing between cooperation and competition, one should remember that better overall organizational productivity will be achieved through cooperation.

Such values as these serve as an organization's superordinate goals, which are higher level goals influencing the formulation of particular first-order goals. In *The Art of Japanese Management*,[98, p. 178] Richard Pascale and Anthony Athos stress the value of these higher level goals:

> Superordinate goals play a pragmatic role by influencing implementation at the operational level. Because an executive cannot be everywhere at once, many decisions are made without his knowledge. What superordinate goals do, in effect, is provide employees with a "compass" and point their footsteps in the right direction.

18

As an example of an organization's statement of values, Pascale and Athos[98, p. 184] list IBM's basic beliefs:

- **Respect for the Individual.** Respect for the dignity and rights of each person in the organization.
- **Customer Service.** To give the best customer service of any company in the world.
- **Excellence.** The conviction that an organization should pursue all tasks with the objective of accomplishing them in a superior way.

GOALS OF THEORY Z MANAGEMENT

Every organization needs a clear statement of mission — a central purpose that captures its essence. For an industrial or a business enterprise, the mission should be to provide a quality product or service to consumers at a reasonable price. For a hospital, it should be to provide quality health care for patients at a reasonable price. For a school system, it should be to provide quality educational services to students at a reasonable price. The mission statement should be a statement of purpose *to which every employee in the organization can relate.*

Many industrial or business enterprises consider their central mission to be the generation of profits. Granted that every such enterprise must generate profits to stay in business, this should not be given as the central purpose. As stressed by Peter Drucker,[23] profits are *the reward bestowed upon an organization for carrying out its central mission in an effective and efficient manner.*

A clear statement of goals should support the organization's mission. With the mission being the central purpose of the organization, the goals are the broad statement of purpose that support the mission. To illustrate goals of Theory Z management, it would be difficult to improve upon those formulated by Hewlett-Packard, an electronics firm that William Ouchi identified as a Theory Z company:[96, p. 226f]

1. **Profit.** To achieve sufficient profit to finance our company growth and to provide the resources we need to achieve our other corporate objectives.

19

2. **Customers.** To provide products and services of the greatest possible value to our customers, thereby gaining and holding respect and loyalty.
3. **Fields of Interest.** To enter new fields only when the ideas we have, together with our technical, manufacturing, and marketing skills, assure that we can make a needed and profitable contribution to the field.
4. **Growth.** To let our growth be limited only by our profits and our ability to develop and produce technical products that satisfy real customer needs.
5. **Our People.** To help HP people share in the company's success, which they make possible; to provide job security based on their performance; to recognize their individual achievements; and to insure the personal satisfaction that comes from a sense of accomplishment in their work.
6. **Management.** To foster initiative and creativity by allowing the individual great freedom of action in attaining well defined objectives.
7. **Citizenship.** To honor our obligations to society by being an economic, intellectual, and social asset to each nation and each community in which we operate.

STRATEGIES OF THEORY Z MANAGEMENT

Strategies are means used by management to achieve the goals. It is important that the means be consistent with the ends; theory Z goals call for Theory Z strategies.

Theory Z management has been defined as a uniting of scientific management and human relations management. The most significant development to emerge from scientific management in the past 25 years is management by objectives. The most significant development to emerge from human relations management during the same time period is participative management. These are the two key strategies of Theory Z management.

Management by objectives, as introduced by Peter Drucker in the mid-1950s, should be viewed as a comprehensive strategy of management. The focus is on results. However, as a systems approach to management, it encompasses input, process, and output. Management by objectives provides the foundation and direction for carrying out all of the management functions: planning, organizing, staffing and staff development, motivating, and evaluating and controlling. When used as intended by Drucker, management by objectives provides a hierarchy of objectives for the entire organization, starting at the top and moving down to all successive levels. The result is that each person in the organization should have a clear understanding of how his or her objectives relate to the objectives of the work unit and how the objectives of the work unit relate to higher level objectives. Even though there are many critics of management by objectives, it should be noted that the criticism usually is directed toward the way in which the system is implemented, not toward the concept *per se*. There are some who believe that management by objectives is the most powerful tool of managing that has so far been put into practice.

As a second strategy of Theory Z management, participative management is a means of involving employees in those decisions that influence them. It should be noted that participative management is not management by committee, which usually involves the establishment of *ad hoc* groups as recommending bodies that have insufficient resources and authority to be effective. Moreover, participative management is not pure democratic management, which implies voting on each major issue. In essence, participative management means a group of employees working together as a team and guided by a leader. The group members genuinely participate in those decisions that influence their work, but the leader of the group is held accountable for the quality of the decisions and their execution. Thus, the challenge for the leader is to build his or her people into an effective team that can make good decisions and then implement those decisions successfully. In assessing the effectiveness of participative management at this stage in its evolution, it seems clear that it is not simply another management fad. Participative management is an empirically based approach that generates results in the form of higher quality decisions and greater commitment on the part of employees. Both results contribute substantially to overall productivity.

Uniting these two management strategies — management by objectives and participative management — gives us "participative management by objectives." The key idea here is a group of employees working as a unified team to achieve common objectives. This par-

21

ticipative group then becomes *the basic unit of an organization.* Given that the group's objectives are challenging and attainable and that the group is guided by an effective leader, it would be difficult to find a better strategy for achieving a high level of productivity.

SUMMING UP

The purpose of this chapter has been to present a Theory Z philosophy of management. This philosophy of management is a uniting of scientific management and human relations management and consists of values, goals, and strategies. Its cornerstone postulate is that the blending of concern for production (Theory X) and concern for people (Theory Y) will produce a form a management (Theory Z) that will excel all other forms of management in terms of long-term productivity.

The implementation of Theory Z management on a large-scale basis throughout a given organization will not be a small task. It is important to realize that the practice of this philosophy is tied closely to the personality of the managers in the organization. It would be difficult, for example, for an authoritarian or abrasive personality to practice Theory Z management. It would be equally difficult for an insecure manager who needs to be loved by all his or her employees to practice this form of management. It also is important to appreciate that some employees will not respond to Theory Z management. Employees at the lower levels of the human development scale — at the survival and safety levels — may view Theory Z management as weak management and may respond only to a more authoritarian approach. The intent here is not to end on a gloomy note but rather to report a realistic view of our expectations.

It seems evident that the potential benefits of Theory Z management far outweigh the limitations. Assuming that the barriers can be overcome, the benefits of Theory Z management will be in the form of more effective use of human resources, fewer absences, lower voluntary turnover, higher employee morale, greater job satisfaction, and, most important, higher productivity. That is what management is all about.

Exercise I
Developing Your Philosophy of Management

A.   As a manager, what are your chief *values*?

B.   What *goals* will help you actualize these values?

C.   What is your *strategy* for achieving the goals?

II

The Manager As An Effective Human Being

From the emperor down to the common people, all must regard the cultivation of the personal life as the root or foundation. There is never an orderly upshoot or super-structure when the root or foundation is disorderly.

Confucius
Lin Yutang— *The Wisdom of Confucius* [128, p. 140]

Introduction • Theoretical Framework • Identity • Authenticity • Open-mindedness • Independence • Responsibility • Communication • Reason • Problem Solving • Concern for Others • Zest for Life • Summing Up

---

INTRODUCTION

In the course of conducting management workshops, the author has given participants this assignment:

> Assume that you are interviewing job candidates for the purpose of finding someone to replace you in your present job assignment. Importance is to be given to three areas: (1) Personal Characteristics, (2) Technical Knowledge, and (3) Management Skills. Please distribute 100 points over the three categories to reflect their relative importance for achieving success in your job.

25

The results of this survey are informative. Averaging the responses from some 1000 supervisors and managers shows roughly an equal distribution of points across the three categories. It was found, however, as we moved from first-line supervisors to top management, there is a decrease in number of points assigned to Technical Knowledge. However, the points assigned to Personal Characteristics and Management Skills remain *approximately equal* for all levels of management.

To achieve success in their jobs, managers are reporting that the category of Personal Characteristics — the personality and character of the manager — is at least as important as Technical Knowledge and Management Skills. Thus, it is rather puzzling that so little attention is given to this subject in the management texts. Such texts typically concentrate on the basic principles associated with carrying out particular management functions. It is as though these functions might be carried out by a ghost or phantom.

The character of the manager is the root or foundation of Theory Z management. In the words of Confucius: "There is never yet a tree whose trunk is slim and slender and whose top branches are thick and heavy."[128, p. 140] Using this metaphor, we may view the trunk of the tree as the Personal Characteristics of the manager and the branches as the Management Skills. In addressing the subject of effective management, we must be concerned with the development of the total tree, not merely the branches.

The purpose of this chapter is to present a model or paradigm of the manager as an effective human being. This model is essentially a synthesis of the ideas of a number of psychologists who have used such designations as the "self-actualizing person," the "fully functioning person," the "productive character," or the "healthy personality" to refer to what we have chosen to call the "Effective Human Being."

THEORETICAL FRAMEWORK

In *The Fullness of Life*,[66, p. 55] Paul Kurtz provides a cornerstone for constructing a theoretical framework for the effective human being:

> Compassionate feeling is an essential human good that has
> a rightful place in human affairs. But it should not be in
> opposition to reason, rather in unity and harmony with it.

26

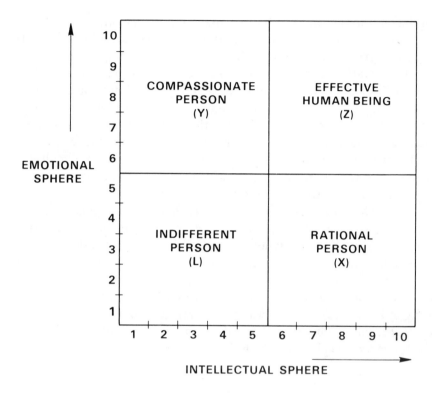

Figure 3. Two dimensions of human existence

These two human characteristics — reason and compassion — are found in full measure in the effective human being. Reason is a manifestation of the intellectual sphere of existence, and compassion is the manifestation of the emotional sphere. In many persons, these two spheres appear to be in conflict. The Effective Human Being, however, is able to bring the two into unity and harmony.

A theoretical framework for describing the effective human being is shown in Figure 3. Here the two spheres are designated as the "Intellectual Sphere" and the "Emotional Sphere," with the numbers from 1 to 10 indicating the degree to which a particular sphere is manifested in a person's life. The resulting diagram reveals four types of persons as "pure types": (1) the indifferent person, who is deficient in both the intellectual sphere and the emotional sphere; (2) the rational person, who is strong in the intellectual sphere but weak

27

in the emotional sphere; (3) the compassionate person, who is strong in the emotional sphere but weak in the intellectual sphere; and (4) the effective human being, who is strong in both spheres.

The relation between this diagram and the one presented in Figure 2 in Chapter I should be clear. Laissez-faire management (Theory L) calls for only an indifferent manager. Production-oriented management (Theory X) requires a rational manager. People-oriented management (Theory Y) needs a compassionate manager. And finally, productivity-through-people management (Theory Z) calls for a manager who is blessed with both reason and compassion — the essential traits of the effective human being.

With this theoretical framework as the point of departure, the following sections elaborate on ten characteristics of the effective human being: (1) identity, (2) authenticity, (3) open-mindedness, (4) independence, (5) responsibility, (6) communication, (7) reason, (8) problem solving, (9) concern for others, and (10) zest for life. The development of each characteristic is described in terms of a "five-rung ladder," *with the successive rungs representing successive stages of development for the individual manager.* It should be noted that the top rung of each ladder includes the desirable features of the lower rungs.

IDENTITY

In his book, *The Quest for Identity,*[125, p. 19] Allen Wheelis gives us a lucid definition of identity:

> Identity is a coherent sense of self. It depends upon the awareness that one's endeavors and one's life make sense, that they are meaningful in the context in which life is lived. It depends also upon stable values, and upon the conviction that one's actions and values are harmoniously related. It is a sense of wholeness, of integration, of knowing what is right and what is wrong and being able to choose.

Identity is one's ability to look at oneself in a mirror and say "I"— and this "I" has real meaning. It is the inner self of the individual, the active center around which all of one's experiences and actions revolve. The "I" is the center core for one's beliefs and values. Identity, then, is the basic foundation on which all of the other personal characteristics are based. Without a firm sense of identity, the individual is unable to become an effective human being.

Some individuals experience considerable difficulty in developing a firm sense of identity. When people in highly specialized technical fields become first-line supervisors, for instance, they may be uncertain as to whether they are technical specialists or supervisors. And this blurring may exist for several years — until the individual either becomes a full-fledged manager or else decides to return to his or her technical speciality on a full-time basis. Similarly, as more women enter the ranks of management, we are finding no small number who are both mothers and managers. Some of these women are expressing concern about their identity problems. Large numbers of managers — men and women alike — find themselves in positions in which they feel compelled to "assume countenances contrary to their inner nature" in order to advance to higher levels of management. Their organizations expect them to display particular appearances that may be contrary to their inner selves. Through these unwritten sanctions of the organization, managers learn to "play the game," perhaps without realizing the long-term detrimental effects on the development of their own identities.

Some managers become aware of their identity problem and seek to correct the problem. They begin to ask such questions as: Who am I? What are my goals? What is my ultimate concern in life? How do I "get my act together"? As the Delphic oracle said, "The first step to wisdom is to know thyself." Knowing that one has an identity problem and then taking steps to correct the problem may be the first step to wisdom.

Understanding our fundamental beliefs and values is a useful step in developing a firm sense of identity. For most persons, these beliefs and values simply have evolved over one's lifetime with little reflection on their nature, their origin, or their significance for one's life. Drawing up a list of values and examining them one by one can prove to be a useful exercise. With regard to each value, one may ask: To what extent can I accept this particular value? To what extent would I want to consider this particular value as a defining characteristic of my self? Socrates expressed it well when he said: "Every man should expend his chief thought and attention on the consideration of his first principles — are they or are they not rightly laid down? And when he has duly sifted them, all the rest will follow."[43, p. 470]

It is not sufficient merely to generate a list of values to guide our lives. These values must be integrated into a meaningful whole to

29

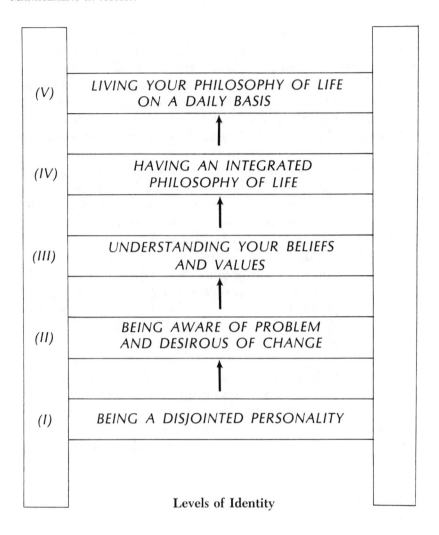

(V)   *LIVING YOUR PHILOSOPHY OF LIFE ON A DAILY BASIS*

(IV)   *HAVING AN INTEGRATED PHILOSOPHY OF LIFE*

(III)   *UNDERSTANDING YOUR BELIEFS AND VALUES*

(II)   *BEING AWARE OF PROBLEM AND DESIROUS OF CHANGE*

(I)   *BEING A DISJOINTED PERSONALITY*

Levels of Identity

form a philosophy of life. In evaluating a particular philosophy, the one criterion agreed upon by practically all philosophers is internal consistency. Are the basic values embedded in our philosophies of life mutually reinforcing or contradictory? Satisfying the criterion of internal consistency requires an in-depth analysis of our values with the aim of making appropriate adjustments to form a truly integrated philosophy of life that possesses unity and coherence.

Moving to the top rung of the ladder involves actually living our philosophies of life on a daily basis. Many are the persons who have developed elegant philosophies of life (comprised of clearly articulated values that are internally consistent) that only lie on the drawing board. Because these philosophies are not put into practice, they remain as "castles in the air." The ultimate achievement in developing a firm sense of identity is to actually live one's philosophy of life on a daily basis. Here we find two kinds of consistency: first, consistency among the values themselves and, second, consistency between the internal values and the overt actions. Achieving both types of consistency leads to a firm sense of identity, which is the foundation stone for all of the remaining characteristics of the effective human being.

AUTHENTICITY

The true meaning of authenticity was grasped by Confucius[128, pp. 179-80] when he observed:

> A man who has a beautiful soul always has some beautiful things to say, but a man who says beautiful things does not necessarily have a beautiful soul.

Each person has two selves—the inner self and the outer self. Authenticity may be defined as consistency between inner self and outer self. The phrase "That person is for real" essentially refers to a consistency between the person's inner self and outer self. In the words of Abraham Maslow, "Authenticity is the reduction of phoniness toward the zero point."[83, p. 183]

A common human tendency is to "play roles"—to pretend to be something that one is not, to act a part that is different from what one really is. When this occurs, the individual acting the part may feel guilty. On the other hand, when the individual says what he or she really thinks and feels, there often follows a feeling of pride.

Suppose we decide to stop living phony lives and to stop "playing roles." Suppose that we want to achieve the satisfaction that comes from "being for real." Assuming that we have been only personages rather than real persons, bringing about major changes will be no easy task. Nevertheless, there is a way to the top of the ladder.

First, we can become aware of our own thoughts and feelings.

31

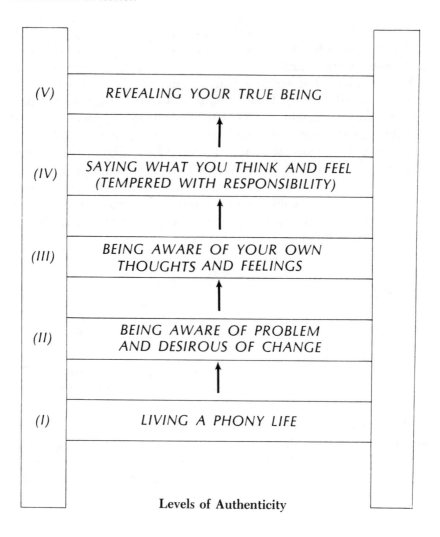

(V)	*REVEALING YOUR TRUE BEING*
(IV)	*SAYING WHAT YOU THINK AND FEEL (TEMPERED WITH RESPONSIBILITY)*
(III)	*BEING AWARE OF YOUR OWN THOUGHTS AND FEELINGS*
(II)	*BEING AWARE OF PROBLEM AND DESIROUS OF CHANGE*
(I)	*LIVING A PHONY LIFE*

Levels of Authenticity

What are *my* thoughts about this particular matter? What are *my* feelings about this particular matter? It is important to appreciate the wide range of our thoughts and feelings without evaluating them as "good" or "bad." At this stage, we should just attempt to understand them and appreciate them.

After becoming better aware of our thoughts and feelings, we can learn to express them. At the beginning, we should work in the nonthreatening areas — nonthreatening either to ourselves or to others. Then, we can begin to express ourselves on more important issues. It is imperative that this expression be tempered with control and responsibility. Programs in sensitivity training led some graduates to believe that they were to express whatever thoughts and feelings they might have, regardless of the consequences. The results were sometimes disastrous. Effective human beings, on the other hand, have learned to express their thoughts and feelings tempered with responsibility and consideration for the thoughts and feelings of others.

The highest rung on the authenticity ladder signifies that we have decided to live authentic lives by revealing our true beings to others with whom we have personal relations. Consistency between our outer selves and our inner selves becomes our watchword. This does not mean that in responding to "How are you today" we give a complete elaboration of our aches and pains. It does mean, though, that we endeavor to express ourselves honestly and openly on more important matters.

If authenticity becomes our preferred mode of behaving, we will find that it is not without risks. There are some individuals, including persons in positions of power, who are threatened by authentic people. If we can persevere in the face of these risks, the gains for personal development may be substantial. For one thing, we will feel better about ourselves — we will feel a sense of pride. Second, by living as authentic persons, we will discover that we are more successful in developing a firm sense of identity — we have a better understanding of who we actually are. Third, if we are working in an organization that values authentic behavior, we will discover that we can truly make a greater contribution to the organization by being ourselves rather than by merely parroting the ideas of others.

OPEN-MINDEDNESS

In the book, *How We Think*,[21, p. 30] John Dewey provides a clear definition of open-mindedness:

> Open-mindedness may be defined as freedom from prejudice, partisanship, and such other habits as close the mind and make it unwilling to consider new problems and certain new ideas.

33

Open-mindedness is the willingness to try to understand different points of view. It does not mean necessarily that we agree with them.

Karl Jaspers suggests that humans beings, with the years, tend to "enter into a prison of conventions and opinions, concealments and unquestioned acceptance." [51, pp. 10-11] This prison of convictions becomes the individual's reality, and he or she tends to reject any

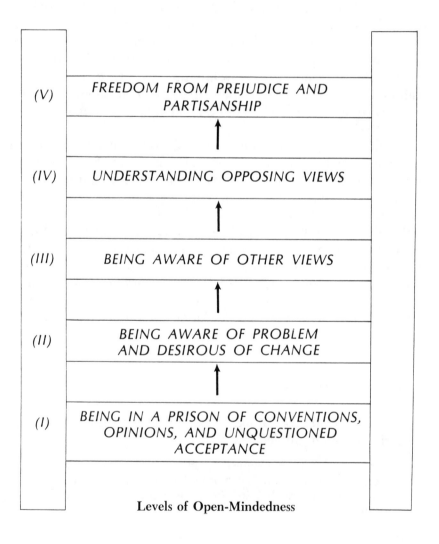

(V)	FREEDOM FROM PREJUDICE AND PARTISANSHIP
(IV)	UNDERSTANDING OPPOSING VIEWS
(III)	BEING AWARE OF OTHER VIEWS
(II)	BEING AWARE OF PROBLEM AND DESIROUS OF CHANGE
(I)	BEING IN A PRISON OF CONVENTIONS, OPINIONS, AND UNQUESTIONED ACCEPTANCE

Levels of Open-Mindedness

opinions that might contradict these convictions. Such persons become one-channeled thinkers. They cannot accept the idea that truth is multi-channeled. These are the truly closed-minded people. These are the persons who say, "Don't bother me with the facts; my mind is already made up."

Perhaps we can change. Perhaps we can appreciate the problems associated with our one-channeled thinking — lack of genuine dialogue with others, lack of creativity, and lack of intellectual growth. Unless we make a serious effort to break loose from our prison of conventions and unquestioned acceptance, we will be at a standstill in terms of personal development.

The first step in this effort to become open-minded persons is to become aware of other views. We can be sensitive to the fact that there are diverse views on every major issue — religion, politics, leadership, productivity, success, etc. We can become aware of these views simply by being attentive, that is, by reading and by observing. We can seek out persons who hold views different from our own. We should not attempt to evaluate any particular view as being either "right" or "wrong" but simply be perceptive to the diversity and richness of these views.

Next, we can endeavor to understand truly these diverse views. What is this person really trying to say? Why does the person view the situation in this particular way? In all truthfulness, is my own view on this issue any more valid than my adversary's view? A sincere effort to answer these questions will help us become more open-minded persons.

After a reasonable amount of experience in becoming aware of other views and sincerely trying to understand these views, we may be able to move to the highest rung on the ladder — freedom from prejudice and partisanship. On this rung we discover that the earth does not crumble when we toss aside certain of our own cherished views that we have held so dearly.

In this context, we can heed the wisdom of that great orator, Marcus Aurelius Antoninus: [58, p. 21]

> Suppose a man can convince me of error and bring home to me that I am mistaken in thought or act; I shall be glad to alter, for the truth is what I pursue, and no one was ever injured by the truth, whereas he is injured who continues in his own self-deception and ignorance.

35

INDEPENDENCE

In his book, *The Self*, [94, p. 274] Clark Moustakas captures the meaning of independence in these words:

> The real individual moves toward increased autonomy, and increasingly feels that the locus of direction lies within himself. His development and continued growth are dependent on his own potentialities and latent resources.

From the classic sociological studies of David Riesman, many of us have become attuned to the concepts of inner-directed and other-directed social character. Riesman, in *The Lonely Crowd*, [100] describes inner-directed persons as ones who are guided by internal gyroscopes that keep them "on course" and help them withstand the buffeting of the external environment. In contrast, other-directed persons use their contemporaries as their source of direction — either those known personally or those known indirectly through friends or the mass media. Other-directed persons pay close attention to the signals from others.

The challenge for all of us is to look within ourselves and ascertain where we are with respect to the other-directed — inner-directed continuum. If we truly want to be our *selves* and realize our own unique potentialities, we should endeavor to move toward the inner-directed end of the continuum. But this decision obviously is fraught with risks. If we are successful in making this transition, we may lose the psychological protection of the group with which we have identified. We may find ourselves alone in our thinking, and this aloneness may result in rejection by some of our closest associates. Moving from "group think" to "individual think" can indeed be a threatening move; it requires a fairly brave soul to take the risk.

Assuming that we do make the decision to be independent thinkers, a reasonable first step is to have some thoughts of our own. As we study the various issues of the day, we can begin to analyze them and explore how various authorities view the issues. We can then make up our own minds on each issue. We can begin to be independent thinkers by putting our *selves* into the balance — evaluating, weighing, and deciding. This will start us on the road to becoming independent thinkers.

After we achieve some degree of success in having thoughts of our own, we can then begin to develop our own plans. In each im-

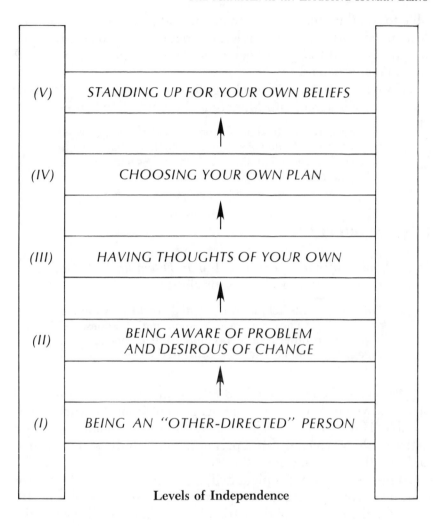

(V)	*STANDING UP FOR YOUR OWN BELIEFS*
	↑
(IV)	*CHOOSING YOUR OWN PLAN*
	↑
(III)	*HAVING THOUGHTS OF YOUR OWN*
	↑
(II)	*BEING AWARE OF PROBLEM AND DESIROUS OF CHANGE*
	↑
(I)	*BEING AN "OTHER-DIRECTED" PERSON*

Levels of Independence

portant area calling for a plan, we can formulate our own goals and the means for achieving them. We will find satisfaction in knowing that these are *our* plans and not merely plans that were passed on to us by others. We will discover to our delight that we are both "sculptor and marble," that we possess the necessary raw material and that we ourselves can mold this raw material into something of our own liking. This is freedom in the best sense of the term.

Then, finally, to reach the top rung of the ladder, we must be able to stand up for our own thoughts and plans. To have some effect on the world around us, it is not enough merely to have thoughts of our own and to develop our own plans. We must be willing to promote and defend them.

If we are successful in reaching the top rung of the ladder, then we surely will agree with Mahatma Gandhi[9, p. 127] when he says:

> If I also, perhaps, stood before the prospect of finding myself in a minority of *one* voice, I humbly believe that I would have the courage to remain in such a hopeless minority. This is for me the only truthful position.

RESPONSIBILITY

In the book, *Psychology and the Human Dilemma*,[86, p. 175] Rollo May focuses on the root word of "responsibility":

> This inseparable relation of self and world also implies *responsibility*. The terms mean "responding," "response to." I cannot, in other words, become a self except as I am engaged continuously in *responding* to the world of which I am a part.

We human beings are indeed related inseparably to this world of which we are a part. Total disengagement from the world is impossible. However, all of us have a choice: to continuously *respond* to this world of which we are a part or to sit passively on the sidelines and let others respond for us.

Why are so many people unwilling to accept responsibility for their own lives? They ask their physicians to prescribe their health plans for them; they ask their friends how they should vote in the next election; they ask their gurus to think for them. The responsibility for guiding one's life frequently is pushed "out there," seldom accepted "within here."

By shifting the burden of responsibility to others, some individuals will discover that they are sacrificing something very precious — the potential for becoming their *selves*. Therefore, if this loss of *self* development is perceived as an undesirable consequence, the individual must make every effort to correct the situation. And this alteration can be brought about through courage and effort.

First, we can start with the foundation stone. We can begin to accept our lives as our own responsibility. Importantly, we cannot

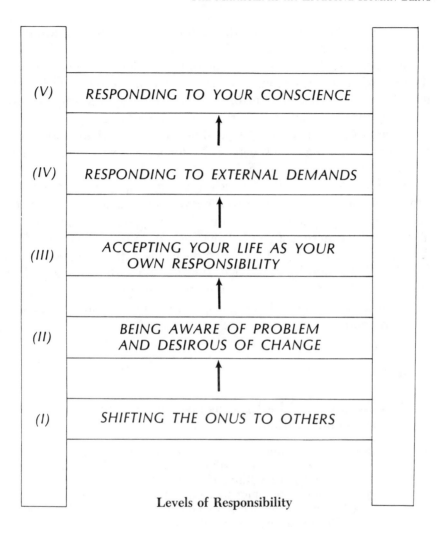

(V) RESPONDING TO YOUR CONSCIENCE

(IV) RESPONDING TO EXTERNAL DEMANDS

(III) ACCEPTING YOUR LIFE AS YOUR OWN RESPONSIBILITY

(II) BEING AWARE OF PROBLEM AND DESIROUS OF CHANGE

(I) SHIFTING THE ONUS TO OTHERS

Levels of Responsibility

limit our attention to only the big things in life. We also must attend to the little things, what others may view as trifles. We must commit ourselves to being responsible for our own thoughts and actions, whether they are minor or momentous. This *I* believe, and this *I* will be responsible for. No longer do we shift the burden to others. Sören Kierkegaard,[56, p. 209] the Danish philospher, puts the point nicely

39

when he says: "The doctor and the pastor ask about your health, but eternity makes *you* responsible for your condition."

We can advance to the next rung of the ladder by responding to the external demands around us. Here we truly respond with our total beings. A situation confronts us, and *we* respond—our selves respond, our innermost beings respond. We will react to the external demands placed upon us; we will not sit on the sidelines as mere observers of an interesting spectacle. No longer will we put our heads in the sand as the ostrich does.

Then, finally, responding to one's conscience represents the highest rung of the ladder. As most persons know, there is a delicate balance between responding to external demands and responding to one's conscience. When there is a conflict between the two, we will opt for the latter. We are able to make such decisions with little hesitation because of our internal gyroscopes that guide us. Regardless of the outcome of these decisions, there will be no later regrets. We simply did what seemed to be right and proper according to conscience and that's the end of it.

COMMUNICATION

In his *Philosophy*,[49, p. 54] Karl Jaspers gives us a succinct description of genuine communication:

> Existential communication is not to be modeled and is not to be copied; each time it is flatly singular. It occurs between two selves which are nothing else, are not representative, and are, therefore, not interchangeable. In this communication, which is absolutely historic and unrecognizable from outside, lies the assurance of selfhood.

Martin Buber, the philosopher of dialogue, identified three distinct types of communication: (1) monologue, which is one-way communication but is often disguised as two-way communication; (2) technical communication, which is two-way communication but is limited to the exchange of information; and (3) dialogue, which is honest and open two-way communication between two authentic persons. To appreciate the meaning of dialogue, it is helpful to understand that the root word of "communication" is "commune." To commune means "to share"—to share our selves.

Why do we find so little genuine dialogue in our everyday lives?

Why is it that so many people engage in monologue and confuse it with dialogue? Why do people act as though they are listening, but are merely reveling in their own thoughts? Buber suggests that lack of genuine dialogue is the most serious problem of the modern age.

In analyzing our own communication patterns, we should judge where we lie on the monologue-dialogue continuum. If we discover that our typical mode of communication indeed is found lacking, we can resolve to bring about a change. We are likely to discover that improvement in interpersonal communication brings about positive changes in our total beings. We become not only better communicators but also better persons.

As a first step in this planned growth experience, we must grasp the significance of the two essential dimensions of communication: speaking and listening. Most of us have been taught how to speak, but few of us have been taught how to listen. More than 2000 years ago, Plato observed that there were three main reasons for poor interpersonal communication. First, people want to be right at all costs; second, people refuse to stick to the subject; and third, people do not know how to listen. It seems that humankind has advanced very little over the past two millennia. Thus, to be better communicators, first we must resolve to be better listeners. Listening requires that we be "truly present" in each dialogue. Our thoughts cannot be preoccupied with matters irrelevant to those at hand.

Assuming that we have achieved some degree of success in learning how to listen, we can then proceed to improve our ability in expressing our thoughts and feelings. While the expression of thoughts is an accepted mode of communication in many quarters, the expression of feelings is not. Though the expression of feelings probably is not actually taboo, it is often assumed to be. Perhaps this is a rationalization on the part of the person who is apprehensive about revealing his or her feelings. Whatever the reason, we must deal with the problem and overcome it if we want to be effective communicators. Certainly this expression of feelings should not be done in a cantankerous manner but, rather, in a caring and constructive manner.

Making a genuine commitment to a life of dialogue will move us to the top rung of the ladder. Dialogue is genuine communication between a person and a person, between a self and a self. The personages or masks are tossed aside, and only the persons remain — two authentic human persons interacting with each other from the

41

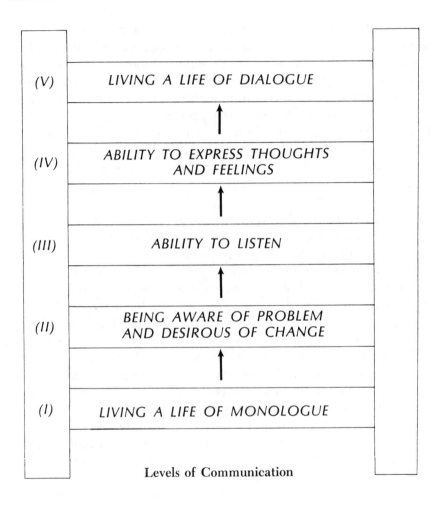

Levels of Communication

cores of their inner beings. Buber and other serious students of human communication have highlighted some of the salient features of dialogue: both participants are "fully present" . . . both participants are spontaneous and unrehearsed . . . both listen with understanding and avoid evaluation . . . each participant helps the other to clarify thoughts . . . the participants deal with conflicts in a constructive manner . . . and even when they stand in opposition, each confirms the other as an existing human being of worth . . . essentially the two partners are in a loving struggle for truth. "In this communication," Jaspers tells us, "which is absolutely historic and unrecognizable from outside, lies the assurance of selfhood."

As we reflect on the significance of the life of dialogue, we may be challenged by the words of Martin Buber[8, p. 92]:

> This fragile life between birth and death can nevertheless be a fulfillment — if it is a dialogue.

REASON

In his book, *Reason and Anti-Reason in Our Time*,[50, pp. 38-39] Karl Jaspers provides a capsule description of reason:

> Let me try to characterize reason. Reason has no assured stability: it is constantly on the move. Once it has gained a position, it presses on to criticize it and is therefore opposed to the tendency to free oneself from the necessity for all further thought by once and for all accepting irrevocably fixed ideas. It demands a careful thoughtfulness — it is therefore the opposite of mere capriciousness.

Reason is the search for truth through logical thinking. Logical thinking involves such activities as separating facts and opinions, stating assumptions, and using good judgment. Reason is able to transform an obscure situation into one that is clear and coherent. In the search for truth, reason is "constantly on the move."

Human beings vary considerably in their ability and desire to incorporate reason as a major factor in their lives. Karl Jaspers[50, pp. 67-68] suggests that "There is something inside all of us that yearns not for reason but for mystery . . . not for penetrating clear thought but for the whisperings of the irrational . . . not for science but for wizardry disguised as science . . . not for rationally founded influence but for magic." Each person is faced with an important decision: to decide either for or against a life of reason. If the decision is affirmative, there is a way to climb the ladder.

First, we can learn how to be logical thinkers. Research has shown that the study of such subjects as mathematics and science can help improve one's ability to reason. To move to advanced levels of reason, one might pursue the study of logic and philosophy. On a daily basis,

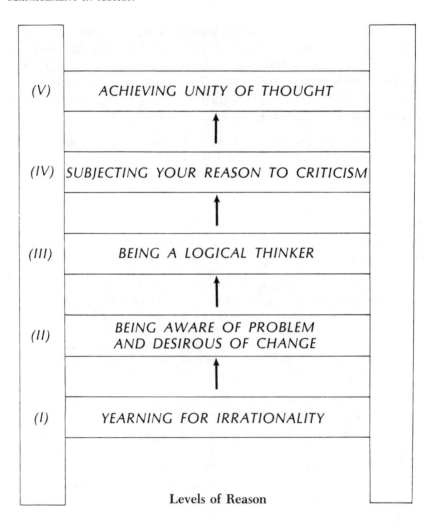

(V)	*ACHIEVING UNITY OF THOUGHT*
(IV)	*SUBJECTING YOUR REASON TO CRITICISM*
(III)	*BEING A LOGICAL THINKER*
(II)	*BEING AWARE OF PROBLEM AND DESIROUS OF CHANGE*
(I)	*YEARNING FOR IRRATIONALITY*

Levels of Reason

one can practice thinking in a logical and systematic manner. The basic tools of reason are not mysterious; they can be learned.

Next, we must be willing to subject our reason to criticism. When looking for reactions to our ideas, many of us will seek out only our friends and supporters. We know in advance that our comrades will endorse our ideas and give us the desired praise. However, we know implicitly that an automatic endorsement of our ideas will contribute little to their development. Persons who are genuinely committed to a life of reason will seek out their adversaries. Viewing reason as the pursuit of truth, these persons desire every possible insight.

Achieving unity of thought represents the highest rung on the ladder. The majority of thinking people have a diversity of ideas and concepts on all sorts of matters—from the profane to the sublime. Some individuals seem unable to achieve any sense of unity among these ideas and concepts, which remain as a mass of unrelated elements. The effective human being, however, is able to bring the diverse and contradictory into a unity. This unity of thinking contributes substantially to unity of personality.

PROBLEM SOLVING

In their *Experimental Psychology* textbook,[127, p. 814] Robert Woodworth and Harold Schlosberg offer a general definition of problem solving:

> A problem exists when (a person's) activity has a goal but no clear or well learned route to the goal. He has to explore and find a route. When he has found a route, he has achieved a solution though not necessarily the best solution.

We humans are faced with problems throughout our lives. Some problems are momentous, and some are trivial. Some deal with our work lives, and some deal with our personal lives. But, regardless of the magnitude or the context, a problem exists when there is some type of barrier between us and the goal. We must find a way around, over, or under the barrier. This is the essence of problem solving.

Many of us humans tend to run away from problems—the ostrich dynamic appears more natural than coping. We are threatened by problems; they simply overwhelm us. Happiness would be a life without problems! We find to our dismay, however, that this reluctance to cope with a problem only increases the magnitude of the problem. We now realize that most problems will not "fade away"—they must be confronted. We must realize that the only way to become an effective human being is to become an effective problem solver.

A first step in moving up the ladder will be to cultivate a responsible attitude toward problems. We realize that a life without problems would be very boring indeed. We also realize that the presence of problems may be the chief reason for the existence of our jobs; if there were no problems, the organization probably would not need us. Thus, rather than viewing problems as threats, we can view them as opportunities — opportunities to test our mettle. Such an attitude can transform a threatening situation into a challenging situation — from "problem" to "opportunity."

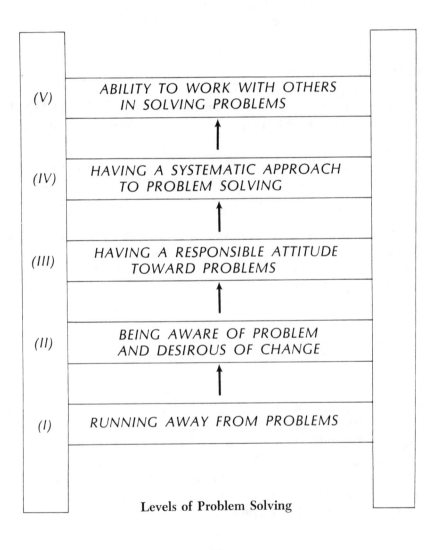

(V) ABILITY TO WORK WITH OTHERS IN SOLVING PROBLEMS

(IV) HAVING A SYSTEMATIC APPROACH TO PROBLEM SOLVING

(III) HAVING A RESPONSIBLE ATTITUDE TOWARD PROBLEMS

(II) BEING AWARE OF PROBLEM AND DESIROUS OF CHANGE

(I) RUNNING AWAY FROM PROBLEMS

Levels of Problem Solving

Assuming that we have cultivated a positive and responsible attitude toward problem solving, we can then proceed to sharpen our problem-solving skills. Based essentially on the scientific method, these well known skills include: a systematic approach, seeing the total problem, clearly defining the problem, identifying the causes, getting the facts, separating idea generation and idea evaluation, and formulating a plan of action. These skills can be learned by any person desirous of learning them.

Building on a responsible attitude toward problems and basic problem-solving skills, we can advance to the highest rung on the ladder by developing the talent for working with others in solving problems. Many problem situations call for interacting effectively with other persons who have a stake in the problem and its solution. Some persons possess the analytical skills needed for solving problems but are inept at working with other persons in *joint* problem solving. Considerable experience and practice may be required for developing the necessary human interaction skills needed for engaging in cooperative problem solving. The acquisition of these skills will be a "plus" for the manager.

CONCERN FOR OTHERS

In a beautiful little book entitled *The Art of Loving*,[33, p. 26] Erich Fromm begins with this definition of love:

> Love is the active concern for the life and growth of that which we love. Where this active concern is lacking, there is no love.

The salient features of love have been identified by a number of humanistic writers. It involves communication between two persons, and this communication occurs between one self and another self (Erich Fromm). It involves treating a person always as an end and never merely as a means (Immanuel Kant). It involves giving of yourself, not merely of your possessions (Kahlil Gibran). It involves providing a helping relationship that will assist the other person in growth and personal development (Carl Rogers). It involves quickening the other person with gladness (Martin Buber). All of these astute observers of human love agree that the benefits of love are reciprocal — both parties benefit from the relationship.

47

In *The Fullness of Life*,[66, p. 101] Paul Kurtz vividly describes what happens to a person who is unable to develop mutual relationships:

> Unless one develops mutual relationships and thus experiences the joys of life, whether with a beloved, a parent, a child, a friend or colleague, one's heart tends to close, one's roots become dry.

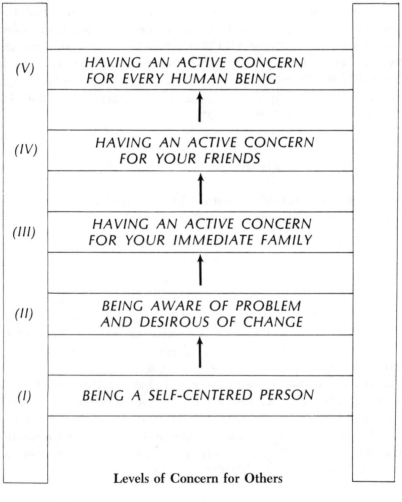

(V)	*HAVING AN ACTIVE CONCERN FOR EVERY HUMAN BEING*
(IV)	*HAVING AN ACTIVE CONCERN FOR YOUR FRIENDS*
(III)	*HAVING AN ACTIVE CONCERN FOR YOUR IMMEDIATE FAMILY*
(II)	*BEING AWARE OF PROBLEM AND DESIROUS OF CHANGE*
(I)	*BEING A SELF-CENTERED PERSON*

Levels of Concern for Others

Should we find ourselves drifting toward the state or condition described by Kurtz, we can decide of our own free will to change the course. We can decide to build interpersonal relationships with others. Achieving success, of course, will depend on much more than simply the decision. In the final analysis, success will be based on our daily actions.

For many people, there may be no better starting point for building strong mutual relationships than with one's immediate family. Perhaps we have been lax in the past. Perhaps those relationships that were so real to us at some previous time have not been nourished over the years, and, consequently, they have slowly died. The family is the true testing ground for building mutual relationships.

After achieving some degree of satisfaction in cultivating close relationships with individual members of the family, we can begin to expand our horizons to encompass our close acquaintances. These are persons we have known for years; but have we really *known* them? Have we ever really established genuine dialogue with them? Have we ever really provided a helping relationship? There are so many opportunities!

When we have climbed to the highest rung on the ladder, we will be able to demonstrate a genuine concern for every human being with whom we come into contact. Perhaps there is time for only a glance or a smile, but we can acknowledge each human person as a significant other. We can acknowledge each individual that we encounter as a person of worth. Here we can benefit from the wisdom of Kierkegaard[57, p. 89] when he says:

> At a distance one's neighbor is a shadow which in imagination enters every man's thought and walks by—but alas, one perhaps does not discover that the man who at the same moment actually walks by him is his neighbor.

ZEST FOR LIFE

In his book, *Joy*,[109, p. 17] William Schutz elucidates the meaning of "zest for life":

> Joy is the feeling that comes from the fulfillment of one's potential. Fulfillment brings to an individual the feeling that he can cope with his environment; the sense of confidence in himself as a significant, competent, lovable per-

49

son who is capable of handling situations as they arise, able
to use fully his own capacities, and free to express his
feelings.

Zest for life means enthusiasm for living. There is great joy in
living life on a daily basis. Persons who experience joy for life not
only achieve a great deal of personal satisfaction, they also have a
positive effect on those around them. Enthusiasm begets enthusiasm.
Peak experiences emerge in large numbers. It seems as though this
is what life is all about.

Sad indeed are those persons who remain at the bottom rung of
the developmental hierarchy. Each day is as dismal as every previous
day. There are no goals, there is no plan, and life becomes mean-
ingless. If this condition remains for an extended period of time, the
individual moves into a state of despair. Here we see the waste of
so much human potentiality.

Admittedly, all of us humans experience high and low points in
our lives. We all experience certain "peaks and valleys." But the thing
that we now realize about human psychology is that we, of our own
free will, can lift ourselves out of the valleys. Some of us will need
a helping hand in the process, but it is possible for each person to
continue to advance in the developmental hierarchy. It is indeed possible for each person to transform latent potentiality into actuality.

A *sine qua non* for zest for life is to be working at something important. The importance of an activity is in the eyes of the one performing the activity — be he or she a company president, a foreman,
or a secretary. If it is not possible to work at something important
in the work context, then the individual would be wise to choose
something outside the job situation (parenting of children, volunteer-
ing to work for a social agency, engaging in an absorbing hobby, etc.).
Whatever it is, it must be viewed as important, satisfying and fulfilling
to the individual. The individual's self becomes absorbed in the be-
loved activity and, in a sense, the self transcends itself. This is the
cornerstone and foundation for a joyous life.

Moving to the next rung on the ladder, we can learn to develop
our capacity to enjoy the present moment. As Ralph Waldo Emerson noted in his essay on prudence,[27, p. 171] "Tomorrow will be like today. Life wastes itself while we are preparing to live." Many are those
who see happiness as being "out there." It is as though they live their
complete lives waiting and hoping for happiness. They seem convinced that, even though today is just another day, tomorrow will

surely bring happiness. These persons are doomed to disappointment. A key to the good life is to develop the capacity to enjoy the present moment — to see the rich possibilities for meaning in the here and now.

We reach the top rung of the ladder when we feel that we are moving steadily forward in realizing our potentialities. Perhaps there is no greater satisfaction than that which we experience when we are truly fulfilling our potential. We are moving *toward* something.

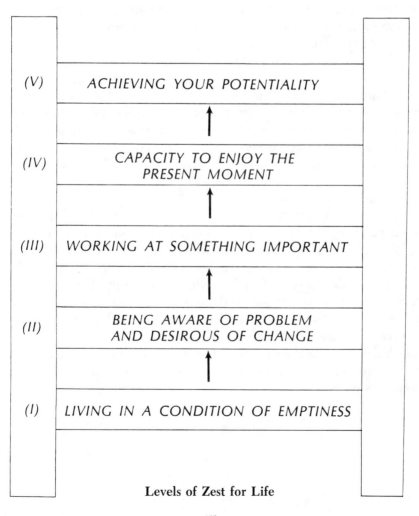

(V)	ACHIEVING YOUR POTENTIALITY
(IV)	CAPACITY TO ENJOY THE PRESENT MOMENT
(III)	WORKING AT SOMETHING IMPORTANT
(II)	BEING AWARE OF PROBLEM AND DESIROUS OF CHANGE
(I)	LIVING IN A CONDITION OF EMPTINESS

Levels of Zest for Life

We have a commitment to important goals, and we enjoy the process of working toward the goals just as much as actually achieving them. To our delight, we discover that *the path and the goal become one*.

SUMMING UP

This chapter has presented a brief description of the manager as an effective human being. Certainly there are important characteristics in addition to those listed here, which also could be defined and illustrated in different ways. Nevertheless, an attempt has been made to summarize many of the ideas used by the great humanists to describe the effective human being.

The basic thesis of this chapter has been that the effective manager must be proficient in three areas: (1) personal charcteristics, (2) technical knowledge, and (3) management skills. It is taken for granted by most management theorists that many supervisors must be proficient in technical knowledge in order to supervise the employees who report to them. These theorists then proceed directly to the third area — the development of management skills — while ignoring, or at least minimizing, the importance of personal characteristics to the effectiveness of the manager.

We must appreciate that any person carrying out the functions of management is *a living human being*. The significance of this statement is highlighted in the following logic: (1) the personal characteristics of the manager will influence the choice of a particular leadership style; (2) the leadership style will determine how the person carries out the management functions; and (3) how the individual manager carries out the management functions will have a profound influence on the overall productivity of the organizational unit for which the manager is responsible. The logic appears irrefutable. Thus, our conclusion is that Theory Z management calls for effective human beings as managers.

Exercise II

Becoming a More Effective Human Being

A.   Evaluate yourself on each of the 10 characteristics of the effective human being by circling the Roman numeral on each ladder that best represents where you now are in your own personal growth. (If you believe that you are between two rungs, you may indicate that position accordingly.)

B.   What do you consider to be your chief strengths and chief weaknesses as an effective human being?

Strengths	Weaknesses

C.   List five personal goals for becoming a more effective human being during the next 12 months.

III

Leadership Styles*

Leadership is generally defined as influence, the art or process of influencing people so that they will strive willingly toward the achievement of group goals. This concept can be enlarged to imply not only willingness to work, but also willingness to work with zeal and confidence.

Harold Koontz and Cyril O'Donnell
Management [64, p. 661]

Introduction • Theoretical Framework • The Theory L Leader • The Theory X Leader • The Theory Y Leader • The Theory Z Leader • An Illustrative Example • Results of Different Leadership Styles • Common Questions About Leadership Styles • Summing Up

---

INTRODUCTION

It would be difficult to improve upon this definition of leadership provided by Harold Koontz and Cyril O'Donnell. The key concept is *influencing people so that they will strive willingly toward the achievement of group goals.* This ability to influence others might

---

*This chapter is based largely on the work of Robert Blake and Jane Mouton, as reported in *The New Managerial Grid* (6).

be exhibited by any member of the organization — be it a secretary, an engineer, or a manager. For purposes of this chapter, however, we are looking specifically at the leadership exhibited by managers in an organization.

Leadership effectiveness can be assessed through systematic field research. In conducting such studies, a three-step strategy is often used. It is first necessary to define and measure criteria of organizational effectiveness, such as quality of product or service, customer satisfaction, growth, profits, return on investment, employee turnover, etc. The next step is to assess the behavior of the organization's leaders in terms of different leadership styles manifested. Then, correlations between leadership style and the criteria of organizational effectiveness can be calculated. The results of such studies have provided many insights into the relative effectiveness of different leadership styles.

An appreciation of the overall impact of leadership can be gained through a review of an analysis reported by Koontz, O'Donnell, and Weihrich.[65] A summary of their analysis of a number of specific studies dealing with leadership effectiveness is shown in Figure 4. With "leadership ability of the manager" constituting the independent variable, and "employee utilization of capability," the dependent variable, the authors conclude that the leadership ability of the manager has the potential for contributing at least 40 percent of the total variance in employee utilization of capability.

In essence, Koontz, O'Donnell, and Weihrich are saying that, if managers simply go into their offices each day and "put their feet on their desks," the employees reporting to them can be expected to perform at about 60 percent of their potential. The 60 percent figure results from social pressure, need for a job, and the authority of the superior. But through effective leadership, it is possible to add 40 percent to the 60 percent base. Of course, these figures are averages, and the actual percent of contribution by the leader in any given situation would depend on a number of factors, such as maturity level of employees, degree of self-motivation of employees, need for linkages across employees, etc. Nevertheless, regardless of these qualifying remarks, a potential average contribution of 40 percent is no small amount!

The purpose of this chapter is to discuss leadership effectiveness. Specifically, we will be looking at different leadership styles and what effect these different styles have on organizational productivity.

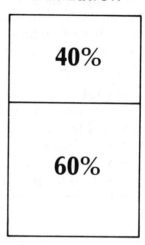

Contribution induced by leadership ability of the manager

Normal expectancy of capability utilization induced by social pressure, need for a job, and authority of superior.

Koontz, O'Donnell, and Weihrich — *Management*, 1980, McGraw-Hill, pp. 661. Reprinted, by permission of the publisher.

Figure 4.   Impact of leadership on employee utilization of capability

THEORETICAL FRAMEWORK

In his book, *Eupsychian Management*,[82, p. 28] Abraham Maslow highlights the importance of two basic dimensions of management:

> In general, we may say that management theory can stress roughly two products, two consequences: one is the economic productivity, the quality of products, profit making, etc.; the other is the human products, that is, the psychological health of the workers, their movement toward self-actualization, their increase in safety, belongingness, loyalty, ability to love, self-respect, etc.

These two dimensions of management—"concern for production" and "concern for people"—were identified back in the mid-1950s as an outcome of the Ohio State Leadership Studies.[46] Through systematic empirical research, psychologists identified the two

57

primary dimensions of leadership as "Initiating Structure" and "Consideration."

The dimension of Initiating Structure means that the leader is task-oriented or concerned primarily about getting the job done. To appreciate the meaning of this dimension, it is useful to consider some of the original questionnaire items used in the Ohio State Leadership Studies assessment:

- Works with a plan.
- Lets staff members know what is expected of them.
- Sees to it that the work of staff members is coordinated.
- Emphasizes the meeting of deadlines.
- Maintains definite standards of performance.
- Sees to it that staff members are working up to capacity.
- Criticizes poor work.

Quite different in nature, the dimension of Consideration means that the leader is concerned primarily about people and is desirous of playing a supportive role for his or her staff. Again, to better appreciate the meaning of this dimension, the following are some questionnaire items used to assess the dimension of consideration:

- Does little things to make it pleasant to be a member of his/her staff.
- Finds time to listen to staff members.
- Looks out for the personal welfare of individual staff members.
- Consults with staff before acting on important matters.
- Is friendly and approachable.
- Makes staff feel at ease when talking with them.
- Puts suggestions made by staff into operation.

As shown in Figure 5, these two dimensions of leadership are orthogonal, which means that they are independent of each other, not opposite. With Initiating Structure increasing from low to high on the horizontal axis, and Consideration increasing from low to high on the vertical axis, it was found by the Ohio State group that leaders in organizations are distributed throughout the diagram. Those in the lower-left quadrant of the diagram are found lacking in both dimensions; those in the lower-right quadrant are high on Initiating Structure but low on Consideration; leaders in the upper-left quadrant

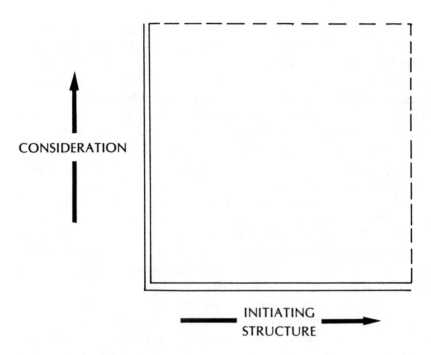

Figure 5.   Ohio State leadership factors

are high on Consideration but low on Initiating Structure; and those in the upper-right quadrant score high on both dimensions.

In evaluating leaders in organizations, the Ohio State group found that considerably different weights were assigned to these two dimensions by the leader's immediate supervisor and by the employees reporting to the leader. Rather consistently, the immediate supervisor would give primary weight to Initiating Structure, whereas the employees would focus primarily on Consideration. Thus, being an effective leader is like balancing oneself on top of a rubber ball — the leader must look in one direction toward what is important to his or her superiors (Initiating Structure) while simultaneously looking in a different direction toward what is important to his or her employees (Consideration). Inasmuch as these two dimensions sometimes come into conflict, it would be easy to lose one's balance. The effective leader, however, is able to maintain his or her balance on top of the rubber ball.

Building on the results of the Ohio State Leadership Studies, Robert Blake and Jane Mouton developed the well known Managerial Grid. Translating Initiating Structure into "Concern for Production" and Consideration into "Concern for People" yields a two-dimensional diagram. With each of the two dimensions established on a 9-point scale, there are 81 possible leadership styles. For ease of communication, Blake and Mouton highlighted five specific leadership styles as "pure types": Impoverished Management (1,1), Authority-Obedience Management (9,1), Country Club Management (1,9), Organization Man Management (5,5), and Team Management (9,9).

There have been numerous studies conducted on the Managerial Grid. The basic question posed by many of these studies is: What is the relative effectiveness of the various leadership styles? On the basis of more than 20 years of research, one answer appears definitive: in terms of the effect on long-term organizational productivity, the 9,9 leadership style is the most effective.

Translating the Managerial Grid into a framework consistent with that used throughout this book results in the diagram shown in Figure 6. Again, using "Concern for Production" and "Concern for People" as the two basic dimensions of leadership, we can identify four distinct types of leaders: The Theory L leader (laissez-faire), the Theory X leader (autocratic), the Theory Y leader (benevolent), and the Theory Z leader (team).

We look next at the characteristics of these four types of leaders— as "pure types." Each type will be described in terms of the leader's management philosophy and how the philosophy is put into practice in carrying out the functions of management. We will let our four hypothetical leaders speak for themselves.

THE THEORY L LEADER

Philosophy of Management. "My philosophy of management is essentially one of noninterference: 'Leave them alone.' Working in a bureaucratic organization, there is not much that I can actually do to influence the overall operation. The policies and procedures of our organization are established by top management, and my job is to make certain that these policies and procedures are carried out. The best description of my function is that of 'information transmitter.' My job is to convey information from upper management to my

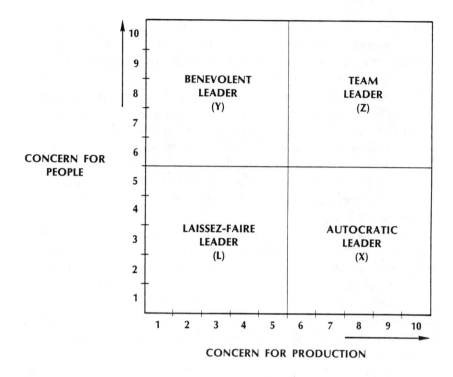

Figure 6. Two dimensions of leadership

employees. I believe that I should be evaluated on the basis of my being a good information transmitter."

Planning. "Any planning that affects my unit is done by top management. Beginning in July of each year our top management begins the annual planning process for the coming calendar year. This process is then completed in December, at which time I receive a summary of the annual plan. I then give copies of this summary plan to my people. But, in actuality, we do pretty much the same thing year after year, so the plan has little bearing on our actual operation."

Organizing. "We have an organizational structure that is established by top management. The organizational chart shows the chain of command and reporting relationships. We also have written job descriptions that describe the duties and responsibilities of every job. Authority for approvals and decision making are spelled out in the operations manual. My role in this area is to make certain that my people have all the written documentation that pertains to their jobs."

Staffing and Staff Development. "With regard to recruiting people for my unit, I pretty much accept the people assigned to me. These decisions are made by my management and the Personnel Department. With regard to training and staff development, I really don't see this as part of my job. It's up to the Personnel Department to provide training programs. With all of the paperwork I have to handle, I don't know how I would find time to do any staff development even if I were instructed to do so. But I do pass on a lot of information to my people; maybe this could be viewed as one form of staff development."

Motivating. "There is very little that I can do about motivating my employees. I believe that people are either motivated or they aren't. Motivation is something they bring with them to the organization. I do find, however, that some of the people in my unit seem to decline in their level of motivation after they have been with the organization for an extended period of time. This must be due to the nature of the overall organization. There's really not much that I can do about it."

Controlling. "My people pretty much know what's expected of them. The jobs are spelled out in writing, so there's no need for me to complicate the situation. Essentially, my employees serve as the controllers or regulators of their own jobs. Of course, if upper management informs me that somebody in my unit is not operating properly, then I do pass on this information to the appropriate party. In this sense I suppose that I serve somewhat as a controller."

"In summary, I would say that my approach to management is one of noninterference. I see to it that my people have the information they need to do their jobs, and then I let them do it. My basic philosophy is 'Don't rock the boat.'"

THE THEORY X LEADER

Philosophy of Management. "My philosophy of management is that I should direct my people toward the achievement of organizational objectives. To this end, I will do whatever is required. There are managers and there are non-managers. The organization pays me to manage, so I will manage. My primary focus is on productivity, and I will do whatever is required to attempt to maximize organizational productivity — insofar as I have some control of the situation."

Planning. "My organization has an annual planning process that begins in July of each year. In developing the plan for my unit, I begin with the guidelines and objectives provided by my immediate superior. I then go through a systematic process of developing a written plan — by stating measurable objectives, generating alternatives means for achieving the objectives, and allocating the budget. After discussing the plan with my immediate superior and making any necessary changes, I review the plan in detail with my people. I tell my people what is expected of the group as a whole and what I expect of each individual in the group. I view this planning process as an essential requirement for high productivity."

Organizing. "I view the organizing function as a logical step that follows the planning. The basic question that I must answer is: What kind of organizational structure do I need to carry out the plan? In answering this question, I develop an organizational structure that should give me the highest level of productivity. I try to adapt people to fit the structure. And when this doesn't work, I get rid of them."

Staffing and Staff Development. "I select people on the basis of their potential for making a substantial contribution to my group's objectives, and I assign them to specific tasks on the basis of the unit's needs. The heart of staff development is through 'stretching' my people through specific job assignments. I always give candid feedback to my employees so they will know what they must do to improve their performance. And, of course, I periodically weed out the weak ones and replace them with people who seem to have greater potential for contributing to my unit's overall productivity."

Motivating. "The only way to motivate people is through the carrot-and-stick approach. This is the approach used by all of the really effective managers in my organization. And it gets results. I hold out the carrot in the form of the possible salary increases and promotions, while at the same time I am carrying a big stick — in the form of KITA. And if neither works on a given employee, I simply get rid of the person. I do not believe in babying employees. If people need that kind of attention, they should get out of our kind of business."

Controlling. "I view controlling as a major part of my job. It is essential that my plans succeed, and the way to assure this is to establish tight controls. I insist on regular reports from each of my subordinates. I use these reports to compare actual performance with planned performance, and I make a careful analysis of any deviations. When subordinates are not performing according to plan, I instruct them on what must be done to effect the necessary changes. I then follow up very closely."

"In summary, I would describe myself as a production-oriented manager. I work hard and insist that my subordinates do likewise. My mission is to achieve the highest possible productivity with the resources that I have at my disposal. And to this end, I will do whatever is necessary."

THE THEORY Y LEADER

Philosophy of Management. "I truly believe that people are our most important resource. My philosophy of management is that I should serve as a facilitator for my people — my primary job is to help them achieve their goals. In my opinion, the most important goal of our organization is to provide employment for people and to help each employee achieve self-fulfillment. I view each employee as a unique human being with many potentialities to be realized. I would like to play a significant role in helping to convert this potentiality into an actuality."

Planning. "Our organization has an annual planning process that begins in July of each year. I first make a study of what resources are likely to be available to my unit. I then work with my people on a one-to-one basis to help them develop their own plans. And I give them a great deal of encouragement throughout the planning process. If one of my people comes up with a plan that is not actually supportive of the organization's overall plan, I do not object. In this way, I can foster initiative and motivation on the part of my people."

Organizing. "I believe that the organizational structure should be adapted to the people, rather than vice versa. Each of my people is a unique human being — with unique abilities, unique aspirations, and unique needs. So why should we try to fit people into molds? It seems to make much better sense to adapt the organization to the unique attributes of each employee."

Staffing and Staff Development. "I try to select people who will find satisfaction in our unit of the organization. In the employment interview, I attempt to find out the applicant's goals and aspirations in life. If there seems to be good fit between the applicant's goals and the opportunities provided by my group, then the chances are reasonably good that I will extend a job offer to the person. And I always try to assign my people to jobs they will like. With regard to staff development, I try to find out the interests of my people and then attempt to obtain the resources that will be needed to support their developmental efforts. I try to give my people encouragement in their staff-development efforts."

Motivating. "I believe that I can motivate people best by giving them encouragement. If I can provide the necessary support through a helping relationship, then I feel confident that each person will do his or her best. I learned years ago that praise is better than punishment, and this is what I practice. All that is needed by most people is a 'pat on the back.' And when this sometimes fails with a particular employee, I try to analyze where I might have gone wrong with this person."

Controlling. "It seems to me that, if given the proper tools, each employee should be able to control his or her own performance. Who is closer to the actual job situation than the employee? I see my job as one of providing the information and tools that each employee needs to carry out this control function. And I give each person a great deal of encouragement along the way."

"In summary, I am truly a people-oriented manager. I believe that every employee has considerable potential. If I can only provide the proper environment — through encouragement and praise — then this potential will be realized."

THE THEORY Z LEADER

Philosophy of Management. "As a manager, I have a commitment to both production and people. To me, there is no inherent conflict between the two. I view the job of management as one of bringing about a marriage between the goals of the organization and the goals of the employees. When this is achieved, we will achieve the highest degree of success — for both the organization and the individual employees. I believe that the best strategy for achieving this aim is *a team approach to achieving organizational objectives.*"

Planning. "Good planning is the cornerstone of our entire operation. Each year, our organization begins planning during July for the coming calendar year. As a first step in developing our unit's annual plan, my senior people and I make a thorough study of the overall organizational plans. Also, I usually ask a member of upper management to review these plans with my staff. My people and I then meet to lay out our unit's plans for the year. We first formulate the unit's goals and objectives and the strategies for achieving these goals and objectives. After receiving approval from upper management on our plan, I then meet with each of the people reporting to me to jointly develop the individual's performance objectives for the year. "

Organizing. "In our organizational unit, structure follows strategy. This means that our organizational structure is designed as a vehicle for carrying out our plans. After receiving approval on our annual plan, I meet with the senior staff of our unit to review the existing organizational structure and to decide what changes might be called for. In addition, we bring our job descriptions up to date each year. On the basis of these job descriptions and the performance objectives, each staff member has a reasonably good understanding of his or her primary responsibilities for the coming year."

Staffing and Staff Development. "Acquiring and building the staff probably is my most important function. In selecting new employees, my senior staff and I interview applicants and then jointly decide whether or not to extend job offers. The main point here is that the staff members who will be working most closely with the new employee participate in making the decision. Our staff development activities are guided by a career development program that involves all of our people. We view career planning as a continual dialogue between the employee and the immediate supervisor. Here we are trying to get a good fit between the present and projected needs of the organization and the aspirations of the individual employee."

Motivating. "The key to employee motivation is to seek a synergistic relation between the goals of the organization and the goals of the individual employee. By 'synergy,' I mean that the whole is greater than the sum of its parts. When the goals of the organization and the goals of the individual are mutually reinforcing, great things can happen. To bring this about, we need to have a good grasp of both the organization's goals and the individual's goals. Perhaps the most important thing about our group is that we have a team of people working cooperatively toward common goals. Here we see motivation at its best."

Controlling. "Controlling is the function that we carry out to make certain that our plans succeed. Underlying this controlling function is a detailed written plan and a management information system that provides us with accurate and timely data on our progress. An important point here is that information is made available to every person who needs it. To carry out the control function, our people meet at least monthly to compare performance with plan. We analyze the deviations and then decide what corrective measures are called for."

"In summary, I believe that my primary function as a manager is to build a team of people who are able to make good decisions and then successfully execute these decisions. I can think of no greater challenge than to build a group of individuals into a productive team — a team in which the members find a great deal of personal satisfaction in contributing to the achievement of organizational goals. To me, this is what management is all about."

AN EXAMPLE

To appreciate better the differences among the four styles of leadership just presented, it is worthwhile to consider an example. The situation is one which involves an important project that is on a tight schedule. The organizational structure for the project includes Marty as Project Leader and Jerry, Charlie, and Mary Lou as the three Task Leaders who report directly to Marty. The three tasks are closely linked: the output of Jerry's task serves as the input for Charlie's, and the output of Charlie's task serves as the input for Mary Lou's.

During the third month of this six-month project, it was necessary for Marty, the Project Leader, to be away for a two-week period. Upon his return, he discovers that the project is one week behind schedule. The delay is in Jerry's output, which was due to be given to Charlie on a specified date.

Now the question: Assuming that they were Marty, how would each of our hypothetical leaders deal with this situation?

The Theory L approach would be to do nothing. Feeling rather powerless and being committed to a doctrine of noninterference, this manager simply would not get involved. This is the ostrich dynamic — put your head in the sand and perhaps the problem will disappear. As most managers know, the problem will not fade away; it will only get worse.

The Theory X approach would be to immediately "ride herd." A quick diagnosis of the situation would be made by the Project Leader and immediate corrective action would be demanded. Perhaps Jerry would be removed from the position of Task Leader. "This will teach those so-and-so's not to fall down on the job when I am away!"

The Theory Y approach would be to play an active part in trying to get the project back on schedule. This leader would be confident that the Task Leaders were trying to do their best and that there must have been something beyond their control that caused the delay. "Perhaps I could come into work over the next several evenings and try to get the project back on schedule."

The Theory Z approach would be to immediately involve all three Task Leaders in a group problem-solving effort. Under the guidance of the Project Leader, the group would address itself to these questions: What is the problem? What is the cause of the problem? What can we do to correct the problem? Emerging from this session would be a concrete plan of action for solving the problem — a plan developed by the group. The Project Leader then would monitor the situation closely until the problem was solved.

Which of these four approaches is likely to be most effective? In this context, "effective" means achieving results by getting the project back on schedule. The answer should be unequivocable. Theory Z will win out for two reasons. By involving the Task Leaders in the problem-solving process, the *quality* of the solution will be upgraded and the *commitment* on the part of the Task Leaders to implement the agreed-upon solution will be substantial.

RESULTS OF DIFFERENT LEADERSHIP STYLES

Numerous empirical studies have been conducted to ascertain the relative effectiveness of different leadership styles. Much of the pioneering work was carried out by Rensis Likert and his associates at the University of Michigan's Survey Research Center.[71] Perhaps the most lucid summary of the extensive research on leadership styles has been presented by Robert Blake and Jane Mouton in *The New Managerial Grid*. It is worthwhile to review some of the key findings of these studies.

Theory L Leadership is found in a number of different settings: government agencies in which the administrators feel overwhelmed by the bureaucracy; hospitals in which the administrators feel dominated by the physicians; public school systems in which building principals assume that all decisions of any significance will be made by the central office; and research laboratories in which the administrators view "management" negatively in terms of regulating and controlling — which obviously will "inhibit creativity." All of these situations may be described as "missing management." The employees are left alone "to do their own thing." This type of management (or better said, "non-management") leads to a number of undesirable outcomes:

- Collaborative efforts between or among employees will probably never occur because there is no one actively promoting or capable of coordinating such efforts.
- Those employees who might find it difficult to obtain other employment may remain in the organization, but high achievers will leave.
- Some employees who have potential for becoming high performers will sink into the Theory L quadrant because whatever they might do with regard to improving their performance "really doesn't make much difference."
- Productivity, however measured, will be low, very low.

Theory X Leadership abounds in the business/industrial setting. In any organization that is profit oriented and has a short-term time perspective, Theory X leadership seems to be prevalent. With short-term financial objectives serving as the chief driving force, it seems only natural to *drive* the employees toward accomplishing these objectives. Theory X leadership is likely to produce the following results:

- The quality of decisions will suffer because the manager did not solicit ideas from his or her staff.
- The commitment of the staff members will be minimal because they were not involved in those decisions that influence their work.
- Job satisfaction of employees will be low.
- Absenteeism and voluntary turnover will be high.
- Some employees will suffer from psychosomatic illnesses as a result of job stress.
- Workers will join together to form unions.

69

Theory Y leadership is found in organizations that are not in a competitive environment and that have kindly managers. Blake and Mouton appropriately use the term "country club" to refer to this type of management because this term suggests a type of organization established simply for the sake of "having fun" rather than for the purpose of achieving concrete objectives. In settings other than country clubs, Theory Y leadership is likely to produce the following results:

- Low-achieving employees may find the environment satisfying because they are never criticized.
- Achievement-oriented employees may be impressed initially with the psychological support they receive from their supervisor, but will then become disillusioned when they discover that little emphasis is placed on productivity.
- Creativity will suffer because the clash of ideas necessary for its realization will be "smoothed over."
- Theory Y leadership will not survive in a competitive environment.

Theory Z leadership is found in a few enlightened organizations. These are the organizations that have a long-term perspective of their goals and responsibilities. These are the organizations that have a genuine concern for both production and people and view these two concerns as mutually reinforcing. Theory Z leadership is likely to produce the following results:

- Absenteeism and voluntary turnover will be relatively low.
- Quality of decisions will be high because of the wide involvement of employees in the decision-making process.
- Commitment and motivation will be high because of the active involvement of employees in problem solving and decision making.
- Creativity and innovation will be higher than that found with any of the other styles of leadership.
- Cooperation rather than competition will prevail.
- In terms of financial measures, short-term productivity may not be impressive because needed investments are made in facilities, research and development, and staff development.
- Long-term productivity will be higher than that found with any of the other styles of leadership.

It is clear from these summary results that Theory Z leadership is superior to the other forms of leadership. This obvious conclusion then raises the obvious question: Why is it that so few managers actually practice Theory Z leadership? This is a good question for the reader to reflect on.

COMMON QUESTIONS ABOUT LEADERSHIP STYLES

In the course of conducting management workshops, the author has been asked a number of thought-provoking questions about leadership styles. The questions most frequently asked and the author's answers are presented below. The reader is encouraged to form his or her own answer to each question.

1. **Are leaders born rather than made?**
   Because a person's leadership style is linked closely to his or her personality, it might appear that leaders are born rather than made. But personality is primarily a function of the environmental forces acting upon the individual. Inasmuch as these environmental forces have their primary impact during the early years of a person's life, personality is fairly well "set" by the time a person enters the world of work. Three genetically-influenced factors — intelligence, physical stamina, and physical height — do contribute to leadership ability. Thus, we must conclude that leadership ability is a function of both heredity and environment. Leaders are both born and made.

2. **Shouldn't one's leadership style be modified to fit the situation?**
   The answer to this question is a qualified "yes." As Maslow says in *Eupsychian Management*, "The best approach to management is that which best fits the objective requirements of the objective situation." But we must make a distinction between the contingency/situational leader and the Theory Z leader.

   The situational leader looks at a particular situation and then decides which leadership style (L, X, Y, or Z) is most appropriate for handling it. The only *strategy* held by the situational leader is to choose the appropriate tactic for a given situation. As an "other-directed" person, the situational leader

71

simply responds to the demands of a given situation. This type of leader is "eclectic" in the best sense of the term.

Now the Theory Z leader also looks at a particular situation and decides which leadership style (L, X, Y, or Z) is most appropriate for handling the situation. But, in contrast to the situational leader, the Theory Z leader is an "inner-directed" person who has a unified philosophy of management. This leader is guided by both the situation *and* his or her own internal gyroscope. Even though the tactics selected at particular times may reflect a variety of leadership styles, the overall strategy is always pointed toward Theory Z. Recognizing that employees are at different rungs on the developmental hierarchy, the Theory Z leader knows that the tactics will have to be appropriate to their positions on the hierarchy. Here is the key point: *The Theory Z leader is constantly trying to help the employees move up the developmental heirarchy so that they will be responsive to Theory Z leadership* (e.g., not be afraid of freedom and be willing to assume responsibility). Thus, while the situational leader is likely to view employees only in terms of where they *are*, the Theory Z leader views them in terms of where they *are* and where they *should be*. By trying to create conditions that will foster responsiveness to Theory Z leadership, the Theory Z leader is confirming employees in the terms of both their actuality and their potentiality.

Here is an illustration of the salient difference between the two types of leaders:

- **Situational Leader:** "My people are behaving like animals. This situation must be corrected pronto. I'll show them that I can be the best Theory X leader in the whole damn organization!"
- **Theory Z Leader:** "Our people are behaving in an undesirable manner. This situation must be corrected immediately. I wonder *why* they are behaving as they are. We must get at the root causes and deal with the causes so that they will begin to act in a more mature and responsible manner."

3. **Can a person function as a Theory Z leader in a Theory X environment?**

After participating in a workshop on leadership styles, many managers would respond to this question by saying, "I would like to be a Theory Z leader but my boss is a pure Theory X." One thing in favor of managers who find themselves in such a predicament is that both types of managers have at least one thing in common: a concern for productivity. Thus, if the junior manager is able to achieve the level of productivity demanded by the senior manager, the junior manager should be able to practice a leadership style considerably different from that practiced by the senior manager.

Though it is possible to function as a Theory Z leader in a Theory X environment, it certainly is more difficult than it would be in a Theory Z environment. It is more physically and psychologically "draining" for the person desirous of being a Theory Z leader. What frequently happens in such situations is that the junior manager tries to serve as a buffer between the senior manager and the junior manager's staff. It obviously would be better for all concerned if a Theory Z environment prevailed throughout the organization.

4. **Why is it that some managers who are clearly Theory X leaders make it all the way to the top?**
   In many cultures, the Theory X model has been accepted implicitly as the most effective leadership style and perhaps as the *only* way to really manage. Many people apparently believe that *autocratic* leadership and *effective* leadership are one and the same. It would follow from this notion that upper-level managers would view Theory X as the preferred mode of functioning. If these upper-level managers function in a Theory X mode, they would tend to select and reward younger managers who function in the same way. Thus, a general Theory X environment promotes and reinforces Theory X management all the way down the line. Only in recent years, primarily because of the impact of Japanese management, have managers begun to ask: Is there a better way of managing?

5. **What should I do to become a more effective leader?**
   It is important to understand that the development of one's leadership ability must be viewed as a long-term, if not life-long, program. It cannot be done overnight. Though it is no easy task to change one's leadership style, it can be done. A

73

recommended strategy involves the following five steps:

- First, attempt to achieve an understanding of your present leadership style through the use of such inventories as the Managerial Grid and assessments by your immediate supervisor and your staff. (As the Greek sage suggested, "The first step to wisdom is to know thyself.")
- Second, form a clear model — or mental picture — of the type of leader you would like to become.
- Third, develop a specific plan for moving from where you are toward the model.
- Fourth, carry out the plan on a daily basis.
- Fifth, review your progress at the end of each day. What did I do well today? Where did I go astray? What should I do tomorrow to bring about improvement?

If this strategy is carried out conscientiously, say for a 12-month period, considerable improvement in one's leadership style could be achieved. During this "early growth" period, it is important not to get down on yourself if you have a bad day. Keep your long-term goal in mind and make a new attempt the next day.

During the early part of this century, the famous psychologist-philosopher William James suggested that the most significant psychological insight of that era was the realization that people could change themselves — that the human person was both marble and sculptor. Now, almost a century later, we must be reminded of this insight. With clear vision and solid determination, it is possible for a manager to alter his or her leadership style. People indeed can change themselves!

SUMMING UP

Following the lead of Koontz and O'Donnell, this chapter has defined leadership as the art or process of influencing people so that they will strive willingly toward the achievement of group goals. This art of leadership can be viewed in terms of two basic dimensions: concern for production and concern for people. Arranging these two dimensions as orthogonal axes produces four types of leaders as "pure types": Theory L (laissez-faire), Theory X (autocratic), Theory Y (benevolent), and Theory Z (team). A summary of these four leadership styles is presented in Table 4.

In terms of effect on overall organizational productivity, the Theory Z leadership style is superior to the other three styles in most situations (but not necessarily in all).

Those enlightened organizations that desire to promote Theory Z leadership should give due consideration to three important requirements: (1) Theory Z leaders are healthy personalities — they are effective human beings in the best sense of the term; (2) the cultivation of Theory Z leaders is facilitated greatly if managers function in a Theory Z environment; and (3) young managers need role models to emulate if they are to become Theory Z managers.

In our efforts to cultivate Theory Z leadership, we should heed the wisdom of Peter Drucker[23, pp. 462-63] when he says:

> For the spirit of an organization is created from the top. If an organization is great in spirit, it is because the spirit of its top people is great. If it decays, it does so because the top rots; as the proverb has it, "Trees die from the top." No one should ever be appointed to a senior position unless top management is willing to have his (or her) character serve as the model for his (or her) subordinates.

Table 4. A Summary of Leadership Styles

	THEORY L LAISSEZ-FAIRE	THEORY X AUTOCRATIC	THEORY Y BENEVOLENT	THEORY Z TEAM LEADER
(1) PHILOSOPHY OF MANAGEMENT				
(2) PLANNING	Passes plans from upper management to staff.	Develops the plan and instructs staff how to execute it.	Helps staff members develop their plans.	Uses a team approach in developing the plan.
(3) ORGANIZING	Distributes organizational chart and job descriptions to staff.	Adapts people to fit the organizational structure.	Adapts organizational structure to fit the people.	Uses a team approach in establishing an appropriate organizational structure and responsibilities.
(4) STAFFING AND STAFF DEVELOPMENT	Leaves it up to the Personnel Department.	Uses stretch assignments and weeds out poor performers.	Selects people who will find satisfaction in the unit.	Uses a team approach in personnel selection and staff development.
(5) MOTIVATING	Does not get involved in the motivational area.	Carrot-and-stick approach.	Provides a helping relationship and gives encouragement.	Seeks a synergistic relation between goals of the organization and goals of the individual.
(6) CONTROLLING	Allows staff to control their own performance.	Monitors closely and instructs staff in how to take corrective action.	Provides the tools that are needed by the staff.	Uses a team approach in analyzing deviations and deciding upon corrective action.

Exercise III

Becoming a More Effective Leader

A. Write a brief description of your typical leadership style (in reference to Theory L, Theory X, Theory Y, and Theory Z).

B. List five personal goals that will help you become a better Theory Z leader.

IV

Participative Management

Over the past fifteen years, the role of the manager has changed significantly in many organizations. The strong manager capable of almost single-handedly turning around an organization or department, while still a folk hero in the eyes of many, has given way to the recent demands of increasingly complex systems for managers who are able to pull together people of diverse backgrounds, personalities, training, and experience and weld them into an effective working group.

William Dyer
Team Building[25, p. xi]

Introduction • Theoretical Framework • Organizational Climate • The Productive Team • Productive Meetings • Participative Decision Making • Team Problem Solving • Conflict Resolution • Team Development • Summing Up

---

INTRODUCTION

In recent years, there have been significant changes in the demands on management. We have seen changing expectations in the labor force, rapidly changing technology, an oscillating economy, and evergrowing governmental regulations. If it is to survive, the modern-day organization must stay abreast of these changing demands and cope with them.

The autocratic manager cannot cope with these changing

demands single-handedly. The job of management is too complex to be carried out effectively by a single person at the helm. The times are calling for an alternative approach to management.

Participative management is the proposed alternative to autocratic management. The idea of truly sharing the management function has considerable merit. Rather than a single person attempting to manage a group or an entire organization, why not share the management function?

The purpose of this chapter is to present the salient features of participative management. We will begin with a theoretical framework, including a definition of participative management, and then discuss specific ways in which the theoretical framework can be put into practice.

THEORETICAL FRAMEWORK

Participative management has different meanings to different people. It is important first to state what participative management is *not*. It is not management by committee, which involves an *ad hoc* group established to deal with a particular problem or issue but without adequate resources or authority. It is not pure democratic management, which involves putting issues up for vote. It is not merely consultative management, which is a one-to-one approach between the superior and the subordinate.

Participative management is defined here as *a team approach to management*. The members of the team, under the guidance of a leader, actively participate in making decisions and solving problems that influence their work. Responsibility for the outcome of any decision made by the group remains on the shoulders of the leader. The leader has the prime responsibility for building a team that can make good decisions and then successfully execute these decisions.

An illustration of participative management is found in the way in which a project planning activity might be carried out. An autocratic approach would be for the team leader, working alone, to develop the plan and, then, to direct his or her team members to execute the plan. In a participative approach, the leader truly involves the team members in formulating the plan. The members of the team and the leader may spend an extended period of time work-

80

ing together in a conference room to develop the plan. The leader clearly communicates the conditions that must be satisfied in terms of objectives, deliverables, schedule, budget, etc. The members of the team — as a team — then proceed to construct the plan. If the participants get "off track," it is the responsibility of the leader to get them back on course. The product emerging from this effort should be a *team product* in the best sense of the term, created through a joint effort of the team members. Here we find participative management at its best.

The essence of participative management is found in authentic two-way communication. Many are the managers who apparently believe that the mere transmission of information constitutes communication. However, we must be reminded of the root word of communication, which is "commune," and "to commune" means "to share," which is truly a two-way activity.

A framework for participative management may be constructed by focusing on two types of communication — downward communication and upward communication. By representing these two types of communication as orthogonal axes, Figure 7 reveals four types of communication: abstention (Theory L), orders and edicts (Theory X), suggestion system (Theory Y), and dialogue (Theory Z).

"Abstention" means that the members of an enterprise simply abstain from getting involved in any meaningful communication. Each individual goes his or her own way, hardly acknowledging the existence of other persons. Perhaps there are a few enterprises in which this type of behavior is acceptable, but in most, it will prove to be highly counterproductive.

"Orders and edicts" means that upper management transmits to those below specific commands and directives that are to be carried out. Perhaps the only communication on the part of the subordinates is to ask occasionally for clarification and to report when the work is completed. With this type of communication, we can expect the subordinates to do just about what is expected of them, no more and no less. They may comply but without enthusiasm or commitment.

"Suggestion system" refers to a form of upward communication promoted by a number of organizations — namely, the use of a suggestion box in which employees can place their written recommendations. When used sincerely, this form of communication does convey to employees that management has an interest in their ideas and

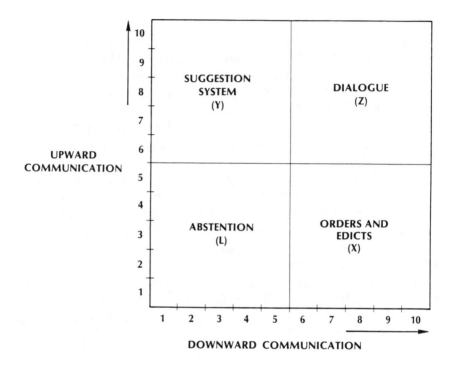

Figure 7.   Two dimensions of participation

recommendations. The problem with the suggestion-box type of communication is that it is impersonal because it simply involves an individual employee sending written communication to some anonymous member of upper management.

"Dialogue" means genuine two-way communication between the members of an organization. Thoughts and feelings are expressed openly and honestly by all members of the organization. The members listen to each other! When observed in practice, this form of communication is beautiful to behold and seems to be a miracle because of its infrequency.

Genuine dialogue is at the heart of participative management. Assuming that the members of an organization are sufficiently mature to function in this type of environment, dialogue will yield greater productivity than any of the other forms of communication.

ORGANIZATIONAL CLIMATE

What are the characteristics of the organization in which participative management prevails? Rensis Likert and his associates at the University of Michigan researched this question extensively for a great number of years. The findings of this research are reported in the book *The Human Organization*.[71] Some of the key points made by Likert in characterizing the participative organization are summarized below:

1. **Confidence and trust prevail throughout the organization.** Management has trust in the employees, and the employees have trust in management. Whenever management presents something in words — either orally or in writing — this communication is perceived by the employees as being true. Because the actions of managers are consistent with their words, managers have considerable credibility in the eyes of the employees. Confidence and trust are an outcome of authenticity.

2. **Staff feel completely free to discuss their job problems with their supervisor.** Employees in a Theory X organization are reluctant to discuss their job problems with their supervisor because they fear that this would be a sign of ineptitude and would make them vulnerable to criticism. Standing in sharp contrast, employees in a Theory Z organization feel completely free to present their job problems to their supervisor without fear of recrimination. The employee has no apprehension about entering the supervisor's office and saying, "I've got a problem. Can you help me out?"

3. **There is group participation in goal setting.** The Theory Z organization is guided by clearly defined goals and objectives. Rather than being defined by the superior, the goals and objectives of an organizational unit are developed jointly by members of the unit. The outcome of this approach is a feeling of ownership on the part of all group members — "These are *our* goals and objectives."

4. **Personnel at all levels feel real responsibility for organization's goals.** In the Theory X organization, only members of upper management feel any real responsibility for the achievement of the organization's goals. The situation is considerably dif-

83

ferent in the Theory Z organization, in which both the employees and the members of management share a feeling of responsibility for achieving the organization's goals. The common feeling is that "We all have a stake in the success or failure of the organization. Each person can make a meaningful contribution to the success of the organization — be it a secretary, a machinist, or a supervisor."

5. **Information flow is down, up, and with peers.** Open and honest communication prevails throughout the organization. Accurate information flows in three directions: from upper management to staff all the way down the line, from employees to management, and across organizational units. Each staff member has access to whatever information he or she needs to get the job done. People are not afraid to ask questions!

6. **There is very substantial cooperative teamwork throughout the organization.** The climate of the Theory Z organization promotes cooperation among all members of the enterprise. The common belief is: "We are in this together. To achieve our common goals, it will benefit all concerned if we work *with* each other rather than *against* each other." A win-win attitude prevails throughout the organization.

7. **Staff members are actively involved in key decisions that influence their work.** Prior to making important decisions that will influence the work of employees, managers actively involve their employees in these decisions. Important issues are presented and discussed — the more important the decision, the more extensive the discussions. Ideas and reactions from the parties that will be affected by the decisions are actively sought. The managers truly listen to the reactions and suggestions offered.

8. **Responsibility for review and control is widespread.** A productive organization is sensitive to the importance of the review and control function to make certain that the plans succeed. In the Theory X organization, the review and control function is carried out essentially by management, which dictates to those below the proper procedures for corrective action. In the Theory Z organization, the responsibility for review and control is shared by all staff — managers and employees alike.

9. **Control data are used for self-guidance and coordinated problem solving.** Theory X managers analyze control data, develop plans for corrective action, and then issue orders for execution of the plans. In contrast, Theory Z managers make the control data available to all concerned parties and then work *with* their people in analyzing the data and deciding on corrective action.

10. **Formal and informal organizations are one and the same.** The formal organization defines how things are *supposed* to be done; the informal organization represents how things *actually* are done. If these two aspects of an organization are at odds with each other, the enterprise is in trouble. In the Theory Z organization, the informal organization is a mirror of the formal organization — each supports and reinforces the other.

These 10 descriptions are an excellent summary of the general climate of the participative organization. The author's own research has used these ten items for assessing organizational climate in a number of different organizations. A simple procedure is to ask the respondents to evaluate their own organization on a 1-to-5 scale, with 5 representing "excellent" and 1 representing "very poor." The item scores are then added to produce a composite score for each respondent. With a perfect score being 50, scores from individual respondents have ranged from a low of 15 to a high of 48. Based upon the author's own observations of the organizations being evaluated, it can be asserted with considerable confidence that there is a close connection between the scores on the inventory and the overall productivity of the organization being evaluated.

THE PRODUCTIVE TEAM

The basic unit of the Theory Z organization is a team of dedicated people working toward common goals. Such teams exist throughout the organization, and there are numerous overlapping teams involving individuals serving on multiple teams. The teams are productive — they get results.

Douglas McGregor was an astute observer of teams in organizations. He was able to identify the salient characteristics of productive teams.[88] It is useful to review these characteristics.

1. **The atmosphere is relaxed; people are involved and interested.** The members of the productive team are truly involved in what they are doing; no one is simply an "observer." Each member manifests considerable interest and enthusiasm in the task at hand. To the outside observer, it appears as though these dedicated persons would prefer to do what they are presently engaged in rather than anything else. They are involved in the task at hand because they *want* to be involved in it.

2. **Virtually everyone participates in goal-directed discussions.** Whenever meetings are held, there is little or no ambiguity concerning purpose and goals. Each meeting has a clearly defined objective and discussion is directed toward achieving the objective. Should an extraneous matter be introduced, the team members gently bring the offender back on track by directing his or her attention to the primary objective of the meeting. Virtually everyone makes a contribution in helping the group achieve the specified objective.

3. **The objectives of the group are well understood and accepted by the members.** The team has clearly defined objectives toward which its activities are directed. Each team member has a clear understanding of the objectives and how his or her activities contribute to the objectives. Because all team members participate in formulating the group's objectives, the objectives are accepted by the members.

4. **The members listen to each other.** Each member of the team truly listens to the other team members. These team members are open-minded persons who desire to understand the different points of view of the other members. They do not merely "hear" their associates; rather, they listen with understanding. An observer of these groups would be inclined to believe that good listening is contagious because every new member who joins the group seems to manifest good listening skills.

5. **Disagreement is openly expressed.** Being independent thinkers, the members of the productive team openly express their disagreements with each other. They feel free to disagree with both their peers and their leader. In fact, they are courageous enough even to disagree with their own ideas put forth at some previous time. The disagreement has a construc-

tive purpose, which is to find the best possible solution to whatever problem is confronting the group.

6. **Most decisions are reached by a kind of consensus.** Whenever an important decision is to be made, the leader actively involves those team members who are likely to be affected by the outcome of the decision. Discussion of the issue at hand is continued until every participant is given the opportunity to express his or her feelings about the issue. Throughout the discussion, the leader intermittently checks for a group consensus. At a certain point in time, the leader decides the time has come for committing to a particular course of action. Those who continue to disagree with the chosen alternative nevertheless will commit themselves to supporting the decision.

7. **Criticism is frequent, frank, and relatively comfortable.** Members of the productive team have "the courage to confront." They feel free to criticize the ideas of their peers as well as those of their leader. But this criticism is constructive! Its sole purpose is to help in the improvement of ideas and actions. It is important to note that the criticism is directed toward ideas and issues, not toward personalities. The individual members of the group realize that they have reached a fairly high rung on the developmental ladder when they can readily accept — and even welcome — criticism from their peers.

8. **People are free in expressing their feelings as well as their ideas.** Members of the team feel free in expressing their own ideas regardless of how "far out" these ideas may seem to be. They realize that most truly creative ideas seem "far out" when they are first introduced. These members also feel free to express their feelings, whether they are positive feelings (such as joy) or negative feelings (such as fear). Members of the productive team understand and appreciate that they can "be themselves."

9. **When action is to be taken, clear assignments are made and accepted.** Whenever action is to be taken, it is crystal clear who is to do what and when. There is no ambiguity regarding assignments and responsibilities. Again, because the affected parties were involved in making the decision that is to be executed, the assignments are fully accepted.

10. **The leader does not dominate the group.** The productive team has a visible leader, and the importance of the leadership function is readily acknowledged by all members. However, the leader of the group does not dominate it; rather he or she leads by helping the group become a productive team. Indeed, there are times when the leader must communicate the conditions and constraints that must be satisfied and occasionally may find it necessary to keep the group on course. In this context, the leader is serving more as a facilitator than as a regulator or controller.

11. **The group is self-conscious about its own operation.** The productive team is sensitive to how it functions as a team. All members understand the close connection between their effectiveness as a team and their effectiveness as individuals. As a result of this awareness, they occasionally review and discuss how they are functioning as a team. The team members are receptive to constructive suggestions for improvement as well as to any ideas that will help them become a more productive team.

This list of attributes is an excellent summary of the productive team. Just as with the previous list of items describing the climate of the participative organization, the author has used these statements formulated by McGregor to construct an inventory of team functioning. Again, each item was evaluated on a 1-to-5 scale. With a perfect score being 55, composite scores recorded by individuals in evaluating their own teams have ranged from a low of 11(!) to a high of 53. Follow-up interviews and observations have revealed a close connection between scores on the inventory and the actual productivity of the team.

PRODUCTIVE MEETINGS

Meetings are an essential activity of the productive team. Inasmuch as people spend such a large amount of their working lives attending meetings, it is important that these gatherings be both effective and efficient — that is, that they achieve their objectives and that they make good use of the participants' time.

There are four basic types of meetings: (1) meetings for information giving, (2) meetings for information collection, (3) meetings for decision making, and (4) meetings for problem solving. In addition to these four purposes, meetings also play an important role in building a diverse group of individuals into a cohesive team.

There are a number of practical guidelines for conducting productive meetings. The conscientious application of these guidelines should increase the effectiveness and efficiency of the bulk of most meetings by as much as 50 percent.

Guidelines for conducting productive meetings include the following:

1. **Write the objective of the meeting.** What is the purpose of the meeting? What is the desired outcome? Why is the meeting being called? Write in one single sentence the objective of the meeting.

2. **Decide what kind of meeting it will be.** The selection of a general approach to be used in the meeting should be based on the objective to be accomplished. The approach might be information giving, information collection, decision making, problem solving, or some combination of these approaches.

3. **Decide who should attend the meeting.** A common mistake is to invite too many people to the meeting by inviting anyone who might have an interest in the subject at hand. Normally, the leader should invite only those persons who are expected to make a significant contribution to the meeting or are expected to be actors in carrying out the decisions made at the meeting. Others who have only a peripheral interest in the subject should be sent minutes of the meeting.

4. **Decide on the time and place of the meeting.** Choose a time for the meeting that will not seriously disrupt a person's day, such as 8:00–9:00 a.m., 11:00–12:00 a.m., 1:00–2:00 p.m., or 4:00–5:00 p.m. Let all participants know in advance the starting time and the ending time of the meeting. Choose a location that provides privacy and is geographically convenient for the majority of participants.

5. **Decide what work should be done before the meeting.** Many meetings fail because of lack of preparation on the part of the leader and the participants. Perhaps certain written materials should be studied by all participants prior to the meeting in order to have fruitful discussion of this informa-

89

tion. It is the leader's responsibility to make certain that this pre-meeting homework is done.

6. **Prepare and disseminate an agenda.** One of the most useful tools for assuring an effective and efficient meeting is an agenda, which should include topics to be covered and estimated time allocations for the various topics. A useful procedure is for the leader to prepare a tentative agenda and request modifications from the participants.

7. **Create a climate for active and responsible participation.** The leader has the responsibility for creating a climate that encourages active participation on the part of all the participants in the meeting (unless, of course, the meeting is being held simply for transmitting information). The leader should not allow one or two aggressive individuals to dominate the meeting. A useful technique is for the leader to say, as appropriate, "Now we've heard from Charlie. What do the rest of you think about this issue?"

8. **Evaluate the meeting.** To improve the effectiveness and efficiency of meetings, it is useful to evaluate them intermittently. At the close of a meeting, the leader might either ask for oral comments or distribute a printed evaluation sheet. The basic question is: "What should we do to have more productive meetings?"

9. **Prepare and distribute minutes of the meeting.** Too frequently the leader of a meeting simply relies on memory to assure compliance with the action items agreed upon during the meeting. Such a casual approach often leads to misunderstandings. Any meeting that generates action items should result in minutes — a brief narrative of who is to do what and when. These minutes should be distributed to all participants within 24 hours after the meeting.

10. **Follow up.** It is important to recognize that a meeting is only the beginning. Something is to take place following the meeting. It is the responsibility of the leader to follow up to make certain that this "something" actually happens.

It is obvious that the leader plays a crucial role in most meetings. Richard Schmuck[105, p. 244] lists the following leadership functions: (1) setting goals, (2) proposing problems, (3) asking for information, (4) giving information, (5) proposing solutions, (6) asking for clarification, (7) giving clarification, (8) testing for consensus, (9) supporting, (10) asking about group progress, (11) summarizing, and (12) evaluating. It is important that these functions be carried out in a Theory Z manner.

In their book *How to Make Meetings Work*,[22, p. 72] Michael Doyle and David Straus point up the importance of meetings for staff morale:

> When people leave meetings feeling good, the transition back to their jobs is easier. And when you feel good about your team and what it can do collaboratively, you tend to work harder on your own. It's a combination of not wanting to let the team down and feeling that your job is meaningful because it is necessary for the group's success.

PARTICIPATIVE DECISION MAKING

Effective decision making is the lifeblood of the productive organization. Managers make decisions every day; some turn out well and some turn out poorly. The question is raised: How should managers go about the decision-making process?

From a purely technical standpoint, the decision-making process should go something like this:

1. Clearly state the objective to be achieved.
2. Develop alternative solutions.
3. Identify the probable consequences of each alternative.
4. Rank the probable consequences in order of their desirability.
5. Select what appears to be the best alternative in view of Step 1 and Step 4.
6. Implement the chosen alternative.

From the standpoint of Theory Z management, managers should consider the framework for decision making provided by Robert Tannenbaum and Warren Schmidt. In their paper "How to Choose a Leadership Pattern,"[115] they present the "continuum of leadership behavior" shown in Figure 8. Boss-centered leadership is 100 percent on the far left and moves gradually to zero percent on the far right. Subordinate-centered leadership is 100 percent on the far right and moves gradually to zero percent on the far left. Along this continuum are seven different approaches for involving staff in the decision-making process. In terms of leadership style, the Theory X leader would be found on the far left of the continuum and the Theory

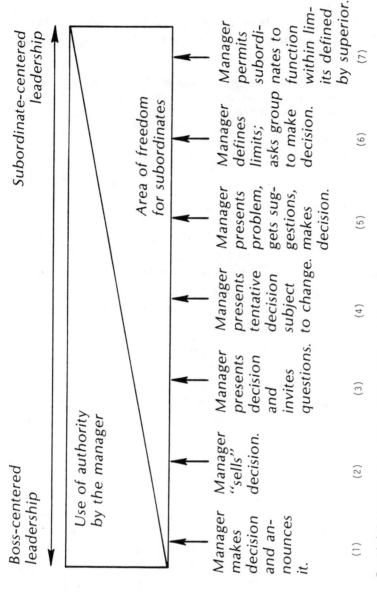

Boss-centered leadership

Subordinate-centered leadership

Use of authority by the manager

Area of freedom for subordinates

(1)	(2)	(3)	(4)	(5)	(6)	(7)
Manager makes decision and announces it.	Manager "sells" decision.	Manager presents decision and invites questions.	Manager presents tentative decision subject to change.	Manager presents problem, gets suggestions, makes decision.	Manager defines limits; asks group to make decision.	Manager permits subordinates to function within limits defined by superior.

Figure 8. A continuum of leadership behavior

L leader on the far right. The Theory Z leader might function at any one of the positions along the continuum, depending on the particular circumstances. Frequently, however, the Theory Z leader would be found functioning in modes 4 and 5.

"Two different dimensions seem to be relevant in appraising a decision's potential effectiveness," says Norman Maier.[78, p. 3] "One of these is the objective or impersonal quality of the decision, the other has to do with its acceptance or the way the persons who must execute the decision feel about it." Maier's classic equation for decision making is:

$$\text{Effective Decision} = \text{Quality} \times \text{Acceptance}$$
$$ED = Q \times A$$

An effective decision is defined as one that is *successfully executed*. To this end, both the quality of the decision and its acceptance by those persons who must execute it are important. With some decisions, the Q in the equation is more significant than the A; in others it may be just the reverse. In either case, the manager should keep in mind the importance of *participative* decision making, which can contribute substantially to both the quality and the acceptance of the decision.

TEAM PROBLEM SOLVING

Successful managers accept problems as "a way of life." That is why they are needed as managers. If there were no problems, they probably would not be needed in their present jobs.

Today there is a generally agreed upon strategy for problem solving. Essentially based on the scientific method, the strategy goes something like this:

1. Clearly state the problem.
2. Collect the facts.
3. Identify the causes of the problem.
4. Generate alternative solutions.
5. Evaluate the alternative solutions.
6. Develop a plan of action.
7. Implement the plan of action.

In carrying out this strategy, there is a significant difference between the approach used by the Theory X leader and that used by the Theory Z leader. The Theory X leader essentially works alone in carrying out Steps 1 through 6 and then instructs his or her people to implement the plan of action. In contrast, the Theory Z leader involves his or her people in the total seven-step process.

In his book *Team Building*,[25, p. vi] William Dyer makes special note of the current trend toward participative problem solving:

> The modern manager has shifted from dealing with problems on a one-to-one basis to solving more problems collectively by involving everyone who has a contribution to make in either solving a problem or implementing actions. In this context, the manager is a coach, a facilitator, a developer, a team builder.

CONFLICT RESOLUTION

The Theory Z manager views conflict as a necessary and important part of life. This manager is well aware of the problems associated with suppressing conflict, which is destructive for both the individual and the organization. The challenge for the manager is to direct the conflict toward creative and innovative solutions to problems, transforming a negative situation into a positive one.

In terms of different leadership styles, we can identify four distinct approaches to conflict resolution:

- The Theory L leader *ignores* the conflict: "If I just ignore the problem, maybe it will go away."
- The Theory X leader *suppresses* the conflict: "I won't tolerate that kind of behavior around here!"
- The Theory Y leader *smooths over* the conflict: "Come on now, we don't have any major differences. We are just one happy family."
- The Theory Z leader uses *problem solving*: "Let's get the problem out on the table and deal with it."

Anyone who has experienced all four of these approaches to conflict resolution undoubtedly will agree that the Theory Z approach is the most effective in most situations (not in *all* situations). As a team builder, the Theory Z leader views conflict resolution as an important part of his or her job. Through practical experiences gained in conflict resolution, this leader becomes an effective mediator between conflicting parties.

The Theory Z leader takes to heart the assumptions underlying conflict resolution as proposed by Roger Harrison in the paper "When Power Conflicts Trigger Team Spirit":[44]

1. Most people prefer a fair negotiated settlement to a state of unresolved conflict, and are they willing to invest some time and make some concessions in order to achieve a solution.
2. If the participants are willing to specify concretely the changes they desire from others, then significant changes in work effectiveness can usually be obtained.
3. Unless behavior changes on both sides the most likely result is that the status quo will continue.

There are times when a confrontation meeting is appropriate. It is better to get the issue out in the open and discussed rather than suppressed. In this situation, the manager's role is that of a mediator between two parties — either two individuals or two groups of people — who are involved in a serious conflict. Richard Beckhard[3] suggests the following agenda for a confrontation meeting:

1. Establish willingness to participate.
2. Get the attitudes and feelings out in the open.
3. Make total information available to all.
4. Develop a plan for resolving the problem.
5. Plan first actions and commitments.

As a management consultant serving in the role of a mediator, the author has made use of Beckhard's agenda in several confrontation meetings. It works! A vital step in the process is to develop with the two parties concrete action steps for the coming week. It is important to follow up with both parties to review progress and to develop additional action steps. Anyone experienced in this area probably would concur with Roger Harrison's observation: "Most people prefer a fair negotiated settlement to a state of unresolved conflict, and are willing to invest some time and make some concessions in order to achieve a solution."

The key to success in conflict resolution is for the two parties to focus on their commonalities. Typically, individuals and groups locked in conflict concentrate only on their differences. The mediator's task is to turn the situation around and get the two parties to focus on what they have in common. The participants should then be able to build on this foundation of commonality to achieve higher levels of creativity and innovation that will benefit both parties as well as the organization as a whole.

In simplistic terms, there are three attitudes toward conflict resolution: lose-lose, win-lose, and win-win. The win-lose attitude is all too common. Each party views the conflict situation in terms of a zero-sum game—if one party gains a certain amount of power, it is then assumed that the other party will lose a corresponding amount of power. A win-win attitude, however, suggests that cooperation between the parties will help both parties gain in power. The overall power circle actually expands! This is the Theory Z attitude.

Whenever we become discouraged by the prevalence of interpersonal or intergroup conflict, we should reflect on the following admonition by Abraham Maslow:[83, p. 34]

> Conflict is, of course, a sign of relative health as you would know if you ever met really apathetic people, really hopeless people, people who have given up hoping, striving, and coping.

TEAM DEVELOPMENT

William Dyer[25, p. 42] defines a team as a unified, cohesive group of people who have special functions, but each person needs the resources and support of others to get the job done. Dyer goes on to define team development:

> Team development in its best sense is creating the opportunity for people to come together to share their concerns, their ideas, and their experiences, and to begin to work together to solve their mutual problems and achievement goals.

The Theory Z manager devotes substantial time and energy to team development. Certainly the primary function of the group — production of goods or services—is very important, but the way in which the group operates as a team also is important because this supports and enriches the primary function. The Theory Z manager gives due attention to both productivity and process.

As a starting point in team development, it is useful to consider the relevant areas of concern noted by James Shonk in his book *Working in Teams.*[112] The five areas are:

1. **Organizational Climate** —To what extent does the organization create a climate for effective team functioning?
2. **Mission/Goals/Objectives** — How are the objectives set? Are they clear? Are they agreed to? Is there commitment?
3. **Roles** — Are roles clearly defined? Do all members know what others expect of them? Do roles overlap or conflict?
4. **Procedures** —What are the procedures for communication? Decision making? Conflict resolution?
5. **Relationships** —What is the nature of the relationships between the various team members and between the members and the leader?

The team-development process proposed by Shonk is presented in Figure 9. Step 1 involves defining the team and gaining an understanding of how team development can help. Step 2 involves making an analysis of existing team performance. The outcome of Step 3 is a specific plan of action for improving team performance. Step 4 involves implementing the plan of action. The purpose of Step 5 is to evaluate team functioning as a result of the actions taken and to determine what else needs to happen. The arrow from Step 5 to Step 3 suggests that team development should be an ongoing process.

On several occasions, the author has served as an outside facilitator for a team-development activity. On those occasions, he has found it beneficial to get the team away from the home site for at least one full day* during which it works through the first three steps of Shonk's strategy. A major outcome of the day's activity is a list of concrete action steps to be implemented during the coming weeks. The author's follow-up of these activities has revealed that teams indeed can bring about significant improvements in their performance if there is a will to do so. Perhaps the most rewarding aspect of working in this area is to find managers who begin to appreciate the importance of team development and to view it as a normal part of their job.

---

*If it is impractical for the team to be absent from the home site for a day, an alternative approach is to conduct the same exercise in three two-hour sessions in a conference room at the home site.

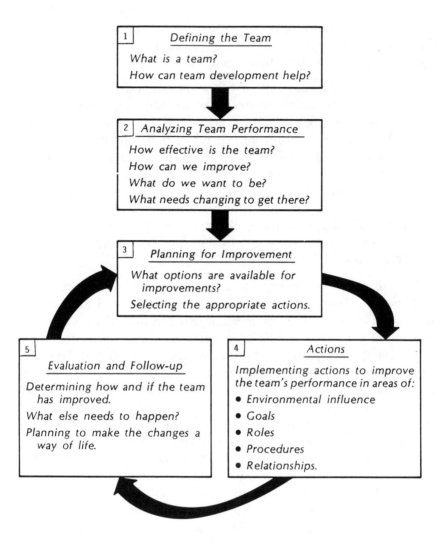

Figure 9.   The team development process

SUMMING UP

This chapter has pointed up the need for an alternative to autocratic management. The alternative proposed is participative management, which has been defined as *a team approach to management.* Members of the team, under the guidance of a leader, actively participate in decisions that influence their work. Responsibility for the quality of any decision and its successful execution remains on the shoulders of the leader. Thus, the leader's prime responsibility is to build a team that can make good decisions and then successfully execute them.

For any manager planning to introduce participative management into his or her group or organization, it is important to *proceed slowly.* If employees have been accustomed to a highly structured environment, a quick shift to a participative environment can be unsettling and counterproductive. To bring about the desired change in a nondisruptive manner, the manager should develop a plan for gradually introducing the concepts and methods of participative management. It is important to note that participative management does not mean that employees are involved in *all* decisions that influence their work. It does mean, however, that they are involved in *key* decisions that are likely to have some effect on their work.

Assuming that the manager is successful in introducing the concepts and methods of participative management, then a number of benefits should be realized. One would expect to find a greater sense of community among the members — an attitude of "We are in this together." Emerging with this sense of community should be improved communication, a higher degree of trust, and greater job satisfaction. Certainly one would expect to find improvement in both the quality and acceptance of decisions. All of which will lead to greater productivity for the organization.

In considering the advantages of participative management, we should reflect on the words of Douglas McGregor:[88, p. 242]

> Fads will come and go. The fundamental fact of (the human being's) capacity to collaborate with (his or her associates) in the face-to-face group will survive the fads and one day be recognized. Then, and only then, will management discover how seriously it has underestimated the true potential of its human resources.

Exercise IV

On the Practice of Participative Management

A.   What is your definition of participative management?

B.   What are some examples of participative management in your organization?

C.   List five things that you might do during the next 12 months to promote participative management in your group.

V

Management by Objectives

Perhaps the most powerful tool of managing that has so far
been put into practice is the system of managing by objectives. It is simple common sense in that it is a reflection
of managing itself. Without clear goals, managing is
haphazard and random and no group or individual can expect to perform effectively.

Harold Koontz
*"Shortcomings and Pitfalls in
Managing by Objectives"* [61, p. 6]

*Introduction • Theoretical Framework • MBO as a Comprehensive Ap-
proach to Management • The Management by Objectives Process • The
Objectives Hierarchy • Key Results Areas • Guidelines for Developing Objectives • Illustrations of Objectives • Summing Up*

INTRODUCTION

Koontz may be correct in his assessment of management by objectives (MBO). Many management tools seem to be merely fads: they
enter the scene with great fanfare, and then, after a few years of being in the limelight, they simply fade away. But management by objectives now has a history of more than a quarter of a century, with
books and articles on the subject running into the hundreds and
possibly thousands. Large numbers of organizations—both private
and public—have introduced some form of management by
objectives.

101

The purpose of this chapter is to describe the salient characteristics of management by objectives — both the theory and the practice. Emphasis will be placed on how management by objectives *should be implemented* in order to make it successful. Many managers would agree with Koontz that, if used according to the guidelines presented in the following pages, management by objectives indeed may be the most powerful tool of managing that has so far been put into practice.

THEORETICAL FRAMEWORK

Management by objectives may be defined as a comprehensive approach to management that includes statements of what is expected of every unit and every person involved and assessment of what is actually achieved. This definition contains three important elements: (1) it is a *comprehensive approach to management*; (2) it includes statements of what is expected of *every unit and every person involved*; and (3) it includes *assessment* of what is actually achieved.

In everyday language, George Odiorne[95, p. 58] has elucidated the value of management by objectives:

1. If you don't have a goal, you have no idea whether you are on the right road or not.
2. You can't assess results without some prior expectations against which to measure them.
3. You don't know when things are drifting if you aren't clear what goal would comprise "nondrifting" or purposive activity.
4. People can't perform with maximum effectiveness if they don't know what goals the organization is seeking (and why) or how well they are doing in relation to these goals.

In developing a set of objectives for an entire organization or for a unit within the organization, it is important to satisfy two important criteria: coherence and commitment. "Coherence" means that there is a logical and orderly relation of objectives. "Commitment" means that the persons responsible are motivated to achieve the objectives. Coherence without commitment is sterile; commitment without coherence is blind; but the uniting of coherence and commitment produces meaningful goals and the will to achieve the goals.

The attributes of coherence and commitment are related to two different approaches to developing objectives: top-down and bottom-

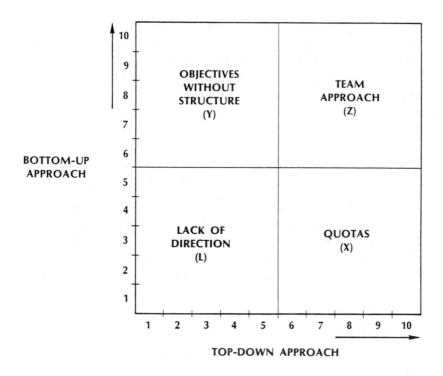

Figure 10. Two approaches to management by objectives

up. In the top-down approach, upper management first develops the organizational objectives and then passes them down to lower levels of management, with each level of management writing its objectives in the light of those written at the preceding level. In the bottom-up approach, first-level managers develop their objectives and then pass them up the ladder, with higher levels of management assuming the role of integrator. It should be noted that the top-down approach leads to greater coherence while the bottom-up approach leads to greater commitment.

The top-down and bottom-up approaches to management by objectives can be related to leadership style. Figure 10 shows the two approaches as orthogonal axes, with the top-down approach represented by the horizontal axis and the bottom-up approach represented by the vertical axis. The diagram reveals four possible organizational conditions: Theory L (low on both top-down and bottom-up approach) leads to lack of direction; Theory X (high on top-down approach but low on bottom-up approach) leads to upper management's establishing quotas for lower management; Theory Y (high on bottom-up approach but low on top-down approach) leads to objectives without structure; Theory Z (high on both top-down approach and bottom-up approach) leads to a team approach to developing objectives.

Based upon the results of empirical research as well as the experience of managerial practitioners, we can estimate the relative effectiveness of the four approaches to developing objectives:

1. The Theory L approach, which lacks both coherence and commitment, will be at the rock-bottom level of effectiveness.
2. The Theory X approach, which reflects coherence but lacks commitment, will be only marginally effective.
3. The Theory Y approach, which reflects commitment but lacks coherence, will be only marginally effective.
4. The Theory Z approach, which reflects both coherence and commitment, will be maximally effective.

The productive management system uses a Theory Z approach in developing objectives. By providing general direction from above, coherence is achieved. By seeking reactions and suggestions from those below, commitment is achieved. By involving all members of the management team in this important activity, the resulting objectives are characterized by both quality and acceptance.

MBO AS A COMPREHENSIVE APPROACH TO MANAGEMENT

An organization can be described and analyzed in terms of three classes of variables: inputs, activities, and outputs. These three terms have been defined clearly by George Odiorne:[95, p. 43]

1. **Inputs** are the resources committed to an idea to make it a tangible, going concern. They include capital (fixed, working, cash, receivables, inventories), labor, and materials.
2. **Activities** are the behaviors of people — designing, making, selling, keeping books, engineering, bargaining, and the like — which *add value* (presumably) to the inputs.
3. **Outputs** are the goods and services, hardware and software, that come out of the system. These outputs are more valuable

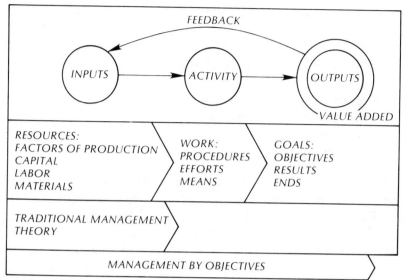

George Odiorne— *MBO II: A System of Managerial Leadership for the 80s.* Belmont, California, Fearon-Pitman Publishers, Inc., 1979. Reprinted, by permission of the publisher.

Figure 11. A systems view of an enterprise

than all of the inputs used up in the making, and a *value added* can be computed.

In terms of these three classes of variables, the introduction of management by objectives has had a profound influence on management thought. Prior to the introduction of MBO, traditional management theory focused on inputs and activities. After its introduction, management theory began to focus on outputs. Today, as indicated in Figure 11, a systems view of an organization calls for focusing on all three classes of variables and their interrelations. This change in management thinking can be attributed primarily to Peter Drucker and his longstanding emphasis on "managing for results."

Within the framework provided by this systems view of an organization, it must be emphasized that management by objectives is *a comprehensive approach to management* that applies to all of the functions of management. Namely:

- **Planning**— MBO forces planning and provides the skeleton outline for the operational plan.

- **Organizing** — MBO provides direction for how the enterprise should be organized and clarifies roles and responsibilities.
- **Staffing** — MBO provides guidance for what kind of people are needed and what knowledge and skills should be developed.
- **Motivating** — MBO provides direction for employee motivation and elicits commitment for action.
- **Controlling** — MBO provides milestones and standards for evaluating performance.

It is unfortunate that so many writers and managers view management by objectives only as a tool for performance appraisal. This indeed is a myopic view. To realize the full benefits of MBO, it is essential that this narrow view be replaced by a broader view that grasps all the ramifications of this powerful tool of managing. Whenever managers are thinking about management by objectives, they should think in terms of *a comprehensive approach to management*.

THE MANAGEMENT BY OBJECTIVES PROCESS

The traditional management by objectives process is fairly well agreed upon by the experts on the subject. Typically, this is a top-down approach that begins with upper management's formulating annual objectives for the organization as a whole. This is then followed by subordinate units — departments, sections, groups — formulating their objectives in the light of the organizational objectives. Next, each manager meets with each of his or her people on a one-to-one basis to mutually agree on the staff member's annual performance objectives. It is stressed by the experts that progress toward the objectives be reviewed periodically throughout the year and that there be a cumulative review at the end of the year. This overall strategy is logical and systematic but it suffers from at least two deficiencies.

One striking deficiency of the traditional approach to MBO has been the singular focus on its use of MBO as a tool for performance appraisal. As stated previously, management by objectives is a comprehensive approach to management that applies to *all* of the functions of management. To limit its use to performance appraisal is a corruption of the basic concept.

A second major deficiency of the traditional MBO approach has been its tendency to reinforce a one-to-one leadership style. The central feature of this approach has been the dialogue between the manager and individual staff members both in developing the annual performance objectives and in reviewing progress toward the objectives. In terms of Rensis Likert's four styles of management (exploitative-authoritative, benevolent-authoritative, consultative, and participative group), the traditional approach to MBO clearly epitomizes *consultative management* — a one-to-one approach that constitutes System 3 in Likert's hierarchy of leadership styles. Although we must agree that the consultative style is superior to either of the two authoritative styles, it nevertheless is one rung below System 4 — the participative group style.

A Theory Z approach to management by objectives can correct the deficiencies embedded in the traditional approach. With Theory Z as a framework, a recommended management by objectives process is outlined in Figure 12. The steps are summarized below:

- **Step 1. Preparation for MBO Process.** Prior to starting the annual MBO cycle, attention should be given to the preparation phase. If this is the organization's initial establishment of an MBO program, orientation and training should be provided for all members of the management team. If it is an annual repetition of a program already established, attention should be devoted to fine-tuning the program and establishing the MBO schedule for the coming year. In either case, the instructions for carrying out the program should be issued from *the office of the chief executive.* These instructions should stress that management by objectives is a comprehensive approach to management and that the sanctioned program is to provide a foundation and framework for carrying out *all* of the functions of management. Furthermore, it should be emphasized that active involvement in the MBO program is an integral part of each manager's job.

- **Step 2. Development of Organizational Objectives.** At the beginning of each new MBO cycle, it is appropriate for members of upper management to review the organization's mission and goals. Are they still relevant? Are any changes called for? After these questions are answered, the next step is to formulate the organization's key results areas for the coming year — based upon both opportunities and problems fac-

107

ing the organization. At least one objective then should be written for each of the key results areas. The compilation of these individual objectives forms the set of organizational objectives for the coming year. This set of objectives should be distributed to all members of the management team.

- **Step 3. Development of Department/Section/Group Objectives.** For the purposes of illustration, we will assume that the hierarchical designations for organizational levels are department–section–group, in that order, going down the hierarchy. After reviewing and discussing the organizational objectives, the departments develop their own key results areas and associated objectives. Next, the sections develop their key results areas and objectives, and then the groups do likewise. Each organizational level writes its objectives in the light of the objectives at the next higher level. A key point here is that each set of objectives is developed through a *participative team approach*. For example, the development of a given department's objectives would involve the department head and all of the section heads reporting to the department head. Similarly, the development of a group's objectives would involve the group leader and at least the senior-level people assigned to that group. The active involvement of the organizational members in this step makes participative management a reality. In addition to improving the quality of the objectives, a major benefit of this active involvement is that the participating members feel a sense of ownership in the objectives.

- **Step 4. Development of Performance Objectives.** In this step of the process every manager develops his or her own performance objectives for the coming year. This is a cooperative endeavor between the individual manager and the manager's immediate supervisor. (How far the MBO process is extended to involve other classes of employees is a question that must be answered by each organization.) The development of performance objectives should be based essentially on two considerations: (1) the objectives of the organizational unit of which the individual is a member and (2) the challenges and opportunities facing the individual staff member in his or her job. These performance objectives should be prepared in writing, and copies of the document should be given to both

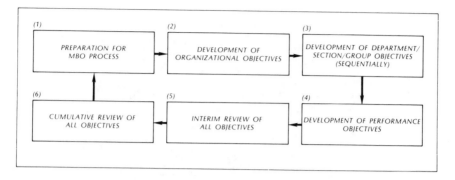

Figure 12. The management by objectives process

the participating member and the member's immediate supervisor.

- **Step 5. Interim Review of All Objectives.** There should be a periodic review (at least quarterly) of progress toward objectives throughout the year. This includes objectives written at all levels: organization, department, section, group, and individual. It is important that the objectives are not viewed as being " cast in concrete." Because of changing conditions, some objectives should be discarded or modified while others should be added. Management by objectives should be viewed as a dynamic process useful for dealing with an ever-changing environment.

- **Step 6. Cumulative Review of All Objectives.** At the end of the year, there should be a cumulative review of all objectives — again, for all levels within the organization. What was achieved? What wasn't achieved? Why wasn't it achieved? What can we do to improve the situation during the coming year? These are the basic questions that need answering.

For this six-step MBO process to be considered a Theory Z approach, a top-down approach must be combined with a bottom-up approach. To this end, Figure 13 depicts Rensis Likert's linking-pin approach to setting multiple-level objectives. Shown in this vertical slice of an organizational structure are managers who serve as linking pins to connect two successive levels of an organizational structure. Each manager in the structure is both a member of one team and a leader of a second. Serving as a linking pin, each manager par-

109

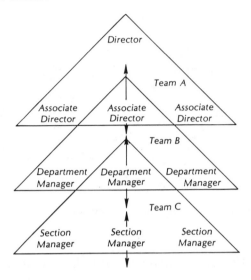

Figure 13.   Likert's linking-pin approach to setting multiple-level objectives

ticipates in developing objectives with the team of which he or she is a member and then discusses these preliminary objectives with the team of which he or she is the leader. Reactions and recommendations are solicited from the team members, and this information is passed to the team at the next higher level. This linking-pin approach has the merit of involving many managers in the development of objectives, which should improve both the quality and the acceptance of objectives. The one disadvantage of the approach is that it is time consuming, because there are both "downward" and "upward" passes before the objectives can actually be established for the coming year. However, to deal with this time problem, it is simply necessary to begin the MBO cycle earlier in the year.

Use of this recommended six-step MBO process along with the linking-pin concept represents a Theory Z approach to management by objectives. The beauty of the process is that it produces both coherence and commitment. This is what Theory Z is all about!

THE OBJECTIVES HIERARCHY

In introducing the concept of the objectives hierarchy, it is necessary to define four important terms: aims, mission, goals, and objectives.

- **Aims** is a generic term that refers to the ends toward which activities are directed.
- **Mission** is the ultimate aim of the enterprise, its reason for existence.
- **Goals** are qualitative statements of aim directed toward the mission.
- **Objectives** are verifiable statements of aim directed toward the goals, clear statements of results to be achieved.

As a comprehensive approach to management, MBO is intended to show the connections between and among mission, goals, and objectives from top to bottom. That all members of the organization should understand these connections is stressed by Abraham Maslow:[82, p. 41]

> It seems clear to me that in an enterprise, if everybody concerned is absolutely clear about the goals and directives and far purposes of the organization, practically all other questions then become simple technical questions of fitting means to the end.

In the development of aims for an organization, it is important to achieve *vertical integration*. As indicated in Figure 14, which is adapted from a paper by Heinz Weihrich,[124] the mission, goals, and objectives of the entire organization should be integrated from top to bottom. Moving downward from the upper levels to those below, aims provide *direction*. Moving upward from the lower levels to those above, aims provide *support*. At the bottom of the hierarchy are written statements of performance objectives, which enable each participating member to understand how his or her objectives contribute to the unit objectives and, in turn, how the unit objectives contribute to higher-level objectives.

In the development of objectives, it also is important to achieve *horizontal integration*. Here we are referring to the integration of objectives *across* organizational units. For example, it is important that the objectives of the Marketing Department mesh with those of the Contracts Department, that the objectives of the Manufacturing Department mesh with those of the Quality Control Department, etc. Without this horizontal integration, it might be found that the achievement of a particular objective by one department is dysfunctional or counterproductive for another department.

A well articulated objectives hierarchy includes both vertical in-

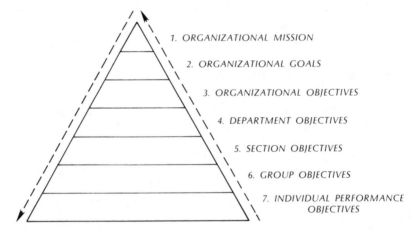

1. ORGANIZATIONAL MISSION

2. ORGANIZATIONAL GOALS

3. ORGANIZATIONAL OBJECTIVES

4. DEPARTMENT OBJECTIVES

5. SECTION OBJECTIVES

6. GROUP OBJECTIVES

7. INDIVIDUAL PERFORMANCE OBJECTIVES

Figure 14.   A hierarchy of aims

tegration and horizontal integration, as suggested by Figure 15. The resulting network of objectives then serves as the roadmap for the entire organization. With such a roadmap, the organization is likely to arrive at its planned destination. Without such a roadmap, however, the organization may end up some place where it does not want to be.

KEY RESULTS AREAS

From a practical standpoint, objectives cannot — and should not — be written to cover all aspects of a unit's responsibilities or a person's job. By including both important objectives and routine objectives, one might generate a list of objectives running into the hundreds. In the development of objectives, it is apparent that we need some points of focus.

The development of objectives calls for a focus on *key results areas*. These are the areas that will truly make a difference in determining the success or failure of the operation in question. Here the question

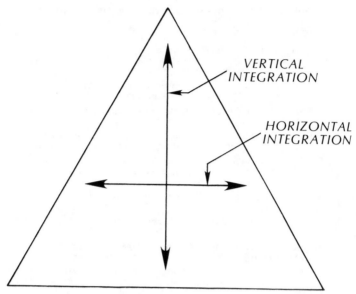

Figure 15.   Vertical and horizontal integration of objectives

is: What are the *critical variables* in this particular operation? To be able to identify the key results areas for a given unit or given job, a systems view is required — meaning that one must understand how the unit or job relates to its larger environment.

In his book *Management by Objectives and Results in the Public Sector*,[92] George Morrisey lists a number of useful guidelines for determining key results areas. These guidelines are presented in Table 5. A few moments of study of this table is recommended.

A research and development organization with which the author is familiar provides instructive examples of key results areas. During recent years, this organization made a major change in its mission — from one involving essentially fundamental research supported by governmental grants to one involving essentially applied research supported by industrial contracts. The key results areas listed below were written during the early stages of the transition from the original

Table 5. Guidelines for Determining Key Results Areas

1. They will identify all major areas within which the accountable manager will be expected to invest time, energy, talent, and other resources during the projected period of commitment.

2. They will include both managerial and operational responsibilities of the accountable manager.

3. They will include both normal work output expectations and innovations or improvement efforts.

4. They will include "soft" or difficult-to-measure areas as well as "hard" or tangible areas that are easier to measure.

5. They will not necessarily cover the entire job, but will identify "the critical few" areas where priority effort should be directed.

6. Each key results area will be limited to a few words.

7. They will not represent activities as such, but rather areas within which activities and, more importantly, results will occur.

8. Each key results area will not be measurable as stated, but will contain elements that can be made measurable.

9. Collectively, key results areas will form a basis for effective communication up, down, and across organizational lines.

George Morrisey — *Management by Objectives and Results in the Public Sector*, pp. 52, 53. Reading, Massachusetts: Addison-Wesley Publishing Company, 1976. Reprinted, by permission of the publisher.

mission to the new mission. For illustrative purposes, we show one "vertical slice" of the organization's key results areas:

1. Organization as a whole
   - Orientation toward applied research
   - Visibility in the industrial marketplace
   - Marketing capability
   - Volume of industrial contracts
   - New facilities
   - Cash flow
2. Energy Department (cost center)
   - Research volume
   - Time on projects
   - Client cultivation
3. Solar Energy Section (technical focal point)
   - Facilities development
   - Staff acquisition
   - Staff technical training
   - Technical publications

4. Solar Housing Project Leader (project focal point)
   - Project quality
   - Project schedule
   - Project budget
   - Follow-on project
5. Senior Researcher on Solar Housing Project (Task Leader)
   - Solar Panels Task
   - Assist in follow-on proposal
   - Publications
   - Work on Ph.D.

The intent of these key results is to focus on the critical aspects of a given unit or a given position — things that will *truly make a difference.* It is recommended that, before writing objectives for either an organizational unit or an individual job position, attention be directed toward the key results areas. This would be followed by the writing of objectives directed toward the key results areas.

GUIDELINES FOR DEVELOPING OBJECTIVES

There is an art to writing good objectives. Over the years, a number of useful guidelines for developing objectives have emerged. This information has been generated by theorists as well as practitioners. It is worthwhile to review some of the more important guidelines:

1. **Individuals responsible for achievement of objectives should participate in their development.** It is important that staff members in an organization feel that "These are *our* objectives." To be truly motivated to achieve objectives, there must be a feeling of ownership. To this end, staff must participate in the development of objectives that influence their work — including their unit objectives as well as their own performance objectives.

2. **Objectives should cover the key results areas for a unit or an individual.** As indicated before, it would be impractical to write objectives for every aspect of a unit's responsibilities or an individual's job position. It is essential to focus on the key results areas — the critical areas that will determine the success or failure of a given unit or given job position. At least one objective should be written for each key results area.

3. **Objectives should be expressed clearly and in writing.** There should be no ambiguity in a written objective: the intended outcome should be clear to anyone reading the objective. An objective usually begins with the word "to" and contains three important elements: (1) a clear action verb, (2) an end result, and (3) a target date.

4. **Objectives should specify "what" and "when," not "why" or "how."** The underlying notion of management by objectives is "managing for results." The primary focus is on results, the ends to be achieved. Thus, the written objectives should include only the end-results to be achieved, not the means for achieving them. Any planning document prepared after the development of objectives, however, should contain both the ends and the means.

5. **Objectives should be verifiable.** "Verifiability" means that two different people observing the outcome of an activity would agree whether or not an objective was achieved. "Verifiability" is a better term than "measurability," because some objectives, such as "meeting the specifications," are verifiable but are not measurable in the strict sense of the term.

6. **Objectives should be challenging yet reasonable.** Objectives that seem to bring about the highest level of motivation are those that are set just high enough to require the unit or person to "stretch" to achieve them but not be out of reach. If objectives are set too low, there will be little challenge and, correspondingly, little motivation. Also, if objectives are set too high, individuals will tend to "give up" at the outset. The task at hand is to estimate accurately what is challenging yet reasonable for a given organizational unit or a given individual.

7. **The number of objectives for a unit or person should be manageable.** A common error made by many individuals in their initial efforts to develop objectives is to write too many. Again, it is important to realize that objectives should focus only on the key results areas. A reasonable number of objectives for a unit or individual would be in the range of five to ten.

8. **The achievement of objectives should be under the control and authority of the responsible unit or person.** Whenever an individual is responsible for achieving a certain objective

116

but does not have sufficient control or authority to make certain that it happens, frustration results. (If such a situation exists for an extended period of time, stomach ulcers may result.) Certainly, by the very nature of organizations, some objectives can be achieved only through the cooperative efforts of two or more units or two or more individuals. However, to the greatest extent possible, efforts should be made to write objectives in such a manner that their achievement is under the control and authority of the responsible unit or individual.

9. **Objectives should be consistent with anticipated resources.** All objectives call for a certain amount of time and effort. Some require an expenditure of funds, and some require certain facilities or equipment. In developing objectives, it is important to give attention to the specific resources that will be needed for carrying them out.

10. **Objectives should be coordinated with other units and managers.** It is highly desirable to achieve both vertical integration and horizontal integration in the development of objectives. To this end, it is a worthwhile practice to first draft a set of objectives and then distribute these preliminary objectives to managers in related organizational units for their review and comments. After receiving comments and suggestions, the preliminary objectives would be revised as appropriate.

These are 10 practical guidelines that have been generated from the experiences and thinking of a large number of people actively involved in management by objectives. The implementation of these guidelines can help make an MBO program a definite asset to the organization.

ILLUSTRATIONS OF OBJECTIVES

To appreciate the nature of objectives, it is worthwhile to review examples of an organization's objectives established in a real-world context. Again, we will consider the R&D organization referred to previously. After a presentation of the mission and goals of the organization, there will be an illustration of objectives written at dif-

117

ferent levels within the organization. One objective has been selected for each of the key results areas previously listed.

The stated mission of the organization is TO HELP SOLVE MAJOR TECHNOLOGICAL PROBLEMS OF THE NATION THROUGH APPLIED RESEARCH AND DEVELOPMENT. In support of the mission are the following goals: (1) to provide quality service to our clients; (2) to be recognized as a national leader in applied research and development; (3) to help our employees achieve self-fulfillment in their work; (4) to be a good neighbor in any community in which we work; and (5) to achieve the profit needed to finance our company growth and the resources needed to support our other company goals.

1. **Organizational Objectives**
   - **Orientation toward applied research:** To prepare and to disseminate to all employees a written statement of the new corporate philosophy by March 1.
   - **Visibility in the industrial marketplace:** To prepare and disseminate to all potential clients a new brochure on organizational capability by June 1.
   - **Marketing capability:** To establish a Marketing Department and hire a Director of Marketing by Feb. 1.
   - **Volume of industrial contracts:** To achieve a dollar volume of $15,000,000 in industrial contracts by year-end.
   - **New facilities:** To expand floor space of laboratory facilities by 50,000 sq. ft. by June 1.
   - **Cash flow:** To solve the cash flow problem by use of advance billing on all new contracts beginning July 1.
2. **Objectives of Energy Department** (cost center)
   - **Research volume:** To achieve a research volume of at least $3,500,000 by year-end.
   - **Time on projects:** To increase staff time on projects from 60 percent to 70 percent by July 1 and maintain the higher level for the remainder of the year.
   - **Client cultivation:** To visit every potential client in the energy field (~ 25) at least once by year-end.
3. **Objectives of Solar Energy Section** (technical focal point)
   - **Facilities Development:** To have the new $500,000 solar energy facility operational by March 1.

118

- **Staff acquisition:** To hire 2 experienced and 3 junior solar energy specialists by June 1.
- **Staff technical training:** To conduct biweekly seminars on solar energy for all professional staff (year-long).
- **Technical publications:** To publish at least 6 professional papers in solar energy by year-end.

4. **Objectives of Solar Housing Project Leader** (project focal point)
   - **Project quality:** To achieve all of the technical objectives of the Solar Housing Project by project end-date.
   - **Project schedule:** To meet all milestones and complete the Solar Housing Project on schedule (Dec 1).
   - **Project budget:** To complete the Solar Housing Project within budget.
   - **Follow-on project:** To prepare a quality proposal for follow-on work to Solar Housing Project by Nov. 1.

5. **Objectives of Senior Researcher on Solar Housing Project** (Task Leader)
   - **Solar panels task:** To complete all scheduled work on solar panels task according to specifications by Nov. 1.
   - **Follow-on proposal:** To complete written input for follow-on proposal by Oct. 15.
   - **Publication:** To complete technical paper on solar panels by Dec. 1.
   - **Work on Ph.D.:** To complete all course work for Ph.D. by Dec. 22.

What is presented above is a vertical slice of an organization's objectives from top to bottom. The intent is to show the form of objectives written at different organizational levels and the linkages between the objectives. Perhaps the form of some of these objectives could be improved, but the basic idea of establishing a hierarchy of clear and verifiable objectives has been illustrated through these examples.

SUMMING UP

The major point emphasized in this chapter is that management by objectives holds great promise as a powerful management tool. In actual practice, however, it is beset with numerous pitfalls. It is important that managers have a good grasp of the possible pitfalls of MBO as well as the strengths.

Unfortunately, the fulfillment of management by objectives has been far short of the promise. When described by the true believers, this approach to management would appear to have a place in every organization that has a mission. (Doesn't every organization have a mission?) Yet there are many managers who want no part in management by objectives; they view it only in negative terms. The question then becomes: With the great promise of MBO, what went wrong?

The author has talked with no small number of managers who hold a negative view toward management by objectives. The following are some of their reactions: "Our company uses MBO only for performance evaluation — MBO is equated to merit pay." . . . "MBO requires a lot of paperwork — my people don't see any value in all this." . . . "My MBOs are passed down from upper management in the form of quotas — I have no part in developing them." . . . "We put our MBOs in writing the first of the year — they are then filed and we don't discuss them until 12 months later." . . . "There is a great deal of variation across departments in our company in how they implement the MBO program — some are completely autocratic while others are participative." . . . "Our managers don't take the MBO program very seriously — because the Director and his Deputy Directors don't establish performance objectives for their own jobs." More examples could be given, but this list should suffice for suggesting some of the major reasons why large numbers of managers hold a negative view toward MBO, why they say they want no part of it.

In assessing management by objectives, it is important to distinguish between the concept itself and the implementation of the concept. It seems evident to most people knowledgeable about the subject that the concept is sound. As Koontz says, "It is simple common sense in that it is a reflection of the purpose of managing itself." The problem is found not with the concept, but in its interpretation and application. In numerous organizations making use of MBO, there seems to be little, if any, connection between the underlying rationale of management by objectives and the actual practice of the rationale. In simple terms: there has been a widescale misinterpretation and misapplication of the basic idea, a corruption of the central concept.

On the positive side, if management by objectives is viewed as a comprehensive approach to management, it offers the following possible benefits:

1. It forces planning and provides a skeleton outline for the organization's operational plan.
2. It provides direction for how the enterprise should be organized and clarifies roles and responsibilities.
3. It provides guidance for what kind of people are needed and what kind of knowledge and skills should be developed.
4. It elicits commitment for effective action.
5. It provides milestones and standards for evaluating performance.

The challenge for each manager is to build on the strengths of management by objectives and avoid its pitfalls. In his paper "Shortcomings and Pitfalls in Managing by Objectives,"[61] Harold Koontz offers some useful guidelines that will help managers achieve this twofold goal. The author's adaptation of these guidelines is as follows:

1. Direct and coordinate the MBO program from the office of the chief executive. (MBO can work if top management commits itself to using the entire concept.)
2. View MBO as a comprehensive approach to management that applies to *all* of the functions of management.
3. Teach the philosophy and the approach of MBO to all members of the management team.
4. Install the MBO program as a uniform system throughout the organization.
5. Promote a team approach to developing unit objectives before developing performance objectives.
6. Promote a joint approach to developing performance objectives.
7. Assure vertical and horizontal integration of objectives throughout the organization.
8. Insist on interim review of objectives.
9. Be willing to change objectives.
10. Recognize that managing by objectives is not all there is to managing.

It would seem that a conscientious application of these guidelines would lead most managers to agree with Koontz[60, p. 51] when he says:

> Management by objectives must be a way of managing, a
> way of planning, as well as the key to organizing, staffing,
> directing, and controlling—it is then a part of managing,
> a summary of what has been done, and not a difficult
> separate operation.

Exercise V

Formulating Your Objectives

A.   What are your five key results areas for the next 12 months?

B.   Write one performance objective for each of these key results areas.

C.   Evaluate each of your performance objectives according to the "Guidelines for Developing Objectives" presented in Chapter V.

VI

Planning

A man who does not think and plan long ahead will find trouble right by his door.

Confucius
Lin Yutang—*The Wisdom of Confucius*[128, p. 182]

Introduction • Theoretical Framework • Principles of Planning • Strategic Planning • Tactical Planning • Project Planning • Summing Up

---

INTRODUCTION

Large numbers of managers — both men and women alike — find trouble right by their doorsteps because they do not give sufficient attention to planning. Many are the managers who remark that they do not have time for planning because they are spending most of their time coping with crises. When they are asked why they are faced with so many crises, they often exclaim, "Because we haven't planned!" And so it goes.

"Every organization is in a continuous state of change," notes Rensis Likert.[71, p. 128] "Sometimes the changes are great, sometimes small, but change is always taking place." Because of this continuous state of change, it is essential that managers devote adequate attention to the planning function. Managers in every organization are faced with two alternatives: they can let change happen to them or they can plan for change. Certainly the second alternative is the preferred one.

125

The implications of unplanned change are not good: managers will find themselves constantly in a reactive mode, constantly "fighting the alligators while they are trying to clear the swamp." In a competitive environment, this mode of operation will lead to the decay and, ultimately, to the death of the enterprise.

The implications of planned change are more desirable. Here managers will find themselves in a proactive mode, being at the helm in plotting a course of action and then pursuing that course of action. Certainly this mode of operation will contribute substantially to the overall productivity of the enterprise.

The purpose of this chapter is to present a Theory Z approach to planning. We will look first at a theoretical framework and basic principles of planning and then at how the framework and principles can be applied to three types of planning: strategic, tactical, and project.

THEORETICAL FRAMEWORK

Harold Koontz and Cyril O'Donnell[64, p. 129] provide us with a practical definition of planning:

> Planning is deciding in advance what to do, how to do it, when to do it, and who is to do it. Planning bridges the gap from where we are to where we want to go. Planning makes it possible for things to occur which would not otherwise happen.

The planning process consists of answering four basic questions:

1. Where are we now?
2. Where do we wish to go?
3. What are the different ways of getting there?
4. How will we know when we are there?

It is important to appreciate that planning is the foundation for the other functions of management. This concept is elucidated by Koontz and O'Donnell in the diagram shown in Figure 16. Here we see that plans (objectives and how to achieve them) are the foundation for determining (1) what kind of organizational structure is appropriate, (2) what kind of people are needed and when, (3) how most effectively to lead and direct people, and (4) what standards of control are needed.

126

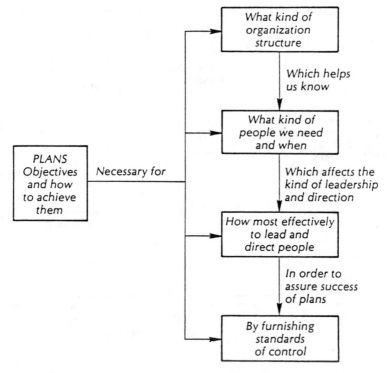

Koontz, O'Donnell, and Weihrich—*Management*, 1980, McGraw-Hill Book Company, pp. 158. Reprinted, by permission of the publisher.

Figure 16.   Plans as the foundation of management

The essence of Theory Z planning is found in the following observation by Margaret Mead:[90]

> But always the surest guarantee of change and growth is the inclusion of living persons in every stage of an activity. Their lives, their experience, and their continuing response—even their resistances—infuse with life any plan which, if living participants are excluded, lies on the drawing board and loses its reality.

Indeed, those persons who are charged with executing a plan must be actively involved in developing the plan. Otherwise, the plan simply will remain on the drawing board and gather dust.

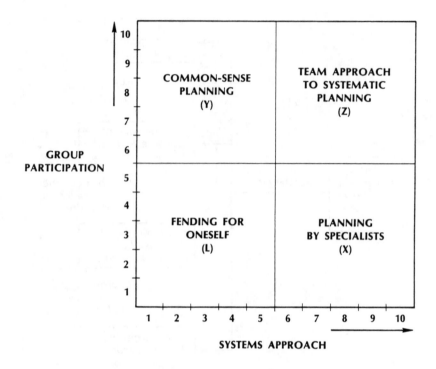

Figure 17.   Two dimensions of planning

The two dimensions of Theory Z planning are: (1) a systems approach to planning and (2) group participation in the planning process. "A systems approach" means a rational and logical approach to planning. "Group participation" means the active involvement of those persons who must carry out the plans.

The two dimensions of Theory Z planning are shown as orthogonal axes in Figure 17. This framework reveals four approaches to planning: (1) fending for oneself (Theory L), which is low on both a systems approach and group participation; (2) planning by specialists (Theory X), which is high on a systems approach but low on group participation; (3) common-sense planning (Theory Y), which is high on group participation but low on a systems approach; and (4) team approach to systematic planning (Theory Z), which is high on both a systems approach and group participation.

128

These four different approaches to planning are likely to produce the following outcomes:

1. **Theory L:** will be at the rock-bottom level of effectiveness; will result in disaster for any enterprise that is in a competitive environment.
2. **Theory X:** will be only marginally effective; may produce elegant plans but there will be a lack of commitment, because the persons responsible for implementing the plans were not involved in their development.
3. **Theory Y:** may prove satisfactory in a small and fairly stable enterprise but will be only marginally effective in a large organization that is in a constantly changing environment; may lead to commitment but will lack the technical depth needed for a plan to be effective.
4. **Theory Z:** will be maximally effective; will produce plans that are technically sound and that have the commitment of those persons who must implement the plans. This approach to planning will make a substantial contribution to the overall productivity of the enterprise.

PRINCIPLES OF PLANNING

The extensive literature on planning provides us with a number of useful principles:

1. **It is essential that those persons responsible for executing the plans be actively involved in developing the plans.** Involving the key actors in the planning process can lead to better plans as well as greater commitment for carrying out the plans. This is true of all three types of planning: strategic, tactical, and project. It is important that people throughout the organization feel that "These are *our* plans."
2. **Planning logically precedes the execution of all other management functions.** Planning provides the foundation and framework for carrying out the other management functions: organizing, staffing and staff development, motivating, and controlling. If the planning is fuzzy, the chances are good that the other functions will be fuzzy. On the other hand, if the

129

planning is crystal clear, the chances are good that the other functions will be clear.

3. **Every plan should be viewed as a tool that can facilitate the accomplishment of enterprise objectives.** Frequently, the development of a plan is viewed by managers as an end in itself. Upon completing the preparation of a written plan, managers have been heard to remark: "We have finished the plan, so now we can get back to work." This attitude contradicts the very nature of an effective plan, which should be viewed as a *vital tool* for achieving enterprise objectives. If the planning process does not satisfy this criterion, it is useless — or even worse than useless, because it is consuming valuable time.

4. **Planning should start with where we are rather than with where we want to be.** In developing organizational plans, it is important that managers have a clear understanding of the baseline from which they are working. A logical starting point in the planning process is to make an assessment of the strengths and limitations of the organization and the environmental forces presently acting upon it. The results of this assessment should then be of considerable value in answering the second question in the process: "Where do we wish to go?"

5. **It is important that the individuals involved in the planning process agree to use consistent planning premises.** Every plan is based upon certain premises, which may be either explicit or implicit. These assumptions may pertain to the marketplace, the economy, the work force, new technology, governmental regulations, and a host of other factors that might have some influence on the plans. It is essential that the planners agree on their assumptions about these forces and that the assumptions be made explicit.

6. **Flexibility must be built into the plans.** Every organization functions in a dynamic environment — some more than others. Consequently, no plan should be "set in concrete." The planners must build flexibility into every plan by viewing it in terms of a "decision tree": If A happens, then we will do B; but if C happens, then we will do D. If something does not work out as planned, the manager should have an alternative strategy. This approach to planning will increase a manager's

batting average in decision making (in terms of outcomes) and, in turn, his or her overall effectiveness.

7. **The plans of an enterprise should be closely integrated.** Just as with objectives, plans should be integrated both vertically and horizontally. The tactical plan should be integrated with the strategic plan, the separate parts of the tactical plan should be integrated, and the separate tasks in a given project should be integrated. The various parts of these different plans should be directed toward common goals, and, rather than being contradictory, they should be mutually reinforcing.

8. **The enterprise's plans should be documented and distributed to all members of the management team.** The documentation of plans should include key information used, planning assumptions, objectives, strategies, schedules, responsibilities, and resources allocated. All members of the management team should receive at least a written summary of the plans.

9. **Planning has value only if it is transformed into action.** Upon retiring as president of the L & K Restaurant chain, Cleo Ludwig was asked to what did he attribute his success. He gave a straightforward reply: "I always developed a plan of work, and I worked the plan." His mode of managing was to develop a detailed plan and then implement the plan. He used the plan to guide his day-to-day activities. He worked the plan. And he was a very successful manager!

10. **Plans should be reviewed periodically throughout the year.** All plans should be submitted to formal reviews. Strategic plans should be reviewed at least semiannually, tactical plans at least quarterly, and project plans at least monthly. The key actors should answer these questions: What is working? What isn't working? Why isn't it working? What should we do differently? On the basis of the answers to these questions, the plans should be modified as appropriate.

These 10 principles can serve as useful guidelines for carrying out effective planning. We will look next at how they can be applied to three types of planning:

1. **Strategic Planning:** Top management's determination of the goals and objectives of the organization and the best way of reaching them in view of the resources currently available and likely to be available in the future.

131

2. **Tactical Planning:** Detailed planning at the division/department/section level that is carried out in the light of the strategic planning.
3. **Project Planning:** Detailed planning for the project and the various tasks included in the project.

These three levels of planning are illustrated in Figure 18.

STRATEGIC PLANNING

The strategic plan is intended to serve as the roadmap for the organization as a whole. Typically, the strategic plan covers a five-year time frame, with a "rolling approach" that involves updating the plan each year. Thus, the organization always has a current strategic plan that covers *the next five years*. Strategic planning is

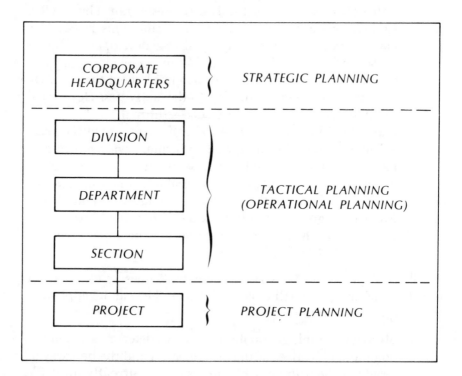

Figure 18.   Three levels of planning in an illustrative organizational structure

132

carried out by members of upper management and, ideally, through the involvement of a spectrum of managers.

In the paper "Can Strategic Planning Pay Off?,"[39] Louis Gerstner presents the strategic planning concept shown in Figure 19. The two key elements in this figure are the description of the organization's present position and the description of its desired position. Feeding into the description of the present position are the assessment of the organization's strengths and weaknesses and the assessment of current environmental forces. Feeding into the description of the desired position are the organization's goals and the assessment of projected environmental forces. In terms of this model, the purpose of strategic planning is to *bridge the gap* between the organization's present position and its desired position.

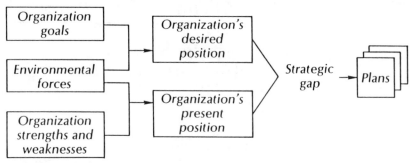

Louis Gerstner, Jr.–"Can Strategic Planning Pay Off? *Business Horizons*, Vol. 15, No. 6, December, 1972, p. 7. Reprinted, by permission of the publisher.

Figure 19.   The strategic planning concept

An approach to strategic planning is outlined in Figure 20. The recommended steps are as follows:

1. **Review the statement of organizational mission and goals.** As an initial step in strategic planning, upper management should review the statement of organizational mission and goals. The mission is the ultimate aim of the organization, and the goals are the qualitative statements of aim directed toward the mission. Sometimes the statement of goals remains stable for a number of years. At other times, however, it is appropriate to make changes. The question here is: "What is the nature of our business?" As Drucker[23, p. 92] stresses,

there also is a need to ask, "What *should* our business be? What opportunities are opening up or can be created to fulfill the purpose and mission of the business by making it into a *different* business?" Managers who fail to ask this question may miss their major opportunity.

2. **Assess opportunities.** Here the question is: What are the op-

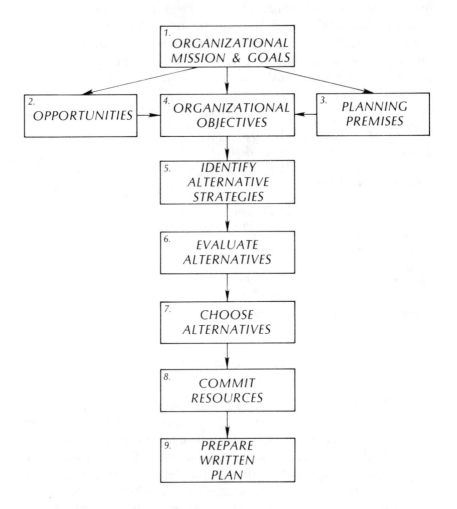

Figure 20.   A procedure for strategic planning

portunities for our products or services in the marketplace? The nature of effective marketing is elucidated by Drucker:[23, p. 64] "True marketing starts out with the customer, his demographics, his realities, his needs, his values. It does not ask, 'What do we want to sell?' It asks, 'What does the customer want to buy?' It does not say, 'This is what our product or service does.' It says, 'These are the satisfactions the customer looks for, values, and needs.'" Drucker stresses that the purpose of marketing is to make selling superfluous. The aim is to know and understand the customers so well that the product or service sells itself.

It is assumed here that the organization's marketing research group has collected and analyzed information about customer needs. And it is further assumed that this group has been able to distinguish between needs and demands, with "need" meaning a discrepancy between the actual and the desired, and "demand" meaning the existence of a need plus the ability to pay for the product or service.

3. **State the planning premises.** The Delphi technique is a useful method for achieving consensus on the planning premises. Here the members of the planning team first agree upon the particular areas for which assumptions must be stated — such as the economy, the marketplace, the labor force, the emergence of new technology, etc. Next, each member of the team individually writes his or her assumptions about each of these areas. The members then meet as a group to present their assumptions and the rationale for making each assumption. After discussing the assumptions and the underlying reasons given, the members, working individually, rewrite their assumptions. Next, the revised assumptions are presented and discussed in the group setting. This process continues until there is a reasonably good agreement among the members regarding the planning premises.

4. **Specify the organizational objectives.** The organizational objectives are written in the light of the mission and goals, the perceived opportunities, and the planning premises. Being stated in verifiable terms, these objectives should be challenging, yet realistic. It would be expected that the achievement of these objectives would make a substantial contribution in

moving the organization from where it is toward where it wants to go.

5. **Identify alternative strategies.** The planning team now raises this question: What are the alternative strategies for achieving our objectives? Requiring considerable vision and imagination, this is the most creative phase of the entire process. To establish a setting conducive to creative thinking, a brainstorming approach may be useful. With this approach, the members of the planning team are encouraged to be truly imaginative — with the stated condition that "far out" ideas are acceptable. Evaluation during this phase is unacceptable because premature evaluation may snuff out the most promising ideas. The result of this phase should be a list of imaginative approaches for achieving the organizational objectives.

6. **Evaluate alternative strategies.** The next step is to systematically evaluate each alternative strategy. Here a general cost-effectiveness analysis is called for. The first step in this analysis is to establish a two-way table with the organizational objectives listed in the columns and the alternative strategies in the rows. By use of a 5-point scale, each member of the team evaluates each alternative strategy in terms of its potential contribution to each of the objectives. The averages of these evaluations are then inserted in the cells of the table. Next, the group estimates the costs associated with each alternative strategy, which are recorded in the last column of the table. With the establishment of the estimated effectiveness measures and the estimated costs, the group now has a reasonable basis on which to judge the alternative strategies.

As a guide for evaluating the alternative strategies, C.Roland Christensen and his associates[12, pp. 136–39] provide a list of practical questions:

a. Is the strategy identifiable and has it been made clear either in words or practice?

b. Does the strategy exploit fully domestic and international environmental opportunity?

c. Is the strategy consistent with corporate competence and resources, both present and projected?

d. Are the major provisions of the strategy and the program

of major policies of which it is comprised internally consistent?

e. Is the chosen level of risk reasonable?

f. Is the strategy appropriate to the personal values and aspirations of the key managers?

g. Is the strategy appropriate to the desired level of contribution to society?

h. Does the strategy constitute a clear stimulus to organizational commitment?

i. Are there early indications of the responsiveness of markets and market segments to the strategy?

7. **Choose alternative strategies.** After conducting the cost-effectiveness analysis and answering the questions suggested by Christensen and his associates, the strategic planning team is ready to select the alternative strategies that will best help the organization achieve its objectives. A key point here is that the alternatives chosen must form a *meaningful whole:* they should be internally consistent and should reinforce one another. Thus, a particular alternative that scored well on all of the individual criteria might be discarded in favor of one that did not score as well, simply because the former does not mesh with the other alternatives chosen.

8. **Commit resources.** Until there is a commitment of resources, a planning document is simply a "wish list." After a commitment of resources, it is appropriate to view the document as a true plan. At this stage in the planning process, the commitment of resources constitutes "top-down budgeting" (as opposed to "bottom-up budgeting"). It involves making a gross estimate of the resources that will be required to implement the various alternatives. The detailed budget analysis — or "bottom-up approach"— would occur during the tactical planning phase.

9. **Prepare written plan.** The strategic plan should be documented. This documentation should include organizational mission and goals, opportunities, planning premises, organizational objectives, selected alternatives, and budget estimates. This written plan — or at last a summary of it — should be distributed to all members of the management team.

137

TACTICAL PLANNING

Tactical planning (or operational planning) is planning that is done for all of the units or programs within the organization. With the strategic plan providing direction for the organization as a whole, the tactical plan provides direction for each component within the organization. The tactical plan is written *in the light of* the strategic plan. In terms of a time frame, the tactical plan might be written in general terms for a five-year time frame and in very specific terms for a one-year time frame. Thus, a new tactical plan is developed each year.

In developing the tactical plan, we assume that a central planning team, under the auspices of the organization's chief executive, has responsibility for coordinating the total effort. However, the detailed planning at the unit or program level should actively involve the key members of each unit or program.

For illustrative purposes, we assume that the strategic planning has been done for the organization as a whole and that the tactical planning is to be carried out for each division within the larger organization. A procedure for tactical planning is outlined in Figure 21. The steps included in this procedure are summarized below:

1. **Review the strategic plan.** As an initial and important step in developing the tactical plan, all members of the division's planning team review the strategic plan. These members need to understand the organization's major opportunities, the planning premises, the objectives, the strategies, and the budgets. To assure this understanding, it is incumbent upon upper management to disseminate copies of the strategic plan and conduct meetings with the members of the planning team to discuss the plan.

2. **Identify the opportunities.** It is important to identify clearly the opportunities now facing the division or expected to face the division during the coming years. Some of these opportunities should be gleaned from a study of the strategic plan, while others will emerge from discussions with members of the Marketing Department and other members of the division's management team. The task at hand is to thoroughly explore these opportunities and establish priorities.

3. **Estimate the resources.** The resources referred to here are

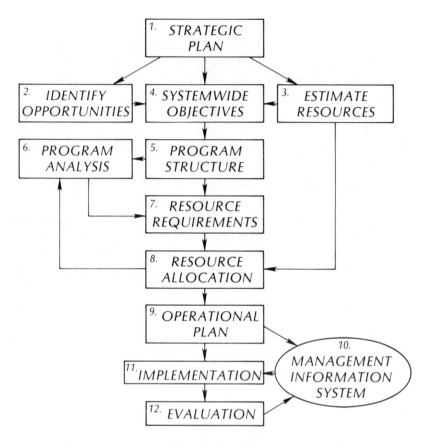

Figure 21. A procedure for tactical planning

essentially the funds that are expected to be available to the division during a given time period. In most organizations, the estimation of resources beyond one year is highly tenuous. Nevertheless, it is appropriate to state the assumptions and make the best guess possible. Even though the error of estimate increases significantly as one goes beyond a one-year time period, this is better than making no estimate at all. The long-term estimates are then updated and revised annually as a normal part of the planning process.

4. **Formulate systemwide objectives.** Assuming that the tactical planning is being done for each division within the larger organization, the systemwide objectives refer to the specific

139

aims of a division for the coming year. These objectives are written in the light of the organizational objectives included in the strategic plan, the opportunities facing the division, and the estimated resources that are likely to be available to the division during the coming year. The set of systemwide objectives would be expected to have an impact on the division as a whole. Achievement of these objectives should help the division advance from where it presently is toward where it wants to go.

5. **Establish program structure.** Many managers may assume that their existing organizational charts are adequate for establishing a breakdown for the components of their tactical plans. Sometimes this is not appropriate, because many significant activities such as interdepartmental projects do not fit neatly into the existing organizational chart. Hence, a more useful approach may be to work from a "program structure" rather than from an organizational chart. A *program* is defined as a set of activities directed toward common objectives (which may refer to either an organizational unit or project that cuts across organizational units). A *program structure* is a hierarchical arrangement of programs showing their interrelations and encompassing all activities within the organization.

An outline for a program structure is shown in Figure 22. Each rectangle in this diagram represents a particular program. "Result-producing activities" are those that contribute directly to the division's mission and goals (such as marketing, engineering, manufacturing). "Support activities" are those that do not contribute directly to the division's mission and goals but do contribute directly to the result-producing activities (such as finance, date processing, personnel). "Housekeeping activities" do not contribute directly to the division's mission and goals and may not contribute directly to the result-producing activities, but they do play a vital role in the total operation (such as maintenance, transportation, food service). The "top-management activities" are established last because only after thinking through the other activities can it be decided what activities top management must carry out to assure the successful accomplishment of the other activities.

140

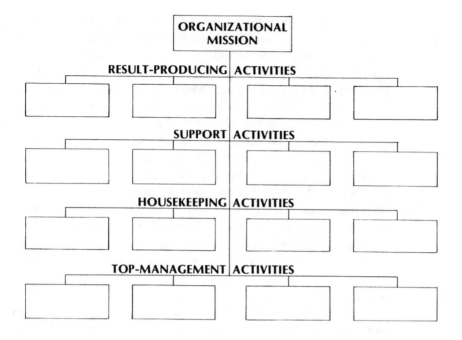

Figure 22. A program structure

This program structure provides the framework for developing the tactical plan. A detailed plan is to be prepared for each of the programs included in the program structure. The sum of these program plans would constitute the tactical plan (or operational plan) for the division.

6. **Conduct program analysis.** Program analysis is the systematic and analytical approach to determining the most appropriate ways to carry out the various programs included in the program structure. It involves the following sequence of steps: (a) review the systemwide objectives; (b) identify program constraints; (c) estimate potential resources available for the program; (d) specify program objectives; (e) investigate alternative approaches for achieving the program objectives; (f) evaluate each alternative approach on the basis of estimated effectiveness and estimated cost; (g) select preferred alternatives; and (h) prepare a program proposal. These program proposals are then submitted to the central planning team.

141

7. **Establish resource requirements.** The purpose of this step in the planning process is to establish resource requirements for all of the programs, individually and collectively. These resource requirements are outlined in a program budget format, which is designed in accordance with the program structure. Both top-down and bottom-up inputs are important in the budget-formulation step. Top-down inputs constitute a rational input based upon systemwide objectives and the corresponding priorities assigned to the various programs. The bottom-up approach uses cost estimates from the program analyses as the basis for the initial program budget.

8. **Allocate resources.** The next step in the process is to allocate the resources to the various programs. This allocation is based on the estimated budget requirements, the estimated resources, and the relative priorities assigned to the various programs. A recommended sequence of steps is to (a) systematically choose a combination of alternatives for the various programs; (b) check the financial and resource feasibility of this combination; (c) if not feasible, choose another combination; (d) if it is feasible in terms of resources, check to see if the estimated effectiveness is satisfactory; (e) if the estimated effectiveness is not satisfactory, choose another combination; (f) if the estimated effectiveness is satisfactory, stop at this point.

   The end product of this step is a set of recommendations for allocating the available resources to the resource requirements established for the various programs. Preparation of a multi-year budget document is appropriate at this point.

9. **Prepare operational plan.** A written operational plan for the division is then prepared. This plan includes the systemwide objectives and the plans for all of the programs. It is important to highlight the vertical and horizontal linkages between and among the programs. This operational plan — or at least a summary of it — should be distributed to all members of the management team.

10. **Develop management information system.** Productive management requires both good planning and implementation of the plans. The former without the latter is sterile. An essential requirement for successful execution of the plan is the availability of an effective and efficient management in-

formation system. This information system must be designed to collect, store, and report all significant information pertaining to the plan during the period of implementation. The major purpose of the information system is to provide the manager with the information needed for evaluation and corrective action. To this end, the information stored in the system must include details about both the planned performance and the actual performance.

11. **Implement the operational plan.** After the plan has been approved, it is put into operation. Each selected alternative is executed according to a specified time schedule. The responsibility for assuring that each selected alternative is implemented according to plan should be assigned to the appropriate manager.

12. **Evaluate.** Program evaluation should take place on a continuing basis. The important questions are: Which objectives are being achieved? Which objectives are not being achieved? Are we proceeding according to schedule? Are expenditures consistent with budget? What are the reasons for the discrepancies? What should be done to improve? Data needed to help answer these questions should be provided by the management information system. Based upon the results of the ongoing evaluation, modifications are made in the implementation of the programs as deemed appropriate.

This 12-step procedure is an effective approach to tactical planning. It provides a roadmap for each unit or program in the organization. All of the smaller roadmaps are integrated into one larger roadmap. Collectively, these roadmaps should be of considerable value in helping the members of the organization reach their destination.

PROJECT PLANNING

A project may be defined as a single nonrepetitive enterprise that has a prescribed end result, time frame, and budget. With regard to organization, a project may be carried out within one organizational unit or may cut across organizational units.

Because it serves as the foundation and framework for all other management functions, planning is central to project success. Good

143

planning is likely to lead to project success; poor planning is likely to lead to project disaster.

A Theory Z approach to project planning calls for (1) a systematic approach and (2) active involvement of the key members of the project team. There is an extensive body of literature dealing with a systematic approach to project planning, but there is little mention in this literature of actively involving the project team members in the planning process. It is important that Project Managers attend to both of these attributes of Theory Z planning.

A recommended procedure for project planning is shown in Figure 23. It is assumed that the key members of the project team will participate as a team in carrying out the following steps :

1. **Study requirements.** The initial step in project planning is to determine client requirements. Every project has a client — the person who will use or judge the results of the project — regardless of whether the project is internally funded or externally funded. It is important to determine *what* is needed by the client and *why* it is needed. (What does the client plan to do with the results?) It also is important to determine what criteria will be used by the client in evaluating the results of the project.

2. **Establish project objectives.** After the client's requirements have been determined, the next step is to state the project objectives. These objectives should be written in terms of the specific aims that are to be achieved as a result of carrying out the project. Written in clear language, the objectives should be verifiable. Further, they should delineate the scope of the project and should be consistent with the existing or anticipated resources that can be mustered. These objectives then serve as the beacon that guides the entire project effort.

3. **Define deliverables.** It is important to state in writing the tangibles that are to be delivered to the client during and at the end of the project. These might include written reports, pieces of equipment, computer software, oral presentations, etc. There should be no question in the minds of the project team as to what is to be delivered to the client as part of the project.

4. **Define tasks.** After the project objectives and the deliverables have been delineated, the next question is: What tasks must

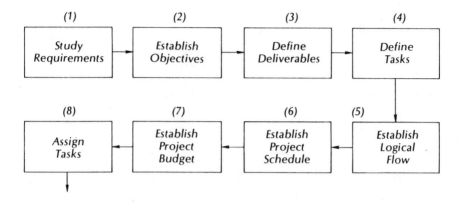

Figure 23. A procedure for project planning

be carried out to achieve the project objectives? A useful technique for answering this question is the Nominal Group Method. With this method, each member of the project team, on an individual basis, first studies the project requirements and lists the tasks that he or she believes must be carried out to achieve the project objectives. The members then meet as a group to discuss the tasks that each has listed and to reach a consensus on a single list of tasks.

These tasks are arranged in a hierarchy that is formally called a work breakdown structure (WBS). A three-level WBS would show the project as a whole at the first level, the major divisions of the project at the second level, and the tasks at the third level. A three-level WBS normally would suffice for a small project, while a five- or even six-level WBS might be required for a very large project. A four-level WBS is shown in Figure 24.[73]

A clearly formulated work breakdown structure has a number of uses: describing the total effort of the project, issuing work authorizations, scheduling, budgeting, and tracking technical performance. It should be noted, however, that the WBS reflects only *what* must be done, not *in what order* the tasks must be carried out or *when* they must be carried out.

145

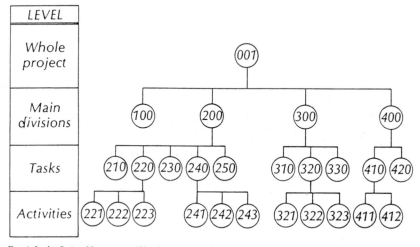

Figure 24.   A work breakdown structure

5. **Establish logical flow of tasks.** Effective planning of the project requires that the project be laid out in a network. What is the proper sequence for carrying out the tasks? Which tasks must be completed first; which second, etc.? Which tasks can be carried out in parallel? What are the dependencies between and among the tasks? These questions are answered through the establishment of a project network.

   A practical approach for laying out a network is appropriately called the "3-by-5 card technique." This technique involves writing each task on a 3-by-5 card. The members of the project planning team then use these cards in deciding upon the appropriate sequence of tasks and the interconnections between and among the tasks. This procedure is carried out by laying out the cards on a large sheet of paper (or sheets of paper) and drawing lines to show the interconnections — such as that shown in Figure 25.[102] Specific techniques such as PERT (Program Evaluation and Review Technique) or CPM (Critical Path Method) can be used then to calculate the critical path in the network.

6. **Establish project schedule.** After the team members decide

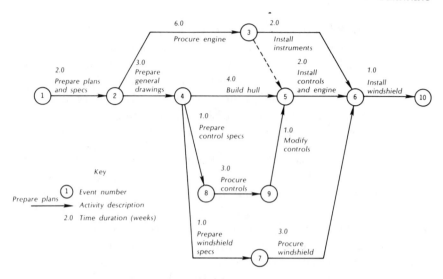

Figure 25. A network for boat-building project

upon the logical flow of tasks, the next step is to decide upon an appropriate schedule for these tasks. Expected start and completion dates are established for each task. It also is appropriate at this time to schedule the assignments of the project personnel. Here it is necessary to work back and forth between Step 5 and Step 6 to achieve a balance between the scheduling of tasks and the anticipated availability of personnel.

7. **Establish project budget.** If the above steps have been carried out with a reasonable degree of accuracy, the establishment of a project budget is a straightforward step. The staff costs are calculated by multiplying the number of scheduled hours for each staff member by salary (or a base that includes both salary and fringe benefits). Additional costs include materials and equipment, use of facilities, travel, project management, and overhead. It is useful to establish the budget breakdown in accord with the work breakdown structure, which aids the Project Manager in both planning and controlling the project costs.

8. **Assign tasks.** If the various project tasks are to be carried out

147

by Task Leaders located in organizational units different from that of the Project Manager, it is important to assign tasks in writing. These brief written assignments should include task objectives, deliverables, important milestones, and budgets. The establishment of these assignments in writing can help prevent misunderstandings from arising during the course of carrying out the project or at the end of the project.

It should be noted that there are a number of feedback loops implicit in the project planning process shown in Figure 21. Assume, for example, that the team members know in advance how much money is available for carrying out the project. After completing Step 7 (Establishing Project Budget), they discover that their estimated costs exceed the total available funds. Here they have several alternatives: (a) meet with the client to discuss the possibility of obtaining additional funds; (b) modify the objectives; (c) modify the deliverables; or (d) modify the sequencing of tasks to achieve greater efficiency. Such iterations should be made until there is a match between the estimated costs and the estimated funds available.

It should be noted also that one should expect the project plan to be modified during the course of carrying out the project. By their very nature, projects bring with them uncertainty. Schedules and budgets cannot be estimated with 100 percent accuracy. Consequently, adjustments must be made in the schedules and the budgets during the conduct of the project. But even though such within-project adjustments are considered essential, the client nevertheless will expect the *total* project to be completed on schedule and within budget.

The procedure described here is an effective approach to project planning. By taking this step-by-step approach, the team members will have a useful roadmap to guide their activities throughout the duration of the project. Furthermore, by involving the key team members in the planning process, a sense of ownership will be realized. This is Theory Z planning at its best.

SUMMING UP

The purpose of this chapter has been to describe a Theory Z approach to planning. Underlying Theory Z is the following key concept: *give the tools of planning to managers throughout the organization so that they can participate actively and responsibly in the planning process.*

The Theory Z approach applies to all three types of planning: strategic, tactical, and project. In strategic planning, there should be a logical and systematic approach and the active involvement of all members of upper management. In tactical planning, there should be a logical and systematic approach and the active involvement of all line managers in the organization. In project planning, there should be a logical and systematic approach and the active involvement of key project team members.

Theory Z planning produces a number of clear benefits:

1. The focusing of action on purposes.
2. Better coordination of efforts throughout the organization.
3. Less reactive management and more proactive management.
4. Fewer crises.
5. Widespread commitment among managers to carry out the plans successfully.
6. Improved employee morale resulting from a sense of purpose and direction.
7. Higher productivity.

These are substantial benefits. They signal the difference between success and failure for any enterprise. It is essential for managers to recognize that failure to devote sufficient time and effort to the planning function will place them in an untenable position. If such a situation prevails throughout an organization, then the enterprise will surely die.

Here we should heed the words of Billy Goetz[41, p. 63] when he says:

> Plans alone cannot make an enterprise successful. Action is required; the enterprise must operate. Plans can, however, focus action on purposes. Without plans, action must become merely random activity, producing nothing but chaos.

Exercise VI

Developing a Plan

Select one of your most important performance objectives listed in Exercise V and develop a plan (in the form of a PERT chart) for accomplishing the objective. Follow these steps:

A. Write the objective and list all of the activities that must be carried out to achieve the objective. (You may use the form on page 151.)

B. Estimate the time required for completing each activity (in terms of weeks, days, or hours).

C. Lay out a network similar to that in Figure 25. (You may use the form on page 152.)

D. Starting with a zero above the first node, do a "forward pass" by *adding* the estimated times from left to right and recording the cumulative times *above* the appropriate node. (If two or more arrows feed into the same node, take the larger or largest of the cumulative times.)

E. You then do a "backward pass" by first taking the total cumulative time and recording it below the last node. You then *subtract* the scores as you move from right to left and place the remainder *below* the appropriate node. (If two or more arrows feed into the same node, take the smaller or smallest of the cumulative times.)

F. The *critical path* is identified by the following rule: For any two connecting nodes, (1) the upper and the lower numbers are the same and (2) the estimated time of the activity is the same as the difference between the two cumulative times. (Draw the critical path with a colored pencil.)

You now know how to construct a PERT chart!

Objective: _____

_____

Activity	Time Estimate

PERT CHART (First Version)

PERT CHART (Revised Version)

VII

Organizing

Moses' father-in-law addressing Moses:

"The thing thou doest is not good. Thou will surely wear
away, both thou and this people that is with thee; thou art
not able to perform it thyself alone. Hearken now unto my
voice, I will give thee counsel. . . . thou shalt provide out
of the people able men . . . and place such over them (the
people), to be rulers of thousands, and rulers of hundreds,
rulers of fifties, and rulers of tens . . ."

Exodus[18:17-21]

---

*Introduction • Theoretical Framework • Principles of Organizing • The
Logic of Organization • Functional Organization • Task Force Organiza-
tion • Matrix Organization • Delegating • A Strategy for Organizational
Change • Summing Up*

INTRODUCTION

According to Scriptures, Moses encountered numerous obstacles in
leading his people out of Egypt to the Promised Land. Contributing
to his problem was his lack of organization: thousands of people
reported directly to Moses. His father-in-law, Jethro, who apparently
was a perceptive person, realized that this lack of organization was
impeding their progress. Jethro advised Moses that the sharing of the
leadership function with able men would expedite the journey and

would make it easier on Moses. Essentially, Jethro was saying, "We must get organized!"

Today, more than three millennia later, managers are still exclaiming, "We must get organized!" These managers are sorely aware that the lack of organization causes frustration for all members of the group and, in turn, leads to lowered productivity. They realize that they must establish orderliness for their activities, that they must "get their act together."

Without effective organization, people are working in a situation of uncertainty and perhaps even chaos. They do not know who is responsible for what. They do not know who has authority for decision making. They do not know how the various jobs are linked together. They do not know what type of coordination is expected. Obviously, such a state of affairs is a serious impediment to individual and group productivity.

Standing in sharp contrast is the group that is well organized. In this situation, all members of the group have a clear grasp of the goals and objectives of the enterprise. The members fully understand their roles and responsibilities, how much discretion they have in decision making, and how their own jobs are linked to other jobs. Such a desirable state of affairs will lead to greater staff morale, greater efficiency, and greater productivity. It is clear that organizing is a vital function of management.

The purpose of this chapter is to present a set of guidelines for effective organization. We will begin with a theoretical framework and general principles of organization. This will be followed by a description of three types of organization: functional, task force, and matrix. Next, the importance of delegating will be stressed. Finally, an outline of a proposed strategy for bringing about change in the organizational structure will be presented.

THEORETICAL FRAMEWORK

The key elements of organizing have been elucidated by Koontz and O'Donnell:[64, p. 71]

> Organizing involves the establishment of an intentional structure of roles through determination of the activities required to achieve the goals of the enterprise and each part of it, the grouping of these activities, the assignment of such

groups of activities to a manager, the delegation of authority
to carry them out, and provision for coordination of
authority and informational relationships horizontally and
vertically in the organization structure.

It is essential that the organization designer appreciate the importance of each of the following elements: (1) determination of the activities required to achieve the goals of an enterprise and each part of it; (2) grouping of these activities; (3) assignment of each group of activities to a manager; (4) delegation of authority to each manager; and (5) provision for coordination. If these various elements are duly instituted, then it is unlikely that members of the group will be exclaiming, "We must get organized around here!" It is more likely that they will be remarking, "We have our act together."

Traditionally, the focus of organization builders and theorists has been on orderliness. Activities must be systematically arranged and carried out. There is clarity of both function and structure. Without such orderliness, it is apparent that the enterprise will be found lacking in both efficiency and effectiveness.

Today, however, many managers realize that orderliness is necessary — but not sufficient — for the design of an effective organization. An enterprise needs orderliness, but, when there is a need for spontaneity and flexibility, an exclusive focus on this one aspect of organization will inhibit the enterprise. The emergence of a unique demand — either a problem or an opportunity — may go unattended because of the rigidity of the organization structure.

In the book *Small Is Beautiful*,[108, p. 229] E. F. Schumacher states it well when he says:

> In any organization, large or small, there must be certain clarity and orderliness; if things fall into disorder, nothing can be accomplished. Yet, orderliness, as such, is static and lifeless; so there must also be plenty of elbowroom and scope for breaking through the established order, to do the things never done before, never anticipated by the guardians of orderliness, the new, unpredicted and unpredictable outcome of a (person's) creative idea.

It seems apparent that an organization structure must be designed for both stability and flexibility. The need for clarity and orderliness is self-evident, but also there is a need for spontaneity and responsiveness to unpredictable demands placed on the enterprise. Thus, the opposite of stability is not flexibility, and the opposite of flex-

157

ibility is not stability. Rather, these are two independent dimensions that should be viewed as complementary aspects of an effective organization.

These two dimensions of effective organization are shown as orthogonal axes in Figure 26. The horizontal axis reflects the degree to which stability is manifested in an organization structure; the vertical axis reflects the degree to which flexibility is manifested. This framework, then, reveals four different types of organization structure: (1) disorganization (Theory L), which is low on both stability and flexibility; (2) functional organization (Theory X), which is high on stability but low on flexibility; (3) task force organization (Theory Y), which is high on flexibility but low on stability; and (4) parallel organization (Theory Z), which is high on both stability and flexibility.

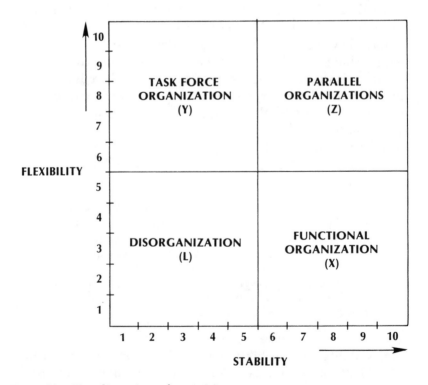

Figure 26.   Two dimensions of organizing

These four different types of organization would be expected to yield the following results:

1. **Disorganization (Theory L)** will lead to crisis management, frustration, psychological stress, psychosomatic illness, low morale, and inefficiency. This type of organization — or better said, "lack of organization"— will be at the rock-bottom level of effectiveness.

2. **Functional organization without task forces (Theory X)** will provide stability without flexibility and will not be effective in dealing with problems and opportunities that cut across organizational units. In a rapidly changing environment, this organization structure will be only marginally effective.

3. **Task force organization without functional organization (Theory Y)** will provide flexibility without stability and will produce uncertainty and insecurity on the part of staff. In any type of enterprise that is expected to be long-lived, this organization structure will be only marginally effective.

4. **Parallel organization (Theory Z)** with the simultaneous operation of the functional structure and task forces will provide both stability and flexibility. If all members *understand* the structure and are *committed* to making it work, this organization structure will be maximally effective.

In considering the importance of the two key dimensions of organization, we must agree with Peter Drucker[23, p. 526] when he says:

> Organization builders (and even organization theorists) will have to learn that sound organization structure needs *both* a hierarchical structure of authority, decision making, and pyramid, and the capacity to organize task forces, teams, and individuals for work both on a permanent and a temporary basis.

PRINCIPLES OF ORGANIZING

Over the years, a number of useful principles of organizing have emerged. These principles serve as useful guidelines in the design of an entire enterprise or in the design of a particular unit within the enterprise. The following are some of the important principles that have stood the test of time:

1. **The key activities that must be carried out to achieve the enterprise objectives should be clearly defined.** Just as with defining the activities for a project, managers must define the activities for an enterprise. Focus should be on *key activities* — those that will make a difference in determining the success or failure of the enterprise. In identifying the activities that must be carried out, it is helpful to think in terms of the following types of activities: (a) key-results activities, (b) support activities, (c) housekeeping activities, and (d) top-management activities. The designer should make certain that no significant activity is overlooked.

2. **The activities should be grouped on some logical basis.** The various activities might be grouped according to similarity in function, similarity in skills and knowledge required, linkages of the activities, geographical location, or other criteria. Whatever criteria are used, it is important to do the grouping on a logical and systematic basis. Certainly it is important not to focus exclusively on homogeneity of tasks or skills, which might result in excessive over-specialization and lack of opportunity for growth. To prevent over-specialization in a given job, the organization designer should think in terms of how best to provide the opportunity for continual learning for each individual in the enterprise.

3. **The responsibilities of each division, department, unit, and job should be clearly defined.** "Responsibility" means accountability for specific activities and results. This is what is expected of the unit or individual. The responsibilities of each organizational unit and each job within the unit should be specified in writing. For the latter, the specification should be in the form of a written job description. Every member of the enterprise should be given a copy of his or her job description.

4. **Authority should be delegated as far down in the organization as practicable.** "Authority" means the power to make decisions and to commit resources. A major determinant in distinguishing between the successful enterprise and the unsuccessful one is the extent to which authority is delegated downward as far as practicable, which means essentially that the enterprise is distributing the leadership function. Unfortunately, many managers are reluctant to delegate — perhaps

because of lack of confidence in their staff or lack of confidence in themselves. But whatever the reason, such managers do a disservice to both themselves and the enterprise.

It is important to be reminded of the truism that authority can be delegated but responsibility cannot. This means that the manager can authorize his or her staff to make certain decisions and commit certain resources, but the manager is still held accountable for the outcome. The manager cannot simply sit back and say to his or her superior, "Well, they blew it." Indeed not. The manager is held accountable for all results under his or her span of control. Thus, it is incumbent upon the manager to exercise proper control over the staff members to whom authority is delegated.

5. **Responsibility and authority should be made equal.** One of the major problems in many organizations is that responsibility and authority are not coequal. Individuals are given a considerable amount of responsibility for achieving certain outcomes but are not given the authority needed for assuring that these outcomes are achieved. Such a situation leads to frustration on the part of the affected parties and, in extreme and prolonged cases, may lead to stomach ulcers. Periodically, upper-level management should review all managerial positions to assure that responsibility and authority are properly aligned.

6. **The number of persons reporting to each manager should be reasonable.** With regard to how many persons should report to one manager, there is no magic number. At the upper levels of management, perhaps there should be no more than five or six individuals reporting to one manager. But in a situation involving a group of employees carrying out essentially the same job in a single location, a first-level supervisor might be able to oversee the work of 20 to 25 employees. Thus, in determining the appropriate number of persons that should report to a single manager, consideration should be given to several factors: the level of experience of the staff, the geographical location of staff, and the amount of linking that must be done by the manager. Then, rather than relying on some arbitrary number of direct reports, a decision should be made on the basis of *what is the appropriate number for this particular situation.*

7. **The organization should be designed to provide stability.** If employees are to have a sense of security about their jobs, the organization must be designed to provide stability. Employees need to feel that the job situation tomorrow will be similar to that which exists today. They need to feel that there is a certain amount of uniformity in roles, responsibilities, and expectations. Even though employees may seek variety in their jobs, they nevertheless want to feel that the organizational environment in which they work is stable. Without this sense of stability, the employees will suffer and their productivity will suffer.

8. **The organization should be designed to provide flexibility.** Practically all enterprises are faced with ever-changing problems and opportunities. The productive organization is able to cope with these changes. Organization designers who focus only on stability are making a serious mistake. They also must focus on flexibility — designing the organization so that it can be responsive to new problems and new opportunities.

9. **The organization structure should be designed for perpetuation and self-renewal.** Organization designers should not limit their thinking and vision merely to the demands of the immediate situation. Rather, they should think in terms of a long-term organization design — the type of design that might be required over the years ahead. The organization should be designed so that it can change and grow to meet the challenges of the future. It should be designed so that it lends itself to an evolutionary change rather than a revolutionary change.

10. **The organization structure should be evaluated on the basis of its contribution to enterprise objectives.** It should not be evaluated on the basis of its beauty or elegance, or its structure or symmetry. Rather, each manager should ask a pragmatic question: Does the existing organization structure for my unit contribute substantially to the achievement of results? If the answer is negative, then the organization structure should be changed.

In addition to these 10 principles, there is another one that has been accepted as gospel for perhaps a century: avoid dual subordination. Underlying this principle is the assumption that reporting to two managers simultaneously causes innumerable problems. It is believed that employees will be in a state of turmoil if they receive competing instructions from their different managers. Today, however, with the introduction of task force organization and matrix organization, this age-old principle is now being called into question. Indeed, it is granted that having two or more bosses can create problems, but this disadvantage may be offset by the advantages of more flexible approaches to organization. Besides, early in our lives, haven't most of us simultaneously worked under two managers — our parents?

With the above 10 principles as a foundation for establishing an organization structure, we will now look at the basic logic of organizing. For managers to be effective organization designers, it is important that they understand this basic logic.

THE LOGIC OF ORGANIZATION

Peter Drucker[23, pp. 601-602] offers the architect of organization some sage advice in this message:

> To obtain both the greatest possible simplicity and the greatest "fit," organization design has to start out with a clear focus on *key activities* needed to produce *key results*. They have to be structured and positioned in the simplest possible design. Above all, the architect of organization needs to keep in mind the purpose of the structure he (or she) is designing.

Drucker[23, pp. 530-31] suggests that organization design start with the following questions:

1. In what areas is excellence required to attain the company's objectives?
2. In what areas would lack of performance endanger the results, if not the survival, of the enterprise?
3. What are the *values* that are truly important to *us* in the company?

When these questions have been answered, the organization designer should proceed to carry out the sequence of steps elucidated by Koontz and O'Donnell:[64, p. 279]

1. Establish enterprise objectives.
2. Formulate derivative objectives.

163

3. Identify and classify the activities necessary to accomplish the objectives.
4. Group these activities in the light of human and material resources and the best way of using them.
5. Delegate to the head of each group the authority necessary to perform these activities.
6. Tie these groupings together horizontally and vertically through authority relationships and information systems.

It can be seen that this logic is grounded in management by objectives. The starting point in the process is to state clearly the objectives of the enterprise. This is followed by the design of the organization structure. It should be clear to all managers that the organization structure is a means to an end, not an end itself. As Drucker repeatedly emphasizes, *structure follows function.*

Assuming that the reader accepts this logic of organization, we will now review three basic types of organization: functional, task force, and matrix. There are more than these three types, but essentially every particular structure may be viewed as a reflection of one of these three basic types. Thus, an understanding of the ones discussed below will give the manager a grasp of the essentials of practically all types of organization structure.

As we consider these different types of organization, we should heed the words of wisdom offered by Dale Zand:[129, p. 65]

> Usually a manager assumes that he (or she) has only one organization, which must be used for all problems. That is like a carpenter who uses a hammer for all jobs. A more effective manager first classifies a problem and then chooses an instrument best suited for it.

FUNCTIONAL ORGANIZATION

Whenever one thinks about an organization structure, it seems only natural to think in terms of a functional structure. Such a structure delineates the enterprise functions: research and development, engineering, manufacturing, marketing, finance, personnel, etc. These are the functions that must be carried out to achieve the enterprise's objective.

A simplified functional structure is shown in Figure 27. Here we see four Department Managers reporting directly to a General

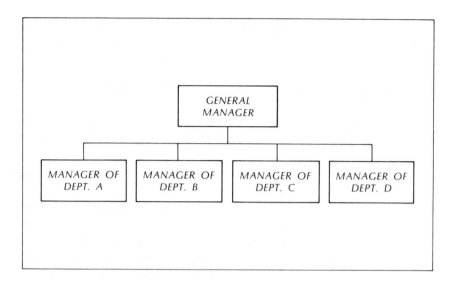

Figure 27.   Functional organization

Manager. Each Department Manager is responsible for a particular functional area. The line of authority is established according to the hierarchy.

The functional structure as we know it today has a long history — going back to the nineteenth century, with its roots established in the bureaucratic organization described in detail by the German sociologist, Max Weber. Weber presented the salient features of bureaucracy in a positive light because this new type of organization met a definite need at the time. Prior to the introduction of bureaucracy, most enterprises in Europe were plagued with patronage: appointments and promotions were based upon personal friendships rather than merit. The bureaucratic organization established a rational basis for appointments and promotions.

Weber[122, p. 214] highlights the technical superiority of bureaucratic organization:

> The decisive reason for the advance of bureaucratic organization has always been its purely technical superiority over any other form of organization. The fully developed bureaucratic mechanism compares with other organizations exactly as does the machine with the nonmechanical modes of production.

165

In *The Theory of Social and Economic Organization*,[123, pp. 333-34] Weber delineates the essential elements of a bureaucratic organization:

1. Required organizational activities are described as official duties.
2. The organization is arranged in a hierarchy of offices, with each office under the control and supervision of the next highest.
3. Operations are governed by a consistent set of rules and policies.
4. Employees are appointed on the basis of their technical qualifications and are not subject to arbitrary terminations.
5. A system of promotions exists according to which an employee may advance by virtue of seniority, achievement, or both.
6. Employees are subject to strict and systematic discipline and control in the conduct of their impersonal official duties.

The praise that Weber[122, pp. 215-16] lavished on bureaucracy would now make the Theory Z manager cringe:

> Bureaucratization offers above all the optimum possibility for carrying through the principle of specializing administrative functions according to purely objective considerations. The objective discharge of business primarily means a discharge of business according to *calculable rules* and "without regard for persons." . . . Its specific nature, which is welcomed by capitalism, develops the more perfectly the more the bureaucracy is "dehumanized," the more completely it succeeds in eliminating from official business love, hatred, and all purely personal, irrational, and emotional elements which escape calculation.

These are harsh words indeed. It appears as though "soul" was to be replaced by "system." But it must be appreciated that the introduction of structure and orderliness into a situation that was very disorderly was viewed as a major contribution at that time. In retrospect, however, we can see that a 180-degree swing of the pendulum may have been excessive.

With its roots firmly established in bureaucracy, the functional structure typifies the organization structure of the modern-day enterprise. It is clear that such a structure has both advantages and disadvantages.

The functional organization offers the following advantages:

1. Functions can be grouped on a logical basis.
2. Responsibility and authority can be clarified.
3. It provides a means of control from the top.
4. It facilitates the flow of communication.
5. It follows the principle of occupational specialization.
6. It simplifies training.

The disadvantages of the functional structure have been elucidated by Drucker:[23]

1. Responsibility for profits is only at the top.
2. The structure is rigid and resists adaptation.
3. Functional specialists become narrow in their vision and skills.
4. It does not prepare people for tomorrow.

In view of these advantages and disadvantages, Barry Stein and Rosabeth Kanter [113, p. 372] stress the importance of supplementing the functional structure:

> We believe that these trends in the 1980s will show that the issue will not be how to *replace* bureaucracy but will be how to *supplement* it. There are some tasks and conditions for which a conventional line hierarchy is better suited than any alternative. The task in the '80s is to permit bureaucracy to function well where it can while a different structure, capable of dealing effectively with the tasks and conditions for which bureaucracy is not suitable, is sought.

TASK FORCE ORGANIZATION

The task force organization emerged as an effective means for overcoming some of the shortcomings found in the functional organization. While the functional organization stresses orderliness and stability, the task force organization stresses flexibility and adaptability.

The task force (or team) has been defined clearly by Peter Drucker [23, p. 564]:

> A team is a number of people — usually fairly small — with different backgrounds, skills, and knowledge, and drawn from various areas of the organization (their "home") who work together on a specific and defined task. There is usually a team leader or team captain. His (or hers) is often a permanent appointment for the duration of the team's assignment. But leadership at any one time places itself ac-

167

cording to the logic of the work and the specific stage in
its progress. There are no superiors and subordinates; there
are only seniors and juniors.

Dale Zand, in the paper "Collateral Organization: A New Change
Strategy,"[129] highlights the key characteristics of the task force
organization:

1. Its purpose is to identify and solve problems not solved by
   the formal organization.
2. It creatively complements the formal organization.
3. It operates in parallel or in tandem with the formal
   organization.
4. It consists of the same people who work in the formal
   organization.
5. The outputs of the collateral organization are inputs to the
   formal organization.
6. It operates with norms that are different from the norms in
   the formal organization.

In the paper "Building the Parallel Organization,"[113] Barry Stein
and Rosabeth Kanter point up the chief differences between the functional organization and the task force organization:

- Functional Organization:
    Routine operations—low uncertainty
    Limited "opportunities" (e.g., promotion)
    Fixed job assignments
    Competency established before assignment
    Long chain of command
    Objectives usually top-down
    Rewards: pay/benefits
    Functionally specialized
    Leadership a function of level
- Task Force Organization:
    Problem solving—high uncertainty
    Developmental assignments
    Flexible, rotational assignments
    Short chain of command
    Objectives also bottom-up
    Rewards:
        Learning

Recognition/visibility
Different contribution
Bonus possibility
New contacts
Diagonal slices — mix functions
Leadership drawn from any level

The task force organization is indeed an effective tool for providing the organization with flexibility and adaptability. Whenever it is necessary to cope with a problem or project that cuts across different departments or organizational units, the task force organization should be considered as a practical alternative to the formal organization. The team members work on a particular problem or project while still being assigned to their administrative "home bases." Assignments might be on either a full-time or part-time basis, but, when the problem is solved or the project completed, the task force is disbanded.

A few enterprises have established a *pure task force organization*, using it to replace the functional organization. Here the members of the enterprise are assigned to task forces on a full-time basis; their only "home base" is the task force itself.* When the work of one task force is completed, the members are then assigned to another task force. This movement from task force to task force may continue throughout an employee's career in the enterprise.

An example of a pure task force organization is found in an R&D division that is organized by projects. As indicated in Figure 28, the various Project Managers report directly to a General Manager. The members of the various project teams report to the Project Managers who have considerable authority in decision making and resource allocation. This form of organization has been used in a number of R&D enterprises that are responsible for conducting a small number of very large projects. Obviously, it would not be effective in enterprises that are responsible for carrying out a large number of small projects.

Thus, it can be seen that the task force organization is considerably different from the functional organization, and just like the func-

---

*The task force organization would exclude supportive groups such as finance, personnel, etc.

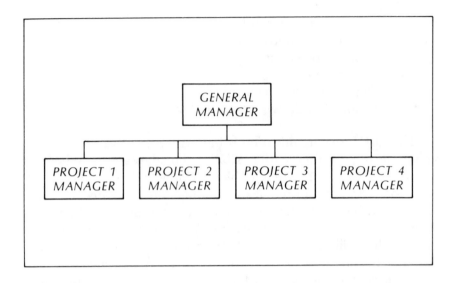

Figure 28. Task force organization

tional organization, the task force organization has both advantages and disadvantage:

The following are the advantages:

1. It provides the enterprise with flexibility and adaptability.
2. It is possible to assemble an inter-departmental team to deal with a given problem.
3. It is open to new ways of doing things.
4. It offers new opportunities for growth and development.
5. It tends to motivate employees.
6. It provides upper management with a means for identifying future leaders in the enterprise.

However, if used exclusively — without the stability provided by a functional organization — the task force organization has the following disadvantages:

1. Frequent organizational change tends to produce anxiety and insecurity in staff.
2. Staff may feel insecure because of lack of contact with a long-term "home base."

3. It does not lend itself to long-term career planning for individual employees.
4. Professionals usually prefer to be located organizationally with their professional group.
5. It frequently leads to inefficient use of human resources.

Considering the strengths and weaknesses of both the functional organization and the task-force organization, the question arises: How can we build on the strengths of the two approaches?

MATRIX ORGANIZATION

Matrix organization may be viewed as a special case of parallel organization. Story has it that, sometime during the early 1960s, an aerospace engineer found himself on an organization chart reporting vertically to his functional manager and horizontally to his project manager. Seeing himself at one of the intersections of the two-way array, he commented, "Here we have a matrix organization." So the term was coined.

In their book entitled *Matrix*, [20, p. 3] Stanley Davis and Paul Lawrence define matrix organization as "any organization that employs a *multiple command system* that includes not only a multiple command structure but also related supported mechanisms and an associated organizational culture and behavior pattern." It is important to consider each of the three features included in the definition.

A "multiple command system" means that authority is given to both the functional structure and the task-force structure. We always have known that the functional structure has authority, but now we have a new twist: the task-force structure also has authority. This point highlights the difference between a committee and a task force: the committee normally is only a recommending body, whereas the task force is given the authority to make decisions and commit resources.

"Related support mechanisms" refers to such processes as a dual accounting system and a dual personnel-evaluation system. A formal accounting system must be established to provide both arms of the matrix with budgets and periodic financial reports. Also, a performance evaluation system must be established to allow managers on both arms of the matrix to participate in the evaluation of individual employees — with the task force managers making inputs to

171

these evaluations and the functional managers coordinating the effort.

"An associated organizational culture and behavior pattern" refers to the organizational climate and the attitudes of managers and employees functioning in the matrix. As mentioned previously, the task-force organization operates with norms that are different from those of the formal organization. This condition applies equally to the matrix organization. Functional managers must be willing to share their power with project managers. Individuals must be willing to report to two or more managers simultaneously. Individuals must be willing to work on projects or task forces in which the leader is junior to them in the functional hierarchy. Without the presence of such attitudes, matrix organization will surely fail.

Davis and Lawrence have identified the three chief conditions that lead to matrix organization: (1) pressure for dual focus (e.g., for both advancing the state of the art and using the existing state of the art to solve current problems); (2) pressure for high information-processing capacity (e.g., the need to write a large inter-disciplinary research proposal that involves people from different units within the organization); and (3) pressures for shared resources (e.g., people, equipment, and facilities).

Matrix organization contains these following key features:

1. It is designed to provide both stability and flexibility in the organization.
2. It provides for the simultaneous operation of the functional organization and task forces.
3. The selection of task force members cuts across different levels and units of the functional organization structure to select the most appropriate team members.
4. Each individual staff member has a "home base" in a functional unit but then may be assigned to one or more task forces on a temporary basis.

An illustration of a pure matrix organization is shown in Figure 29. In this example, both the Department Managers and the Project Managers report directly to the General Manager. Individual employees are located at the lines of intersection in the diagram. If the organization follows a policy of "shifting the people," then individual employees working on the project report to a Project Manager while maintaining their "home bases" in an administrative unit. On the other hand, if the organization follows a policy of "shift-

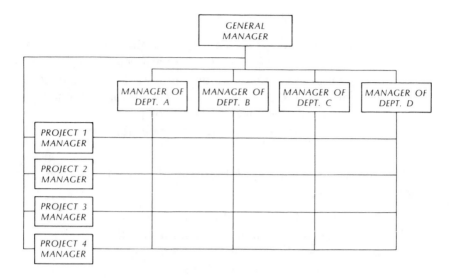

Figure 29. Matrix organization

ing the work," then individual employees are supervised by their functional managers in completing work packages, with the Project Manager assuming the responsibility for integrating all of the work packages. Either of these two approaches can be effective, but it must be made clear at the outset which course is to be followed.

Matrix organization has been used in a variety of enterprises: research organizations, manufacturing organizations, service organizations, and professional organizations. Matrix may be a useful tool in any enterprise in which there is a continuing need to assemble interdepartmental teams to work on a temporary basis.

Davis and Lawrence stress the importance of three key functions of the general manager to make matrix work: (1) power balancing (making certain that there is a balance of power between the functional managers and the task force managers); (2) managing the decision context (establishing guidelines and procedures for decision making); and (3) standard setting (establishing standards that must be met by managers in both arms of the matrix). The success of the matrix will depend greatly on how well these three key functions are executed.

A dispassionate view requires that we consider both the advantages and disadvantages of matrix organization.

173

Matrix offers the following advantages:

1. Provides the enterprise with both stability and flexibility
2. Provides the individual employee with considerable opportunity for growth and development in working with different task forces while still having the security of a "home base"
3. Tends to minimize routine aspects of job
4. Makes efficient use of resources — including people, equipment, and facilities

The following are some of the chief disadvantages of matrix organization:

1. Authority and responsibility are not clear.
2. It imposes new demands for communication.
3. More decision makers add to complexity.
4. It may lead to duplicate efforts.

In view of these disadvantages, it is important that managers do not move headlong into converting their existing organizations into matrix organizations. It is most important to keep in mind an admonition offered by Davis and Lawrence: *a successful matrix must be grown rather than installed.*

It seems clear that matrix can be an effective form of organization *for those enterprises that need it.* However, an enterprise should not attempt to establish a matrix organization unless the participating managers fully understand it and are committed to making it work. It is a very complex type of organization.

DELEGATION

Regardless of the type of organizational structure, one of the major problems found in most organizations is the lack of delegation of authority. Whether it be a functional structure, a project structure, or a matrix structure, one frequently hears complaints about the lack of delegation. Supervisors and managers at practically all levels charge that they have considerable responsibility but not the authority to go with it. If this situation continues for an extended period of time, it can result in considerable frustration and even stomach ulcers.

The purpose of delegation is to distribute the leadership function and to make organization possible. Without effective delegation, it is impossible for an organization of any size to function effectively and efficiently. Effective delegation and effective management are highly correlated.

If these truisms seem almost too obvious to state, why is it that so many managers are reluctant to delegate? In the book *The Time Trap*,[76a] Alec Mackenzie is perceptive in identifying the barriers to delegation. He groups them into three categories: (1) barriers in the delegator, (2) barriers in the delegatee, and (3) barriers in the situation. Some of the principal barriers are listed in Table 6.

Obviously, there are no easy answers to the problem of delegation. There are no "quick-fix" solutions. Each manager must study the barriers and decide which ones apply to him or her. This should be followed by development of a plan for overcoming the barriers.

A strategy for effective delegation has been proposed by William Dyer in his *Contemporary Issues in Management and Organization Development*.[24a] The strategy consists of the following steps:

1. Identify the assignment, project, or area of work that is to be delegated.
2. Identify the *appropriate* person to whom the work will be delegated.
3. Discuss the proposed task to be delegated with the one who is proposed to do it.
4. Make sure the person doing the task has the appropriate resources (time, money, equipment, assistance, etc.) and necessary authority to do the work.
5. Provide the needed training, orientation, or direction the person may need to do the delegated activity.
6. Allow the person to move ahead with strong support, encouragement, and positive reinforcement.
7. Agree in advance on times to review programs.
8. Upon completion of the task, critique the total experience.

The successful execution of this strategy will produce a number of beneficial results. With regard to the delegators, they will find that they have more time to do the things that they should be doing. With regard to the delegatees, they will find that they are growing more rapidly in their fields of endeavor. With regard to the organization, it will be found that effective delegation results in greater effectiveness and efficiency for the total enterprise. In essence, we can conclude that effective delegation is simply good management.

Table 6. Barriers to Delegation

A. Barriers in the Delegator

- Preference for operating
- "I can do it better myself" fallacy
- Insecurity
- Refusal to allow mistakes
- Lack of confidence in subordinates
- Uncertainty over tasks and inability to explain

B. Barriers in the Delegatee

- Lack of experience
- Lack of competence
- Avoidance of responsibility
- Overdependence on the boss
- Disorganization
- Overload of work

C. Barriers in the Situation

- One-man-show policy
- No toleration of mistakes
- Criticality of decisions
- Crisis management - urgency, no time to explain
- Confusion in responsibilities and authority
- Understaffing

Alec Mackenzie—*The Time Trap*, Adapted, by permission of the publisher.

A STRATEGY FOR ORGANIZATIONAL CHANGE

In his book *Designing Complex Organizations*,[35] Jay Galbraith elucidates different strategies for organizational change. Two radically different strategies are illustrated in Figure 30. One approach is simply

176

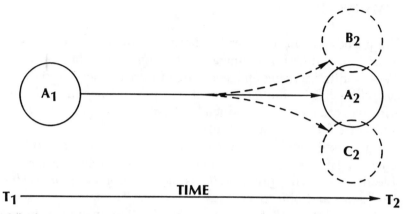

Jay Galbraith—*Designing Complex Organizations*, Reading, Massachusetts: Addison-Wesley Publishing Company, 1973, Reprinted, by permission of the publisher.

Figure 30. Planned and unplanned organizational change

to let organizational change "happen": the organization moves from being an A_1 at time T_1 to being either a B_2 or a C_2 at time T_2. The manager then exclaims, "How on earth did we ever get here!" Quite different in nature is a systematic strategy involving planned change: over time, the organization moves logically and systematically from being an A_1 to becoming an A_2. Certainly, the latter change strategy is the preferred one.

What has been learned from the past is that an effective organizational structure is systematically planned. Managers cannot simply sit back and expect such a structure to emerge of its own volition. As stressed by Drucker, the manager should always carry two organizational structures in his or her head: the present organizational structure and the desired organizational structure.

A systematic strategy for bringing about a change in organization structure consists of the following five steps:

1. Clearly define the goals and objectives of the enterprise.
2. Define the existing organizational structure.
3. Define the desired organizational structure.
4. Develop phase plans.
5. Communicate the plans.

SUMMING UP

The purpose of this chapter has been to provide a framework and general guidelines for organizational design. From the time of Max Weber's initial writing on the nature of bureaucracy up to the present, there has been almost a century of experience in establishing principles of organization. Much has been learned about the dos and don'ts of effective organization.

One thing that has been learned is that structure should follow function. This means that managers must first establish the goals and objectives of the enterprise and *then* design the organization to achieve these goals and objectives.

A second thing that has been learned is that an enterprise needs both stability and flexibility. It is realized that a functional structure is necessary for stability and that the use of task forces — as a parallel organization — is an effective means for achieving flexibility.

Still a third thing that has been learned is that the redesign of an organizational structure should be done in a rational and systematic manner. Every manager should carry in his or her head two organizational structures — the actual and the desired — and then develop systematic phase plans for moving from the former to the latter.

We also know that organization is a means to an end rather than an end itself. Here we must agree with Drucker[23, p. 602] when he says:

> Organization is a means to an end rather than an end itself. Sound structure is a prerequisite to organizational health; but it is not health itself. The test of a healthy business is not the beauty, clarity, or perfection of its organization structure. It is *the performance of people.*

Exercise VII
Defining Your Job

Write a job description for your present job. Include the overall mission, broad functions (numbers), and specific responsibilities (bullets) associated with each function.

Job _____

Mission:

1.
   -
   -
   -

2.
   -
   -
   -

3.
   -
   -
   -

4.
   -
   -
   -

5.
   -
   -
   -

VIII

Staffing and Staff Development

> Many of you have experienced in your manufacturing operations the advantages of substantial, well-contrived and well-executed machinery. If then, due care as to the state of your inanimate machines can produce beneficial results, what may not be expected if you devote equal attention to your vital machines which are far more wonderfully constructed?
>
> Robert Owen
> in Urwick: *The Golden book of Management*[118, p. 7]

Introduction • Theoretical Framework • Principles of Staffing and Staff Development • Human Resource Planning • Personnel Selection • Staff Development • Performance Appraisal • Summing Up

---

INTRODUCTION

Robert Owen, who made the above statement during the middle part of the nineteenth century, is generally acknowledged as "the pioneer of personnel management." As a successful manager in the textile industry in Scotland, Owen fully appreciated the importance of the human factor in industry and was committed to doing something about it. Owen insisted that the personnel function not take a back seat to other functions of management but that it be identified with the purpose of management itself.

181

We frequently hear managers say, "People are our most important resource." But too often these words have a hollow ring to them. The actions of managers belie their words.

During the course of conducting management workshops, the author has asked the participants why managers often commit more resources to maintaining their equipment and facilities than to maintaining their people. A common answer is that the investment in maintaining the material aspects of an enterprise will produce more visible results than a similar investment in people. One can clearly see the results of painting a building, but the benefits of a staff training program are not so apparent.

Theory Z says that staffing and staff development is the most important function of management. Certainly, the other functions are important, but they are secondary to obtaining and building the staff.

The purpose of this chapter is to provide guidelines for staffing and staff development. Emphasis is placed on human resource planning, personnel selection, staff development, and performance appraisal.

THEORETICAL FRAMEWORK

A framework for helping us focus on the essence of staffing and staff development is shown in Figure 31.[17] The two dimensions of this basic structure are "Action Demands" and "Action Capabilities," with the former referring to the demands of the various jobs and the latter referring to the capabilities of the persons in the jobs. The "Flow Channel" signifies the desired situation, in which there is a match between Action Demands and Action Capabilities.

Employee job satisfaction and productivity can be gauged in terms of this diagram. When people are in the Flow Channel, they tend to have high job satisfaction and are productive. On the other hand, when people fall outside the Flow Channel — either below or above — job satisfaction and productivity tend to decline. The obvious challenge for managers is to do everything reasonably possible to get their people in the Flow Channel, which may be accomplished by modifying the job demands, by developing the people, or by a combination of both.

What should be done when someone falls outside the Flow Channel for a significant period of time? Consider, for example, a person

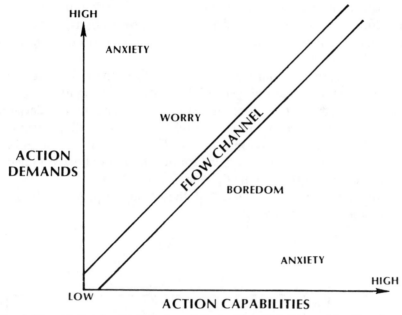

HIGH

ANXIETY

WORRY

ACTION
DEMANDS

FLOW CHANNEL

BOREDOM

ANXIETY

HIGH

LOW

ACTION CAPABILITIES

Journal of Humanistic Psychology, Vol. 15, No. 3, pp. 41–63, adapted from Mihaly Csikszentmihalyi—"Play and Intrinsic Reward." Summer, 1965, Reprinted by permission of the publisher.

Figure 31. A framework for staffing and staff development

who was an excellent engineer but is found to be a very poor first-line supervisor. A Theory L approach would be to simply ignore the situation. Theory X would say to fire the person. Theory Y would say to provide the person with more support. A Theory Z approach is suggested by Peter Drucker:[23, p. 310]

> The nonperformer is often — and perhaps in most cases — not a "dud." He is only in the wrong place — the proverbial square peg in the round hole. He belongs elsewhere, where what he can do is needed and contributes. It is the manager's job to think through where a nonperformer might be productive and effective, and to say to him, "You are in the wrong business — you belong there."

In formulating a theoretical framework for staff development, attention must be given to two critical dimensions: meeting organizational needs and meeting individual needs. The organization has specific needs in terms of skilled personnel in particular fields. The individual employees have specific needs in terms of aspirations for growth and advancement. Both areas of needs must be attended to by the manager.

Shown as orthogonal axes in Figure 32 are the two dimensions of "Meeting Organizational Needs" and "Meeting Individual Needs." The resulting diagram yields four distinct approaches to staff development: (1) indifference to staff development (Theory L); (2) job training without regard for individual needs (Theory X); (3) personalized growth experience without regard for organizational needs (Theory Y); and career development (Theory Z).

The estimated effectiveness of these four approaches to staff development is as follows:

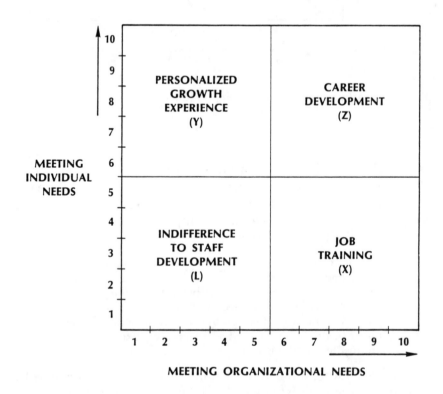

Figure 32. Two dimensions of staff development

1. **Indifference to staff development (Theory L)** can survive only in a low-skills field. In a high-technology industry or in the knowledge industry in general, this approach will prove to be a total failure.
2. **Job training without concern for meeting individual needs (Theory X)** may meet immediate needs for skill development but may have a negative impact on employee motivation because employees will feel that they are being treated as pawns. Overall, this approach will be only marginally effective.
3. **Personalized growth experience without regard for meeting organizational needs (Theory Y)** may contribute to employee motivation because of the individualized concern shown by management but may yield little actual return-on-investment for the enterprise as a whole. Overall, this approach will be only marginally effective.
4. **Career development (Theory Z)** is a marriage between meeting organizational needs and meeting individual needs. The results of this synergistic relation will be maximally effective.

PRINCIPLES OF STAFFING AND STAFF DEVELOPMENT

In most enterprises, there is a crying need for a systems approach to staffing and staff development. Being a shared responsibility between the Human Resources Department and line management, the staffing and staff development function frequently is carried out in piecemeal fashion. Not only do the various pieces not fit together, they actually may be contradictory — with the left hand and the right hand working at cross purposes. If the various elements of staffing and staff development are not integrated and directed toward common goals, this function will be far less effective than it is capable of being. The real challenge, of course, is to fully integrate all of the parts.

A systems approach to staffing and staff development is shown in Figure 33. Included in this diagram are the essential elements of an effective human resources program. The various elements are interrelated and directed toward common goals. In addition to the elements shown in the figure, another important aspect of this systems approach is the systematic evaluation of each element in terms of

185

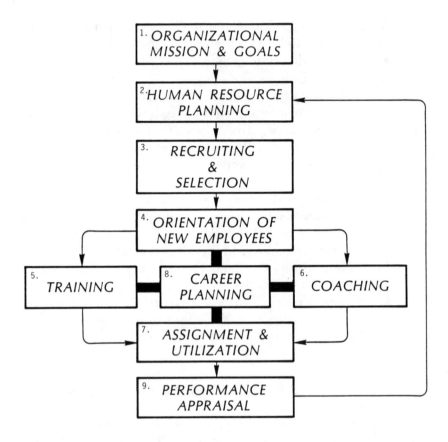

Figure 33. A systems approach to staffing and staff development

its contribution to the goals of the enterprise and its cost.

In the light of this systems view, we can formulate 10 basic principles of staffing and staff development:

1. *A clear statement of organizational mission and goals* should be the beacon that guides the staffing and staff development program.
2. A *Human Resources Plan* should be developed to serve as a roadmap for carrying out the staffing and staff development function.

186

3. An aggressive *recruiting and selection program* should focus on getting the right people for the right jobs at the right time.
4. Every manager should be responsible for the specific *orientation* of each new staff member assigned to him or her.
5. The organization should provide effective *training programs* to meet the need for new knowledge and skills.
6. Every manager should view *coaching* of staff as one of his or her most important job functions.
7. Personnel *assignment and utilization* should be viewed as an effective means for developing staff.
8. *Career development* should not be merely "left to chance"; it should be systematically planned.
9. The primary purpose of *performance appraisal* should be the improvement of job performance.
10. Each element of the staffing and staff development program should be *evaluated* periodically in terms of its contribution to organizational goals and objectives and its costs.

These 10 principles are elaborated on in the following sections.

HUMAN RESOURCE PLANNING

All elements of the staffing and staff development program should be directed toward the accomplishment of organizational goals and objectives. To this end, a comprehensive written plan should be prepared for the program. The plan would include aims, activities, schedules, responsibilities, and budgets. This would be the roadmap.

The importance of the planning phase is highlighted by James Walker in his book *Human Resource Planning*.[119] Walker's elucidation of the human resource forecasting process is shown in Figure 34.

1. The first step in this process is to understand the environmental and organizational conditions. Included here are the external labor supply, legal constraints, and the economy; technological changes, productivity patterns, and trends; management philosophies, policies, and plans; organization structure and job design; and patterns of employee turnover and mobility. Without a clear understanding of these conditions, the Human Resources program would be operating in a vacuum.

187

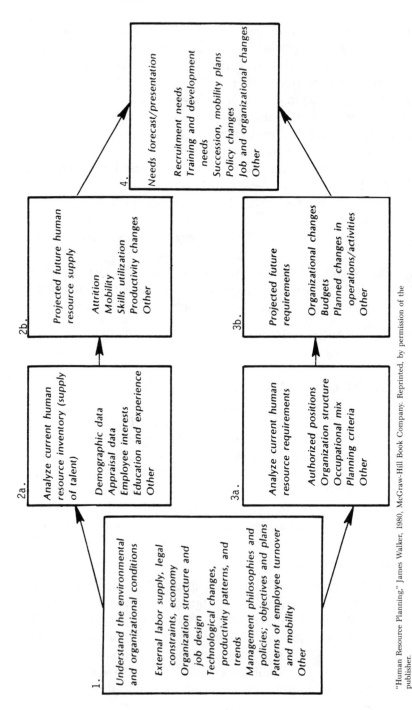

"Human Resource Planning," James Walker, 1980, McGraw-Hill Book Company. Reprinted, by permission of the publisher.

Figure 34.   The human resource forecasting process

2. The second step in the process is to analyze the current supply of talent and to project the future human resource supply. In analyzing the current supply of talent, an appraisal would be made of demographic data, performance data, employee interests, and education and experience. The projected future human resource supply would be based upon an assessment of attrition, mobility, skills utilization, and productivity changes.

3. The third step is to analyze the current human resource requirements and to project future requirements. In the analysis of current requirements, attention is given to organization structure, occupational mix, and authorized positions. In the projection of future requirements, attention is given to planned organizational changes, planned changes in operation and activities, and projected budgets.

4. Building on all of the above information, the final step is to make a needs forecast. This forecast includes recruitment needs, training and development needs, succession and mobility plans, needed policy changes, and needed job and organizational changes.

It is obvious that this human resource forecasting process requires a considerable amount of time and effort. There usually will be a few antagonists who will insist that such forecasting cannot be done with any degree of accuracy. Nevertheless, such human resource planning must be done in the same way that planning is done for marketing, research and development, engineering, and production. The human resource plan should be a vital part of the enterprise's total operation.

PERSONNEL SELECTION

Getting the right people for the right jobs at the right time is the essence of the staffing function. Mistakes are costly both to the individual and to the organization.

Traditionally, personnel selection has relied on three tools: references, psychological tests, and the selection interview. Because of Federal legislation concerning equal employment opportunities, Human Resources Departments are relying less and less on references and psychological tests. Today, the primary selection tool is the interview. Thus, it is essential that all managers responsible for hiring new employees be skilled in conducting a selection interview.

There is an art to effective interviewing, and this art can be learned. The first requirement in learning the art is to recognize that the interview is more than a mere conversation. It is a formal means of exchanging information for the purpose of making a rational decision about the hiring of a new employee.

The selection interview has three purposes: (1) to determine the suitability of a candidate for a specific job opening; (2) to give the applicant information about the job; and (3) to create a feeling of good will toward the prospective employer, regardless of the outcome of the interview.

To achieve the primary purpose of the interview — determining the suitability of a candidate for a specific job opening — it is essential that the interviewee do more of the talking than the interviewer. Experts on the subject recommend that the interviewee do approximately 75 percent of the talking, and the interviewer 25 percent.

Common errors in interviewing include: lack of preparation for the interview, poor interviewing conditions, covering the content haphazardly, poor questions, the "halo effect," invasion of privacy, and premature decisions. Anyone who takes the selection interview seriously will give attention to these common errors and take the necessary steps to avoid them.

In the book *Personnel Interviewing*,[75, p. 31] Felix Lopez stresses that the interviewer must accept the responsibility for guiding the interview:

> You must accept the idea that you are essentially a leader, and that you are fully accountable for the outcome of the interview. You cannot divest yourself of this accountability nor can you attribute interview failure to the interviewee. It is completely up to you to assure a smooth flow of conversation along lines that are congruent with both the implicit and explicit purposes of the interview.

The effective interviewer uses a "patterned interview." Here the dialogue is guided by the interviewer, but the interviewee is encouraged to speak freely and in depth about relevant topics. The interviewer maintains control of the interview to make certain that all relevant areas are covered systematically.

A suggested outline for conducting a patterned interview is presented by Richard Webster[123a] in Table 7, which includes two

Table 7. A Guide for Interviewing

The First Cycle is a discussion of the candidate's present position, interests, and background:

1. Present job, e.g., "Tell me about your present job." What you like, do, don't like, would like to change.

2. Yourself, e.g., "What do you like to do, your interests, your skills and habits (job related)." To find out about the person in the context of his or her job.

3. Others, in the present job situation. "Tell me about your work group, your 'boss', the people who work for you, the people you work with."

4. The organization you work in now, e.g., "Tell me about where you are working now; what kind of an organization are you working with?"

5. Compensation. "Describe your compensation situation, history, needs."

The Second Cycle is a discussion of the same five points; this time with the focus on the interviewer's organization. How good a "fit" is this candidate?

1. This job. "What can I tell you about this job/ opportunity?" "Tell me how this job/situation fits with your objectives."

2. You, the candidate. "What are your objectives? What do you want in a new job?"

3. Others, in the job-offering organization. Introduce the candidate to key people. Give other inter- viewers specific questions to ask -- parts of the cycle to initiate or repeat, and the kind of feedback desired.

4. The (offering) organization. "What would you like to know about our organization?" Other interviewers can easily be asked to cover parts of this one.

5. Compensation, an important element of recruitment. For example: "This job pays in the range of..., and offers other rewards/benefits/opportunities."

Richard Webster—"Interview Cycles." Copyrighted by Management Development Institutes, April, 1982. Reprinted, by per- mission of the publisher.

cycles. The first cycle is a discussion of the candidate's present position, interests, and background. After this first cycle is completed, the interviewer does a quick mental review: "Is this person a possible 'fit' for the job we have?" If the answer is "no," the interviewer terminates the interview. If the answer is "maybe" or "yes," the interviewer proceeds to the second cycle, which is a discussion of the same five areas as in the first cycle but with focus on the interviewer's organization.

This guide can be adapted to each particular situation. In some situations, it may be completely applicable in this form, and in others, it may not be. But whatever the situation, the interviewer should have a general outline to guide the interview to make certain that all relevant topics are covered systematically.

A recommended strategy for carrying out the total interview process is shown in Figure 35. Prior to the actual interview, the interviewer should clearly define the position requirements. What skills, abilities, and attitudes are required for success in this particular position? Also, what will be required for advancement in this particulr career ladder? The next step is to do the pre-interview homework. Here the interviewer should attempt to learn as much about the applicant as reasonably possible — from the application form and any other relevant documents. We next move to the actual interview of the candidate. Successive interviews might include the Human Resources Department, the immediate supervisor, the supervisor's manager, and other employees with whom the employee would be working. Upon completion of this series of interviews, the interviewers would get together to analyze and interpret the information obtained. Then, finally, they would make a decision regarding the hiring of the candidate.

There is a great deal of published information about effective interviewing. Certainly this information has not been codified in a form that would allow for a completely scientific approach. (The humanistic manager would hope that it never will be.) Nevertheless, the available information can provide useful guidelines, and the conscientious application of these guidelines can assure that the interview is carried out in a rational and systematic manner. As a result, the interviewer's "batting average" in the selection process — which will never be perfect — would be expected to improve at least.

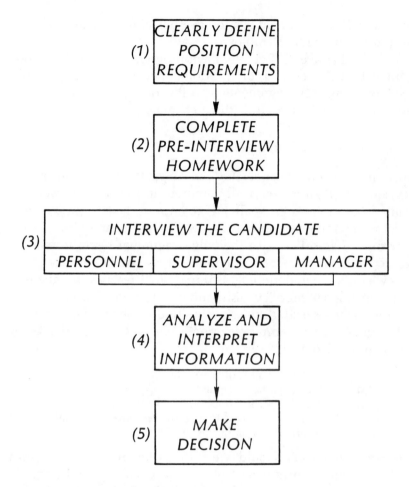

Figure 35.   A strategy for interviewing

STAFF DEVELOPMENT

The Theory Z organization places considerable emphasis on staff development. Employees are viewed in terms of both their *present* skills and abilities and their *potential* skills and abilities. They are viewed as being "in process"— continually moving from the actual toward the potential. Underlying this development is the assump-

193

tion that staff development is a joint responsibility of the organization and the individual employee.

A comprehensive staff development program includes the following important elements: (1) orientation of new employees, (2) training, (3) coaching, (4) assignment and utilization, and (5) career planning. We will look at each of these elements.

Orientation of New Employees

Too often a job applicant gets the "red carpet treatment" during the
interview and then is practically ignored during the first week on
the job. The employer goes "all out" to impress the applicant during
the day of interviewing, and then, once the applicant is hired, places
the person in an office with the only assignment being to read an
outdated company operations manual. In a state of consternation,
the new employee undoubtedly is thinking, "I received so much attention during my interview visit, and now they don't seem to care."
The consequences of this undesirable situation should be apparent.

The importance of employee orientation has been highlighted by
Koontz and O'Donnell:[64, p. 551]

> Every manager is responsible for the specific orientation
> of a new staff member assigned to him or her. It is part
> of the manager's staffing function to take the time and ex-
> ercise the patience required to give the employee essential
> information about his or her assignment.

Indeed, managers should view the orientation of new staff
members as an important part of their job. They should learn all
they can about their new employees; tell them what is expected of
them; tell them how their jobs fit into the overall operation and ac-
quaint them with it; and stress the importance of each job. They
should keep in close contact with their new employees and encourage
them to discuss their job problems with them.

Because of the many demands on the manager, it frequently is
not possible to give the new employee the attention that is warranted.
To deal with this constraint, it often is appropriate to assign a sponsor or mentor for the new employee. This sponsor is selected from
the senior ranks of the unit and is expected to provide much of the
orientation for the new member of the unit. This arrangement usually benefits both the new employee and the mentor.

It must be recognized that the goal of personnel selection is to obtain good people and *retain* them. The retention rate is partially a function of the attention given to the orientation of new employees. The "law of primacy" says that an employee's overall impression of an enterprise is determined greatly by the *first* impression. This first impression is imprinted during the first week on the job.

Training

Many enterprises accept job training as an integral part of their human resource function. Job training refers to the development of specific knowledge and skills through formal means. Certain jobs within the enterprise — either present or projected — require specific knowledge and skills over and above what employees bring to the organization. The organization assumes the responsibility for developing these capabilities in their employees.

Many training programs leave much to be desired. They are developed without a sound rationale. Often, little attention is given to the specification of training objectives, to the selection of appropriate media, or to the adaptation of the program to the target population. Many training programs are conducted year after year without being evaluated systematically. Small wonder that some managers look askance at company training programs!

Over the years, human resource specialists have learned a great deal about the requirements for effective training. In summary, an effective training program has the following features:

1. It is based on organizational needs — either present or projected.
2. It includes clearly stated objectives written in terms of expected learner outcomes.
3. It is tailored for specific audiences.
4. It is directed toward specific on-the-job applications.
5. It is designed for active involvement of participants.
6. It is evaluated and revised as appropriate.

In considering the characteristics of an effective training program, it is important to appreciate the salient factors in adult learning. Adults must want to learn, and they will learn only what they feel a need to learn. A training program must center on problems, and the problems must be realistic. Most important, adults must be able to see the on-the-job applications of the training. Unless these con-

195

ditions are satisfied, an adult may be *physically* present in a training program but not *mentally* present.

Practically all managers need a general understanding of the features of effective training. Even though they themselves may not conduct the training, they should be able to evaluate particular training programs in which their people might be enrolled. The manager should know what questions to ask of the training specialist in order to make an assessment of a given training program and to judge whether or not it seems worthwhile to enroll staff members in the program.

Coaching

While formal training programs may engage staff members anywhere from one to ten days each year, coaching has the potential for being practiced almost every workday of the year — at least whenever the staff member and the supervisor are together in the workplace. Coaching is face-to-face counseling; it is the on-the-job counseling provided by the immediate supervisor. It is assumed that the supervisor is knowledgeable about the job in question and that this knowledge can be passed on to the staff member through face-to-face counseling. This counseling may take place prior to a given job assignment, during the time that the assignment is being carried out, or after the assignment is completed. The basic idea is that the staff member can benefit from the knowledge and experience of the supervisor.

A good "coach" has the following characteristics: (1) is available, (2) is a good listener, (3) is a good communicator, (4) is empathetic, (5) is positive, (6) is enthusiastic, and (7) is patient. Essentially, we can say that the characteristics of an effective "coach" are the same as those of an effective teacher. Here we must agree that the effective manager *is* a teacher.

There is wide variation among managers with regard to how they view their responsibility as a coach. At one extreme will be found managers who accept coaching as a major part of their job, while at the other extreme will be found managers who consider it to be a trivial or insignificant part of their job.

One direct consequence of this variation among managers is the variation in rate of growth among individual employees. One can observe two new college graduates in the same field being hired by the same company at the same time but assigned to two different supervisors. The two graduates are practically equal in ability and potential, but, five years hence, one of them far exceeds the other in ability and performance. Much of this difference can be attributed to coaching: one of the employees had an effective coach and the other did not.

Many are the managers who claim that they simply do not have time to coach their people. Then we should ask about priorities. What is more important than spending time with one's people to help them develop the knowledge, skills, and attitudes needed for success on the job?

Personnel Assignment and Utilization

When an important task must be carried out, the approach used by many managers is to select someone who sometime previously accomplished this task successfully. Certainly, once again, the task is likely to be carried out successfully. But in terms of staff development, one should ask how the assigned staff member will benefit from the experience.

A powerful — and often overlooked — approach to staff development is assignment and utilization of staff for specific tasks. An employee who is assigned to a succession of increasingly challenging tasks has an excellent opportunity for growth and development. To be truly effective, assignment and utilization as an approach to staff development requires systematic planning on the part of the manager. It obviously will not work in an environment characterized by "crisis management."

Sometimes it is useful to match an experienced person with an inexperienced one for carrying out a particular assignment. By assigning the experienced person to the task, the manager has the assurance that the job will be carried out successfully. By assigning the inexperienced one to the task, the manager has the knowledge that an opportunity is being provided for job growth.

It also is useful to consider ad hoc assignments as a means for staff development. Task forces provide the management with a multitude of opportunities for staff growth. Possible assignments to a task force might include task force leader, deputy leader, working team member, or consultant. Such assignments can help "stretch" employees beyond the routine provided by their regular job assignments.

The use of lateral transfers is another means of fostering staff development. If a person remains in the same job for a lengthy period of time, it is likely that he or she will "plateau" on the learning curve. When this plateau is reached, there is little opportunity for growth and little challenge in the job. The predictable result is boredom and a deterioration in performance. To prevent this situation from arising, the alert manager will make use of lateral transfers as an effective means for continually developing staff.

When thinking about staff development, the manager should consider the nature of the learning curve for each job under his or her responsibility. What actions should be taken to assure that the learning curve continues to rise for each of the members of the group? The conscientious use of assignment and utilization is an effective means for making certain that these learning curves continue to rise.

Career Planning

Career planning is at the heart of an effective staff development program. Many people view career development solely as advancement up the organizational heirarchy. But, as stressed by Paul Chaddock,[11] advancement may occur in a variety of ways: (1) being promoted upward in the hierarchy; (2) taking on greater responsibility within a functional specialty; (3) developing into a generalist; or (4) moving from practitioner to innovator.

Career planning should be viewed as a meshing of the needs of the organization and the aspirations and talents of individual employees. The Theory L organization ignores career planning. While the Theory X organization focuses only on the needs of the organization, the Theory Y focuses essentially on the aspirations of individual employees. The Theory Z organization attempts to achieve a marriage between the needs of the organization and the aspirations and talents of individual employees.

Dialogue between the individual staff member and the staff member's immediate supervisor is the cornerstone of effective career planning. The purpose of this dialogue is illustrated by John McMahan and Joseph Yeager[89] by means of the "JOHARI window'" shown in Figure 36. Here the "open area" represents what is known by both the employee and the supervisor regarding the employee's aspirations and talents and the possible job opportunities within the

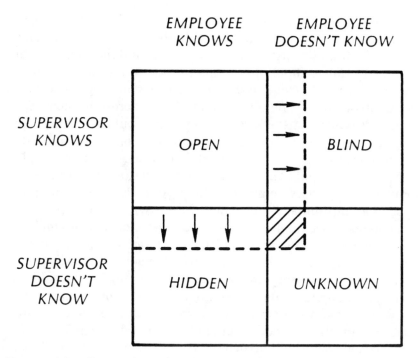

"Manpower and Career Planning," John McMahon and Joseph Yeager, 1976, McGraw-Hill Book Co. Reprinted, by permission of the publisher.

Figure 36.   The Johari window and career planning

organization. The "blind area" represents what is known by the supervisor but not the employee. The "hidden area" is known by the employee but not the supervisor. The "unknown area" covers what is unknown to both the employee and the supervisor. The purpose of the dialogue between the employee and the supervisor is to expand the "open area."

One basic requirement for an effective career planning program is to establish career ladders for the various occupational areas within the organization. Each occupational area should contain a progression of jobs, with a written job description available for each job. Such job progressions should be developed for all occupational areas — be it manager, engineer, technician, or secretary.

199

A second basic requirement for an effective career planning program is that management should establish a policy of posting all job openings within the organization. Vacancies and their requirements and salary ranges should be communicated in a timely manner. If the organization has various divisions in different geographical locations, job openings should be communicated across divisions. Some managers may resist the idea of job posting, but the openness and honesty embedded in the JOHARI window concept require it.

Furthermore, it is recommended that a discussion of career plans be included as an integral part of an annual performance review with individual employees. Inasmuch as many organizations have a policy of conducting annual performance reviews with their employees on a one-to-one basis, this is an appropriate time to discuss the employee's career plans. The employee and the supervisor should jointly complete a brief career planning form, which would be attached to the performance appraisal form. This career planning form would then be updated annually. (See Exercise VIII at end of chapter.)

Why do many employees resign from their jobs on a voluntary basis? Frequently, it is not a matter of pay or fringe benefits. Rather, it is because of a lack of perceived opportunity for growth and development within the organization.

PERFORMANCE APPRAISAL

Perhaps the most difficult aspect of the entire staffing and staff development function is performance appraisal. Many employees are threatened by performance appraisal. Many supervisors and managers dislike criticizing their employees. As a consequence, many people — managers and employees alike — perceive performance appraisal only negatively.

Some of the common problems associated with performance appraisal systems are listed by James Walker[119] in Table 8. After reviewing this list of problems, one can understand why so many people view performance appraisal only negatively.

It is important to recognize at the outset that there are no perfect performance appraisal systems. But there are a number of useful guidelines for developing an acceptable performance appraisal system — one that is acceptable both to the persons being evaluated and to those doing the evaluating.

Table 8.   Problems With Performance Appraisal Systems

- Conflicting multiple uses
- Unclear goals of the system
- Ratings biased by pay considerations
- Lack of clear performance criteria (standards)
- Reliance on ratings of personality rather than performance
- Rater biases such as halo persistence in ratings
- No validation of performance appraisal system
- No conceptual justification of the system
- Managers not trained to administer appraisals
- Managerial dislike for giving feedback
- One-way communication between superior and subordinate
- Rater biases
- No developmental or performance follow-up
- Susceptibility to manipulation by managers
- No built-in reinforcement for doing the appraisal
- Conflicting coach and evaluator roles
- No use of appraisal systems for top management
- No credibility of appraisal systems in the organization
- No impact of appraisal on performance
- Regarding appraisal as an administrative chore not related to business goals.

James Walker—*Human Resource Planning*, 1980, McGraw-Hill Book Co., Reprinted, by the permission of the publisher.

The key to building an effective performance appraisal system is to design it for the purpose of improving job performance. There may be secondary purposes such as determining merit pay and promotions, protecting the Personnel Department, etc. But the primary purpose of a performance appraisal system should be *the improvement of job performance*. The beauty of this goal is that it is one that is shared by both the evaluator and the person being evaluated. This shared goal gives both parties a common reference point and bond.

The key to carrying out the performance appraisal system is to make it a *joint effort* between the staff member and the staff member's immediate supervisor. Performance appraisal involves setting objectives and reviewing progress toward these objectves. Either a pure top-down approach or a pure bottom-up approach is unacceptable. What is called for is a continuing dialogue between the staff member and the supervisor.

The way in which the appraisal interview is conducted is of immense importance. In his book *The Appraisal Interview*,[77] Norman Maier describes in considerable detail three approaches to the appraisal interview: Tell and Sell, Tell and Listen, and Problem Solving. In the Tell-and-Sell method, the supervisor tells the employee how he or she is doing and gains the employee's acceptance of the evaluation and the plan that must be followed for improvement. In the Tell-and-Listen method, the supervisor describes the strong and weak points of the employee's job performance without interruption and then listens to the employee's concurrence and disagreements without any attempt to refute the employee's statements. In the Problem-Solving method, the supervisor and employee jointly identify problems associated with job performance and jointly arrive at approaches for dealing with the problems.

Maier conducted extensive research on these three types of appraisal interviews. With mature, responsible employees, he found the Problem-Solving approach to be superior to the other two approaches. (With immature or irresponsible employees, one of the other approaches may be more effective.) The Problem-Solving approach offers the following advantages: (1) it increases intrinsic motivation; (2) it increases responsibility of the staff member; (3) staff members have more control over their own destinies; (4) it makes greater use of the staff member's capability; (5) it promotes good communication; and (6) the quality of solutions may be upgraded.

Maier[78, p. 73] stresses that the Problem-Solving approach is forward-looking:

> The tendency to blame others is a backward-looking approach. The past is beyond control and cannot be altered. Only the present and the future are subject to change, and hence only they can be controlled through decisions. The problem-solving approach, therefore, must incorporate an attitude that accepts the past and takes up the problem of what to do to reach present objectives.

Building on these basic guidelines, we can now look at a general strategy for performance appraisal. Shown in Figure 37 is a "participative management-by-objectives" approach to staff appraisal adapted from Harold Koontz.[60] The appraisal focuses on developing performance objectives prior to the beginning of the appraisal period and then reviewing progress during the period of appraisal and at the end of the appraisal period. A key point is that the entire process is a *joint effort* of the employee and the supervisor. Experience has shown that this is a sound approach to performance appraisal.

A participative management-by-objectives approach to performance appraisal offers the following benefits:

- All employees know in advance the basis on which they are evaluated.
- The staff member and the manager agree in advance what the job is and what the priorities are.
- It is a self-correcting approach that helps people set objectives that are both challenging and attainable.
- It promotes self-management and individual responsibility.
- It helps identify staff development needs.
- It strengthens the manager-employee relationship.
- It leads to improved job performance!

Most managers undoubtedly would agree that the evolution of performance appraisal systems has been positive: the overall development is at least moving in the right direction. But once again, we can assert that there is no perfect performance appraisal system. Nevertheless, it is indeed possible to develop a reasonably good system — one that is acceptable both to those being appraised and to those doing the appraising.

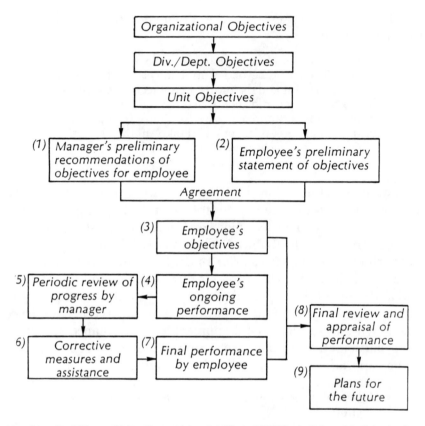

Adapted from Harold Koontz—"Making Managerial Appraisal Effective." © 1972 by the Regents of the University of California. Reprinted/adapted/condensed from *California Management Review*, Volume XV, No. 2, p. 50 by permission of the publisher.

Figure 37. A strategy for performance appraisal

SUMMING UP

The purpose of this chapter has been to present guidelines for the establishment of an effective staffing and staff development program. A comprehensive program includes the following 10 elements:

1. Organizational mission and goals
2. Human resource planning
3. Recruiting and selection

4. Orientation of new employees
5. Training
6. Coaching
7. Assignment and utilization
8. Career planning
9. Performance appraisal
10. Systematic evaluation of all program elements.

These various constituents should be integrated as a total system — as an assemblage of interrelated elements directed toward common goals. The elements should all fit together and reinforce one another. Such an organic approach to staffing and staff development will prove to be far more effective than the traditional piecemeal approach. Certainly, a well coordinated systems approach to staffing and staff development requires close cooperation between the Human Resources Department and the organization's line managers. This is an important responsibility that they must share.

It is essential that both the Human Resources Department and the line managers hold a long-range view of staffing and staff development. A return-on-investment may not be forthcoming this week, this month, or even this quarter. But, in the long run, a well planned and well executed program can be expected to produce substantial benefits.

The following are some of the expected benefits:

- Better qualified staff
- Improved motivation and morale
- Improved job performance
- Increased organizational productivity.

Realizing these benefits is no mean achievement. They can be realized by any organization that is willing to devote sufficient time and resources to the staffing and staff development function. Once again, we should reflect on the words of wisdom offered by the pioneer of personnel management, Robert Owen:

> If then, due care as to the state of your inanimate machines
> can produce beneficial results, what may not be expected
> if you devote equal attention to your vital machines
> which are far more wonderfully constructed?

Exercise VIII

Developing Your Career Plan

(Marion Kellogg — *Career Management*)

1. Long-range career goals:

    _____
    _____
    _____

2. Reasonable next positions or desired changes in the current position:

    _____
    _____
    _____

3. Special talents and experience that qualify you for the desired next position and long-range career goals:

    _____
    _____
    _____

4. Gaps in experience, knowledge, or skill to be minimized if career goals are to be realized:

    _____
    _____
    _____

5. Proposed action plans:

    Action   Approximate Time

    _____   _____
    _____   _____
    _____   _____
    _____   _____

IX

Motivating

Many managers would agree that the effectiveness of their
organizations would be at least doubled if they could
discover how to tap the unrealized potential present in their
human resources.

Douglas McGregor
The Human Side of Enterprise[88, p. 4]

---

*Introduction • Theoretical Framework • Physiological Needs: Freedom from
Excessive Job Stress • Safety Needs: Knowing What is Expected • Belong-
ingness Needs: Being Part of a Team • Self-Esteem Needs: Meaningful Work
• Self-Actualization Needs: Opportunities for Career Growth • Summing Up*

INTRODUCTION

Sagging productivity is a major problem in the United States as well
as in many other countries. From the attention given to the problem
in the news media, declining growth in productivity is clearly of great
concern to managers, economists, and political leaders, as well as
to many citizens. Certainly this attention is warranted; sagging productivity adds to inflation, which, in turn, degrades quality of life.
While productivity growth may still be on the rise in some industrial
nations, ways to further stimulate this growth are equally vital to
their economies. Thus, it affects us all.

The question becomes one of identifying factors causing the sagging productivity. Finding the true cause is vitally important. If one

focuses on the wrong causes and takes corrective action accordingly, the problem will not be solved; quite likely, it will be aggravated.

To identify the reasons for sagging productivity, a number of economists have taken a "macro" approach, which has led them to conclude that sagging productivity can be attributed to three major causes:

- The low level of investment in plant and equipment
- The decrease in R&D expenditures
- Escalating government regulations

Certainly these are significant factors. But are they the *key* to the problem? If so, the problem is out of the hands of most managers in industry.

The contention here is that these factors, while significant, do not hold the key because they are exogenous variables — external factors over which most managers and supervisors have no control in their day-to-day operations. Thus, while these supervisors and managers may spend no small amount of time bemoaning the lack of capital investment and the escalation of government regulations, *there is very little that they can actually do to significantly alter these trends.* Consequently, as a result of emphasizing these factors, apathy develops.

On the other hand, suppose we look at an "endogenous variable"— the management system. Consider this statement by Hideo Suguira, Executive Vice President of Honda Motor Company:[45, p. 5]

> The United States is the most technically advanced country and the most affluent one. But capital investment alone will not make the difference. In any country, the quality of products and the productivity of workers depend on management. When Detroit changes its management system, we'll see more powerful American competitors.

Indeed, the management system is the key causal factor in influencing productivity. And any organization's management system, while guided by the philosophy and policies of top management, is actually put into practice by *all* of the supervisors and managers in the organization — from the supervisor of custodians to the chief executive. Both the nature of the management system and the way in which it is implemented have a profound effect on the motivation and productivity of all employees. This is the key factor demanding attention.

In searching for solutions to the productivity problem, the fundamental question is: As supervisors and managers carry out the functions of management, to what extent are they able to *motivate* their employees and to influence them so that they will strive willingly toward achieving organizational goals?

In the book *Management*,[65, p. 631] Koontz, O'Donnell, and Weichrich state it well when they say:

> Because managing involves the creation and maintenance of an environment for the performance of individuals working in groups toward the accomplishment of a common objective, it is obvious that a manager cannot do this job without knowing what motivates people. The necessity of building motivating factors into organizational roles, the staffing of these roles, and the entire process of directing and leading people must be built on a knowledge of motivation.

Thus, the thesis of this chapter is that *employee motivation is the key factor in productivity.* "Key factor" means the critical variable that warrants the greatest attention in dealing with the productivity problem. This thesis is supported by the following two facts: (1) variation in employee motivation obviously accounts for a large percentage of the variation in productivity, and (2) employee motivation can be dealt with directly, and immediately, by *all* supervisors and managers. The evidence is convincing that improved employee motivation will result in the greatest payoff in improved productivity.

THEORETICAL FRAMEWORK

The essence of employee motivation is captured by Harry Levinson[70, p. 129] in the following observation:

> The highest point of self-motivation arises when there is a complementary conjunction of the individual's needs and the organization's requirements. The requirements of both mesh, interrelate, and become synergistic. The energies of the individual and the organization are pooled for mutual advantage.

The key concept here is "synergy," which means that the interaction of two or more agencies produces a result greater than the sum

209

of the effects taken independently. Here we are saying that "two plus two equals five." This notion may be foreign to mathematicians, but it is well known to successful managers (and to students of thermodynamics). This is what synergy is all about!

Building on the concept of synergy, we can construct a broad framework for analyzing employee motivation in terms of two basic dimensions: (1) concern for organizational goals and (2) concern for individual goals. These two dimensions are shown as orthogonal axes in Figure 38. The diagram produces four approaches for dealing with employee motivation: (1) indifference to employee motivation (Theory L); (2) the carrot-and-stick approach (Theory X); (3) encouraging the employee without giving attention to organizational goals (Theory Y); and (4) achieving a synergistic relation between concern for organizational goals and concern for individual goals (Theory Z).

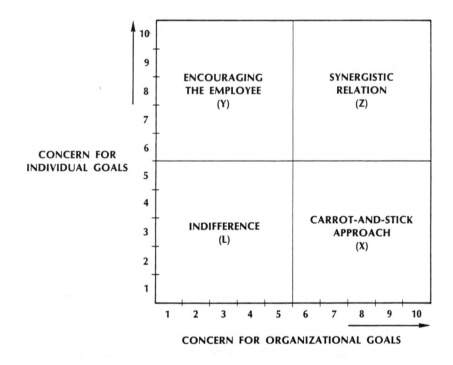

Figure 38.   Two dimensions of employee motivation

These four different approaches to employee motivation are likely to yield the following results:

1. **Indifference to employee motivation (Theory L)** is an approach that cannot sustain itself for any period of time; employee motivation and productivity will be abysmally low. This approach will be at the rock-bottom level in effectiveness.
2. **The carrot-and-stick approach (Theory X)** may produce reasonably good results for a limited period of time, but employees may feel that they are being treated as pawns rather than persons. In the long run, this approach will be only moderately effective.
3. **Encouraging the employee without giving attention to organizational goals (Theory Y)** may motivate many employees, but this motivation may be short-lived if the employees do not see the connection between their efforts and the organizational goals. Thus, this approach will be only moderately effective.
4. **Achieving a synergistic relation between concern for organizational goals and concern for individual goals (Theory Z)** is the condition, as Levinson says, that produces the highest level of self-motivation; this is the ideal toward which all managers should strive. This approach will be maximally effective.

A Theory Z approach to employee motivation is found in the extensive work by Abraham Maslow, who has had a significant influence on management thought in the United States and other countries. His hierarchy of human needs has been described in various management texts and presented in numerous management courses. Our purpose here is to highlight some of Maslow's key concepts and then describe how these concepts can be applied to employee motivation.

Prior to Maslow's landmark work in the area of motivation, most psychologists took a purely behavioral approach to studying motivation. Essentially, this was a stimulus-response approach in which the investigators would carry out a three-step process to: (1) define and measure behavioral aspects of motivation; (2) define and measure environmental stimuli that might affect motivation; and (3) correlate the environmental stimuli and behavioral aspects. Although considered to be a fairly rigorous approach to motivation studies, it bore little fruit.

In sharp contrast to the behavioral approach, Maslow stressed that motivation lies *within* the human organism and can be understood only by viewing it from within. In the book *Toward a Psychology of Being*,[85, p. 22] he says:

> Many of the problems that have plagued writers as they attempted to define and delimit motivation are a consequence of the exclusive demand for behavioral, externally observable criteria. The original criterion of motivation and the one that is still used by all human beings except behavioral psychologists is the subjective one. *I am motivated when I feel desire or want or yearning or wish or lack.*

Maslow defined motivation in terms of *needs*. A need signifies a discrepancy between what the individual *has* and what he or she *desires*. The individual is "driven" or "motivated" to reduce or eliminate the discrepancy. Thus, if there is no discrepancy between what exists and what is desired, there is no motivation.

Maslow postulated that there are basic needs common to all of humankind. These are inborn and are found in all members of the human species, regardless of race or culture. The basic needs are grouped into the following five categories:

1. **Physiological needs**: need for oxygen, water, food, rest, etc.
2. **Safety needs**: need for security, stability, dependency, protection, structure, order, law, limits, strength in the protector.
3. **Belongingness needs**: need for affectionate relations with other people, need for a place in one's group or family.
4. **Self-Esteem needs**: need for self-respect and for the esteem of others.
5. **Self-Actualization**: desire for self-fulfillment, to become all that one is capable of becoming.

According to Maslow, these basic needs are related to each other in a hierarchical order. When one need is satisfied, this does not bring about a state of rest but, rather, it brings into consciousness another "higher" need. Wanting and desiring still continue but at a higher level. As indicated in Figure 39, the hierarchical order of needs progresses from Physiological Needs, to Safety Needs, to Love and Belongingness needs, to Self-Esteem Needs, and finally to Self-Actualization.

Maslow summarizes this hierarchy by saying that one's higher nature rests upon one's lower nature, needing it as a foundation and collapsing without it. He suggests that, for the majority of humankind, the higher nature is inconceivable without a satisfied lower nature; perhaps the only way to develop this higher nature is to fulfill

Figure 39.   The hierarchy of needs

and gratify the lower nature first. One's higher nature clearly rests on the existence of a fairly good environment, both present and past.

With regard to higher and lower needs, one should note Maslow's comments[85, p. 222] on motivation and pay — a matter of great interest to most managers. He gives us the following "food for thought":

> To think of "pay" in terms of money alone is clearly obsolete in the needs hierarchy framework. It is true that the lower need gratifications can be bought with money; but when these are already fulfilled, then people are motivated only by higher kinds of "pay"— belongingness, affection, dignity, respect, appreciation, honor — as well as the opportunity for self-actualization and the fostering of the highest values — truth, beauty, efficiency, excellence, justice, perfection, order, lawfullness, etc.

From his many years of research in human motivation, Maslow found that even though only a very small percentage of the population ever reaches the top rung of the needs hierarchy (that is, achieves self-actualization), the psychologically healthy individual continually advances in the hierarchy. Conversely, the psychologically unhealthy individual is very likely to remain at a lower tier in the hierarchy. Maslow found that when individuals *are not* moving toward self-actualization, they are likely to be characterized by boredom, tension, neurotic anxiety, low frustration tolerance, cynicism and despair, psychosomatic illness, low job satisfaction, and low productivity. On the positive side, when individuals *are* moving toward self-actualization, they are likely to be more open and spontaneous, more tolerant of frustration, more courageous, kinder toward others, more creative, more satisfied with their jobs, and more productive.

Based on Maslow's findings, the message to managers seems clear. They should endeavor to understand each of their employees and to create the proper environment that will help them move up the hierarchy. As a result, the individual employee will have greater job satisfaction and will be more productive. If this happens for most employees in a given work group, then the group itself will be more productive; and so it goes for the entire organization.

It should be recognized that Maslow's theory is not accepted universally among psychologists. Considerable debate continues on two key issues:

1. To what extent are the higher level needs determined by environmental factors rather than genetic or innate factors?
2. Is it necessary for an individual to move up the hierarchy in the exact order proposed by Maslow, or is it quite possible to bypass one or more of the tiers?

Debate on these issues will likely continue for many years, but this does not mean we must postpone applying the theory. Most psychologists probably would agree that:

1. The needs included in Maslow's hierarchy are indeed strong in most cultures and must be dealt with regardless of whether they are determined genetically or environmentally.
2. Even if it has not been proved that the five categories of needs are arranged in a clearly defined hierarchical order, they can serve nevertheless as a useful classification design.

Thus, even though Maslow's theory of needs provides no cookbook solution to the problem of employee motivation and productivity, it does offer a useful framework to help managers deal with the problem in their day-to-day operations.

Within the framework provided by Maslow, the selection of par-

Table 9. Motivation Problems and Proposed Solutions

	NEEDS CATEGORY	MAJOR PROBLEM	PROPOSED SOLUTION
(1)	Physiological needs	Job stress	Stress management
(2)	Safety needs	Not knowing what's expected	Management by objectives
(3)	Belongingness needs	Estrangement from the organization	Participative management
(4)	Self-esteem needs	Meaningless work	Work enrichment
(5)	Self-actualization	Lack of opportunity to achieve potential	Career planning

ticular strategies for improving employee motivation obviously will depend on the particular problems encountered. To illustrate such strategies, Table 9 lists a major problem related to each category of Maslow's needs hierarchy (from the employee's standpoint) and a proposed management approach for dealing with the problem.

This problem-solution matrix obviously oversimplifies the actual situation because each management strategy listed as a proposed approach is applicable to more than one problem category. Likewise, problems are not always easily categorized in the real world and may often overlap needs classes or may be multifaceted. Listed here are the *primary* connections between problems and management strategies. These five problem areas and the proposed solutions are discussed in the following sections.

PHYSIOLOGICAL NEEDS:
FREEDOM FROM EXCESSIVE JOB STRESS

> The physiological needs are the most prepotent of all the needs. For an individual who is missing everything in life in an extreme fashion, it is most likely that the major motivation for this person would be the physiological needs rather than any of the others.
>
> Abraham Maslow[84, pp. 36–37]

215

In the course of conducting management workshops, the author has asked the participants what happens to them when they are subjected to extreme job stress over an extended period of time. With little hesitation and with considerable feeling, they respond: "I get migraine headaches" . . . "My ulcer acts up" . . . "I get a pain in the lower part of my back" . . . "My skin breaks out in a rash" . . . "My hemorrhoids come back" . . . "I have diarrhea for several days." These are examples of psychosomatic illnesses — physical disorders resulting from the mental strain or anguish caused by job stress. Job stress results when certain needs — particularly psychological and physiological needs — are not met.

Cooper and Marshall[15] have identified the major organizational stressors:

- **Physical environment**: temperature, noise, lighting, spatial arrangements, crowding.
- **Job qualities**: work overload, time pressures, work pace.
- **Roles in the organization**: role ambiguity, role conflict, too little management support.
- **Organizational structure**: lack of participation, poor communications, restrictions on behavior, inequities in the reward system.
- **Relationships**: with supervisors, with subordinates, with peers, inability to delegate.
- **Career development**: underpromotion, overpromotion, obsolescence.
- **Change**: organizational, individual.

A useful conceptualization of stress in organizations is shown in Figure 40. Randall Schuler[107] developed this cause-and-effect model that includes environmental stressors, individual characteristics, individual responses, and organizational consequences. Moving from left to right in the diagram, we see that the degree to which various environmental stressors affect employees will differ with experience, ability, life stage, physical well-being, and mental health. Employee responses to stress then fall into three categories: physiological, psychological, and behavioral. Whenever these individual responses occur to any significant degree, the organization is likely to suffer any of a number of undesirable consequences, generally leading to lowered productivity.

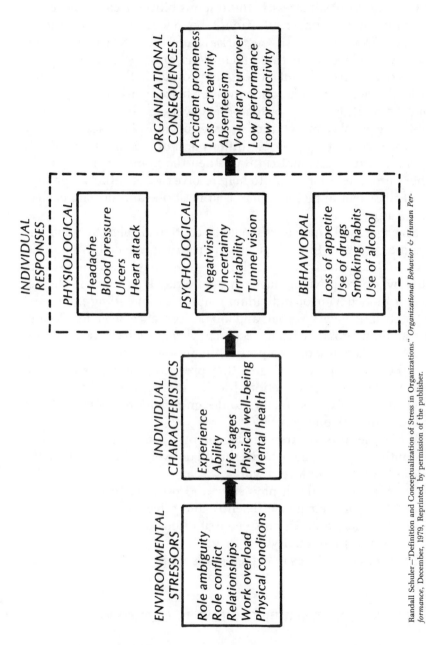

Randall Schuler—"Definition and Conceptualization of Stress in Organizations." *Organizational Behavior & Human Performance*, December, 1979, Reprinted, by permission of the publisher.

Figure 40.   Conceptualization of stress in organizations

Dealing with job stress is the responsibility of each and every supervisor and manager; it cannot be relegated to the Human Resources Department. If stress arises from the physical conditions of the workplace, then these conditions must be improved—not necessarily perfected, but at least improved. If the cause is work overload, then corrective action must be better work spacing, better work distribution, or use of temporary workers. If the cause is role ambiguity or role conflict, then every effort must be made to clarify roles through written job descriptions and oral communication. If the cause is interpersonal conflict, then the manager must use his or her human relations skills to help resolve these conflicts. For each one of these causal factors, there is at least one appropriate corrective measure.

Managers and supervisors should be continually alert to individual responses to stress. Physiological responses are revealed through illnesses and absenteeism. Psychological and behavioral responses are noted by a perceptive manager in day-to-day alterations in the demeanor or behavior of individual employees, including nonverbal (or "body language"), verbal, and job performance behavior. To prevent a small problem from becoming larger, corrective measures should be taken as soon as a potentially serious problem is detected.

Most managers would agree that preventive action is far more effective than corrective action. Ideally, managers should use their knowledge of job stress factors to design a work environment that obviates corrective action.

While the costs for stress management in some situations may be substantial, the accrued benefits should outweigh the costs. Benefits will derive from employees who:
- Are healthy (both physically and psychologically)
- Perform their jobs efficiently and effectively
- Are motivated to make contributions to the organization's overall productivity.

Thus, effective stress management is simply good management.

SAFETY NEEDS: KNOWING WHAT IS EXPECTED

If the physiological needs are fairly well gratified, then there emerges a new set of needs: the safety and security needs. Essentially everything that may be said about the physiological needs is equally true—but to a less degree—about these needs. The human being may equally well be wholly dominated by them.

Abraham Maslow[84, p. 39]

On a number of occasions, the author has asked managers what type of management is practiced in their organizations. Not infrequently the answer is "crisis management." When they are asked for an explanation of crisis management, a typical response is: "Our managers have no plans; they are constantly putting out fires; they move from one crisis to another." The respondents indicate that this approach to management has a disturbing effect on all employees: it engenders anxiety and insecurity. Because employees do not know what is expected, their safety needs are not being met. Indeed, crisis management is dysfunctional to the total organization. There obviously is a better way of managing.

As a means of avoiding or eliminating crisis management, Peter Drucker introduced the concept of management by objectives, or "managing for results." As indicated in Chapter V, this was a radically new concept for much of the management world. Prior to the introduction of this approach, management had focused more on *how* something was done rather than on *what* should be done. Drucker brought about a major change in thinking by emphasizing that managers should focus their attention on *results* rather than process.

The following management by objectives strategy has grown out of Drucker's basic concept:

1. Top management establishes organizational goals and objectives.
2. Middle management establishes unit objectives in the light of organizational objectives.
3. Middle management works with first-line supervisors to jointly formulate each first-line supervisor's performance objectives in the light of the unit objectives.
4. First-line supervisors then work with their employees to agree upon performance objectives for each of the employees.

The complete set of objectives would then constitute the foundation for the organization's plan of action—a roadmap for the coming year. Thus, rather than being plagued with anxiety and insecurity, the employees would have a feeling of confidence and security in knowing where they are headed and what is expected of them. In addition to knowing what is expected of them, all members of the organization would receive periodic feedback on their performance. This approach would be expected to signal the end of crisis management.

In theory, Drucker's concept of management by objectives is excellent; it is viewed by many as the very nature of management. However, while a number of organizations have achieved considerable success in implementing management by objectives, others have encountered serious obstacles and even failure with its implementation. Thus, it is not surprising that many managers look askance at management by objectives. This negativism, though, has resulted from *failures in implementation*, rather than from the nature of the process itself. The experience of many managers witnesses that management by objectives is an effective approach to management *if implemented properly.*

The benefits of management by objectives clearly outweigh the costs. The primary costs lie in the time required for managers to develop objectives and to review and appraise the performance of their staff members. Many managers admit that they spend substantial amounts of time working with employees to develop performance objectives. They feel, however, that this allotment of time is at least offset by the time savings resulting from greater self-management on the part of staff members, who have their own objectives to guide them. This is not to mention the benefit of employee satisfaction derived from knowing where they are headed and what is expected.

If management by objectives is implemented properly, no longer should managers hear any of their employees say, "I really don't know what's expected of me." This would signify that an important safety need had been met.

BELONGINGNESS NEEDS: BEING A PART OF A TEAM

> If both the physiological and the safety needs are fairly well gratified, there will emerge the love and affection and belongingness needs. The whole cycle will repeat itself with this new focus. Now the person will hunger for affectionate relations with people in general, for a place in his or her group or family. The individual will strive with great intensity to achieve this goal.
>
> Abraham Maslow[84, p. 43]

220

Many are the employees who feel estranged from the organizations in which they work. They see themselves as mere objects being controlled and manipulated by management to achieve the financial objectives of the company. They are "Its" rather than "I's"; objects rather than subjects; means rather than ends. As a consequence, there is a rift between the individual employee and the organization. The need for "belongingness" is not fulfilled.

The author has spoken with numerous employees concerning their motivation and job satisfaction, both individually and in small groups. Comments heard during recent years include:

- A secretary: "My boss refers to me as 'bionic fingers.'"
- A technician: "The technicians in our plant are referred to by our professional engineers as 'pairs of hands.'"
- An engineer: "My boss tells me *what* my objectives are, *when* I am to achieve them, and *how* I am to achieve them."
- A production worker: "I made a suggestion to my foreman as to how we could improve our operation, but I was told that it was not my job to come up with suggestions."
- A production supervisor: "My manager assigns completely unrealistic quotas to my group, and I'm not allowed to make any input into what the quotas should be."
- An engineer: "We have weekly meetings with our supervisor, but these meetings are strictly one-way communication. It would save time for everybody if he would just send us a memo."
- A supervisor: "I received my 15-year pin last month; my manager sent it to me through the *interoffice mail*."
- A production foreman: "Our upper-level managers make all of the important decisions around here, and they don't even tell us the *why* of these decisions."

Perhaps if these were isolated cases, there would be no reason for alarm. But they are not isolated; they are all too common occurrences. Small wonder that we find major problems in productivity! Employees in large numbers feel estranged from the organizations for which they work. They view themselves as small cogs in a large wheel, as objects that can be easily replaced.

What brought about this feeling of estrangement on the part of so many employees? The answer probably lies in the establishment of the bureaucratic structure, which has had both positive and negative influences. As indicated in Chapter VII, the bureaucratic structure emerged during the latter part of the 19th century to meet a distinct need for orderliness, rationality, and objectivity, as opposed to the prevailing disorderliness, irrationality, and patronage. Bureaucracy did indeed help achieve at least a semblance of rationality in organizations. On the negative side, however, it sucked the blood of the organization's members. It fostered reason but suppressed feeling. Today the large organization often is like a machine that is devoid of feeling and compassion, like a body without a soul.

It is clear that present-day organizations need an alternative to the purely bureaucratic pattern. Certainly the orderliness and rationality offered by the bureaucratic model are still required, but there is a crying need to bolster this model with concern for people, both individually and collectively.

Participative management has emerged as the solution to many of the problems generated by the bureaucratic pattern. In the simplest terms, participative management may be defined as a form of management that involves a group of employees working cooperatively under the guidance of a competent leader to achieve common goals. These employees actively participate in the key decisions influencing their work. Furthermore, as a prerequisite of all of this, employees are treated as persons rather than objects.

Undoubtedly the greatest success in participative management has been achieved by the Japanese. The salient features of Japanese management have been described by Nina Hatvany and Vladimar Pucik in an article entitled "Japanese Management Practices and Productivity."[45] The authors describe Japanese management practices in terms of philosophy, strategies, and tactics:

1. **Philosophy** is centered on the concept that human assets are to be the firm's most important and profitable assets in the long run.
2. **Strategies** include:
   - Articulating a unique company philosophy
   - Integrating the employee into the company
   - Providing stable long-term employement
3. **Tactics** include:
   - Genuine concern for the employee
   - Emphasis on work groups
   - Open and extensive communication throughout the organization

- Consultative decision making
- Job rotation, internal training, and slow promotion
- A complex appraisal system that focuses on both performance and potential.

Certainly U.S. managers cannot transport the Japanese management model completely intact to this country, but in the area of participative management there is much that American managers can learn from the Japanese.

What are the expected benefits of participative management? It is enlightening to consider the characteristics of persons who participate in decisions that influence their work, as identified by John French and Robert Caplan:[31]

- Low psychological strain
- Low role ambiguity
- High utilization of skills
- Good working relations with others
- Positive attitudes toward work
- High production

Thus, rather than being threatened by participative management, managers should embrace it. In turn, they will discover that they have not lost power: insofar as they are more effective managers, they will have gained power.

SELF-ESTEEM NEEDS: MEANINGFUL WORK

> All people in our society (with a few pathological exceptions) have a need for a stable, high evaluation of themselves, for self-respect, and for the esteem of others. . . . Satisfaction of the self-esteem need leads to feelings of self-confidence, worth, strength, capability, and adequacy, of being useful and necessary in the world.
>
> Abraham Maslow[84, p. 45]

Many employees perform the same tasks day after day, week after week, month after month: the job remains essentially unchanged. As a result, the individual worker becomes disenchanted with a job that initially may have been viewed as interesting and challenging. Rather than being involved and enthusiastic, the worker is bored and stagnant.

We see a close relation between work and self-esteem. If the work is dull and lacks challenge, the employee's self-esteem is dampened. On the other hand, if the work is interesting and challenging, the employee's self-esteem is heightened.

The question then becomes: Assuming that most employees are assigned to particular jobs for periods of 3 to 7 years, what can management do to make their work more interesting and challenging and, in turn, to heighten their self-esteem?

The answer to this question lies in *work enrichment*: modifying the work situation to make it more interesting and challenging to the employee. Much has been written about *job enrichment*, but this focuses only on the job per se. Much has been written about *personal growth experience*, but this focuses only on the employee. Here, the concept of *work enrichment* is intended to encompass both the job and the employee, as well as the relation between the two.

John Hinrichs[47, p. 168] lists certain assumptions underlying the notion of work enrichment:

- Sizable numbers of people are working in jobs that do not fully utilize their abilities and skills.
- People are not inherently lazy; they need to have their abilities and skills more fully utilized in their work.
- Given an opportunity, people will put more effort into their work.
- When this occurs, their productivity will increase, as well as the satisfaction they derive from their work.

There are at least four distinct methods of work enrichment: job redesign, job rotation, the use of temporary task forces, and job training.

Job redesign entails modifying the job to make it more interesting and challenging to the worker. Robert Ford[30] has identified three important aspects of job redesign:

- The module of work — a slice of work that gives an employee a "thing of his or her own."
- Control of the module — as an employee gains experience, the supervisor should continue to turn over responsibility until the employee is handling the work completely.
- The feedback signaling whether something has been accomplished — knowledge of results should go directly to the employee where it will nurture motivation.

224

Extensive research done in such leading companies as AT&T and Texas Instruments shows that efforts in job redesign clearly can produce substantial benefits both to the employee and to the organization: greater job satisfaction for the employee and increased productivity for the organization.

Job rotation involves assigning employees and managers to different jobs to provide them with more stimulating work and to enlarge their job skills. Sometimes called "lateral transfers," this approach to work enrichment has been used extensively by Japanese firms but rarely in American companies.

Because American firms focus more on developing specialists, job rotation is viewed by many as a counterproductive strategy. The Japanese, however, have been successful in the use of job rotation to develop effective generalists: employees and managers who have a wide range of skills, who appreciate the problems of many different functional groups, who are able to communicate across functional groups, and who have a substantial commitment to the goals of the total organization rather than to those of a single specialty. Although the Japanese may suffer in terms of the number of highly specialized employees and managers, the benefits they accrue through job rotation offset this loss.

The *use of temporary task forces* entails assigning individuals to ad hoc teams while they still retain their ties to their administrative units. Inasmuch as this tactic has been discussed in previous chapters, we will only review the benefits:

- Provides more interesting and challenging work for the employee
- Provides opportunities to develop new skills
- Provides opportunities for more people to assume leadership roles
- Fosters collaboration and cooperation across functional groups
- Promotes greater commitment to organizational goals

Job training involves skill development for employees and managers — either to prepare them for carrying out their present job assignments or to prepare them for new assignments.

Companies vary greatly in their commitment to job training. At one end of the spectrum are companies that expend a significant portion of their annual operating budgets for the continual training of their employees; at the other end are companies that expend practically nothing. If training programs are directed toward the specific needs of the company and are well planned and well executed, they can produce a substantial return-on-investment to the enterprise.

These, then, are four methods for bringing about work enrichment. Certainly there are others, but the intent here is not to be exhaustive. It is only to alert the manager to the rich possibilities of using work enrichment as a means of promoting job growth, job satisfaction, and self-esteem for the worker.

SELF-ACTUALIZATION NEEDS: OPPORTUNITIES FOR CAREER GROWTH

> Even if all these needs are satisfied (physiological, safety, belongingness, self-esteem), we may still often (if not always) expect that a new discontent and restlessness will soon develop unless individuals are doing what *they*, individually, are fitted for. Musicians must make music, artists must paint, poets must write if they are to be ultimately at peace with themselves. What individuals *can* be, they *must* be. They must be true to their own nature."
>
> Abraham Maslow[84, p. 46]

One important way in which an enterprise can help its employees move toward self-actualization is through an effective career planning program. While most managers may agree with this statement, they often put career planning on a "back burner" simply because of the pressures of time. Career planning calls for a time perspective of 3 to 5 or even more years, but, as stated before, most U.S. managers limit their thinking to this fiscal year or, even worse, to this quarter. Herein lies the problem. Again, if managers are able to look through the upper lens of their bifocal glasses, they will make the time available for career planning with their employees.

The goal of career planning is to achieve a mutually reinforcing relation between the needs of the organization and the career aspirations of individual employees. Consider the situation in which a given organization has certain manpower needs for meeting its overall objectives, and a given employee in the organization has certain goals and aspirations concerning his or her own job future. Theory X would say that the individual should be adapted to meet the needs of the organization, whereas Theory Y would suggest that the organization should be used as a springboard for facilitating the career growth of the individual. As an integrating concept, Theory Z promotes the idea of achieving a synergistic relation between the needs of the organization and the aspirations of the individual employee. For the majority of situations, the Theory Z approach is certain to yield better results than either Theory X or Theory Y.

In their paper "Manpower and Career Planning,"[89] John McMahon and Joseph Yeager list five important features of career planning:

1. **Dialogue** represents the relation between the individual and the organization.
2. **Guidance** from management is the provision of information about the career milieu in which the individual must function.
3. **Involvement of the employee** requires that means be established to allow individuals to express their career objectives, timetables, values, and other personally meaningful issues.
4. **Feedback** to the individual provides the basis for calibrating his or her plans on the basis of what is learned.
5. **The processes and the techniques** of career planning must interrelate with one another as parts of a functional whole.

The development and implementation of an effective career planning program obviously will require considerable commitment from the entire management team. It would be expected, however, that the benefits to be derived from this effort would far outweigh the costs. Most important, the employees would feel that management has a genuine interest in helping them toward self-actualization.

SUMMING UP

The purpose of this chapter has been to describe the application of Maslow's needs hierarchy to employee motivation and productivity. In summing up, it is important to emphasize at least two points about the hierarchy:

- First, managers must comprehend the hierarchical nature of human needs. For example, an employee at the bottom of the hierarchy — perhaps suffering from extreme job stress — simply will not be interested in those actions relevant to the upper tiers of the hierarchy, such as career planning. Thus, managers must understand the employee's position with respect to the hierarchy and then deal with the situation accordingly.

- Second, managers must relate to their employees on an individual basis. Evidence clearly shows that an approach that is effective for motivating one employee may have no effect, or even be counterproductive, with another.

Giving due attention to employee motivation is no small task. In fact, it may be the central task of the manager. Delmar Landen and Howard Carlson[68, p. 187] state it well when they say:

It is clear that the task of creating a more highly motivated workforce is complex. It is *not* something that can be done with poster displays, campaigns, and across-the-board programs. It is a long-term process. It requires not only tremendous effort, but imagination and deep commitment. Motivating workers is not a special assignment for a group of specialists; it is an integral part of every manager's job.

This point is further emphasized by a discussion that the author had several years ago with a first-line supervisor. An engineer by training, he was the supervisor of 20 engineers and technicians. For almost 50 minutes, he described (in considerable detail and with intense emotion) his many problems concerning employee attitudes, employee motivation, and interpersonal conflicts. After elaborating on these problems, he concluded his discourse by lamenting: "If it weren't for the *human* problems in my group, I would really enjoy my job." Indeed, if it weren't for the human problems! But this is what management is all about.

In dealing with these human problems, each manager faces a great challenge. Standing between the manager and organizational productivity is the intervening factor of employee motivation, which may be viewed as either a problem or an opportunity. In either case, the manager must understand this factor and how to deal with it. When managers clearly comprehend how they can achieve harmony between the goals of the organization and the goals of the individual, they have the potential for reaching the highest levels of employee motivation and organizational productivity.

Even though there is no definitive theory or any handbook answer to the many questions concerning employee motivation, there is considerable knowledge in the form of practical guidelines. The challenge is to act *now* in applying these guidelines on a day-to-day basis, to benefit both the employee and the organization.

Exercise IX

On Self-Motivation and Life Planning

A. With regard to your life as a whole, evaluate the degree to which your personal needs are being satisfied at the present time.

	Excellent	Good	Fair	Poor
(1) Physiological Needs	___	___	___	___
(2) Safety Needs	___	___	___	___
(3) Love and Belongingness Needs	___	___	___	___
(4) Self-Esteem Needs	___	___	___	___
(5) Self-Actualization Needs	___	___	___	___

B. What are your plans for meeting your needs in each of these areas during the next 12 months?

(1) Physiological: _____

_____

(2) Safety: _____

_____

(3) Love and Belongingness: _____

_____

(4) Self-Esteem: _____

_____

(5) Self-Actualization: _____

_____

_____

X

Controlling

People can't perform with maximum effectiveness if they don't know what goals the organization is seeking (and why) or how well they are doing in relation to those goals.

George Odiorne
MBO II [95, p. 58]

Introduction • Theoretical Framework • Principles of Controlling • The Management Information System • Controlling Quality • Controlling Schedule • Controlling Budget • Quality Control Circles • Controlling Your Time • Summing Up

---

INTRODUCTION

Many are the managers who continually seek an answer to the question, "How are we doing?" Some would like to obtain an answer on a daily basis, some on a weekly basis, some on a monthly basis, and perhaps others on a longer-term basis. But regardless of the time frame, the job of management demands that the question be answered.

Answering this question is what controlling is all about. The control function involves determining the difference between actual performance and planned performance, and, if they are not congruent, deciding what corrective action must be taken to bring them into harmony.

Controlling is a vital management function. Presenting this function last does not mean that it is least in importance. Controlling is just as critical as the other functions of management.

Consider a hypothetical enterprise that has done a satisfactory job of planning, organizing, staffing and staff development, and motivating. But it has failed to establish an effective control system. Because of this deficiency, the enterprise will surely flounder. It would be like a commercial pilot attempting to fly a plane from point A to point B without a control system. Certainly no rational person would want to be a passenger on this plane.

It is recognized that many managers face obstacles in their efforts to obtain a satisfactory answer to the question, "How are we doing?" Perhaps the enterprise is attempting to operate without the benefit of a clearly defined plan, which means that the managers are unlikely to have a clear picture of the desired state of their particular operation. Perhaps the enterprise is attempting to operate without the benefit of an effective management information system, which means that managers are unlikely to have access to the information they need for gauging their progress. Perhaps the enterprise is attempting to operate with an autocratic leadership style, which means that honest and open upward communication will not be forthcoming. These are real problems, and they must be dealt with by any organization desirous of establishing an effective control system.

The purpose of this chapter is to present guidelines for effective controlling. Special emphasis will be placed on a Theory Z approach to carrying out the control function.

THEORETICAL FRAMEWORK

Koontz and O'Donnell[63, p. 527] provide us with a succinct definition of controlling:

> Controlling is the management function of making sure that plans succeed. The controlling process is regarded as one of establishing standards against which performance can be measured, measuring performance, and correcting deviations from standards or plans.

This definition points up three key aspects of controlling: (1) the establishment of standards against which performance can be measured, (2) measuring performance, and (3) correcting deviations from the standards or plans. These three interrelated steps constitute a feedback control system.

To grasp fully the meaning of control, it is necessary to understand the meaning of three basic terms:

- Measure — to quantify
- Evaluate — to place value on
- Control — to take corrective action

These three concepts are interrelated and serve as successive building blocks. We first measure; we next evaluate; and then we take corrective action. It is difficult to evaluate unless we first measure; it is difficult to take corrective action unless we have evaluated. Most important, the manager must realize that evaluation *per se* does not constitute control. Controlling has not taken place unless corrective action has been executed (unless, of course, no corrective action is called for).

With the definitions of these basic terms as a starting point, we can now consider a broad systems view of the control process. Figure 41, taken from Robert Anthony and John Dearden,[1] portrays the flow of information in a model control system. This systems view includes several key elements:

- A clear definition of the "responsibility center" (any organizational unit or program within the overall enterprise)
- Detailed plans and objectives feeding into the responsibility center
- A report that compares actual performance and planned performance
- Feedback in the form of either reward (if performance is satisfactory) or guidelines for corrective action (if performance is not satisfactory)
- Corrective action to bridge the gap between the actual performance and the desired performance

This general control model applies to all levels of management. With upper-level management, it would apply to the execution of the organization's strategic plan. With middle management, it would apply to the implementation of the tactical plans. With project managers, it would apply to the execution of the project plan. No manager can function effectively without a control system.

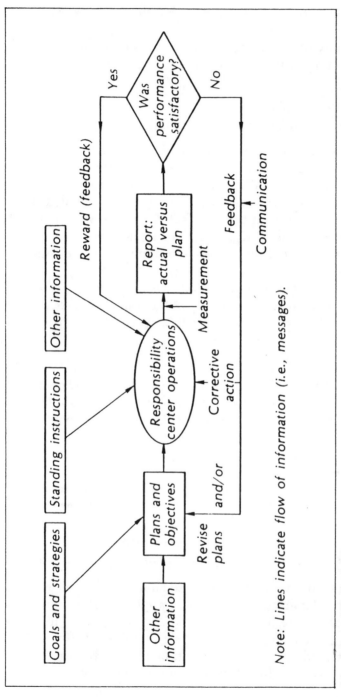

Note: Lines indicate flow of information (i.e., messages).

Robert Anthony and John Dearden – *Management Control Systems*, fourth ed. 1980, Homewood, Illinois,
Richard D. Irwin, Inc. Reprinted, by permission of the publisher.

Figure 41.   A systems view of the control process

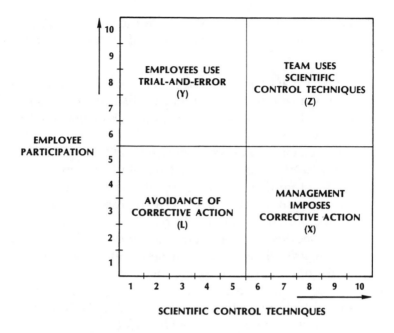

Figure 42.   Two dimensions of controlling

We assume, then, that every reader appreciates the need for an effective control system. The question then becomes: How should the control function be carried out?

In deciding how best to carry out the control function, attention must be given to two different aspects of control: (1) the use of scientific control techniques and (2) employee participation in the control process. Regarding the first aspect, there are a multitude of texts on scientific control techniques — covering PERT, MIS, PPBS, etc. Regarding the second aspect, there is a considerable amount of research pointing up the value of participative management in the control process.

These two aspects of controlling — scientific control techniques and employee participation — are shown as orthogonal axes in Figure 42. The diagram yields four distinct approaches for carrying out the control function: (1) corrective action is avoided (Theory L); (2) management imposes corrective action (Theory X); (3) employees use trial-and-error in attempting to carry out the control function (Theory

235

Y); and (4) the team uses scientific control techniques (Theory Z).

We can estimate the effectiveness of these four different approaches:

1. **Corrective action is avoided (Theory L):** If used throughout the organization, this approach will lead to disaster. The Theory L approach will be at the rock-bottom level of effectiveness.

2. **Management imposes corrective action (Theory X):** This may be fairly effective in the short run, but, because employees will feel that they are being treated as pawns, it will lead to many undesirable side effects. Overall, the Theory X approach will be only moderately effective.

3. **Employees use trial-and-error (Theory Y):** This may yield some degree of employee satisfaction as a result of the high degree of employee participation, but it will be inefficient because employees are not given the benefit of the many tested control techniques in existence. Overall, the Theory Y approach will be only moderately effective.

4. **The team uses scientific control techniques (Theory Z):** This will lead to employee satisfaction and achieve results; will enhance both the quality of the control function and the acceptance by those members who must actually carry it out. The Theory Z approach will be maximally effective.

Within this theoretical framework, it is important to appreciate fully the sharp distinction between the Theory X approach to controlling and the Theory Z approach. With Theory X, upper management serves as the controller, and those below are the "controllees." With Theory Z, however, all members of the organization assume some of the responsibility for carrying out the control function; every member of the organization is a controller.

It is fairly easy to understand why the Theory Z approach is more effective than the Theory X approach. With the Theory X approach, the employee is treated as a thing or an object, a pawn who is expected to comply with instructions passed down from above. With the Theory Z approach, the employee is treated by management as a responsible person, a person who can be trusted to take necessary corrective actions. Anyone who has been on the receiving end of both of these approaches can understand why they yield significantly different results.

PRINCIPLES OF CONTROLLING

The 10 principles of controlling presented below have been taken from the extensive literature on the subject. In each case, the primary source of the principle is indicated.

1. **Controls require a clearly defined organizational structure.**[63]
   The control process focuses on responsibility centers. These centers must be established within a clearly defined organizational structure. Normally, this would be done within the functional structure of the enterprise, but, if an enterprise has established both a functional structure and a task force structure, then the task-force side of the organizational structure also should be viewed in terms of responsibility centers. For example, various projects or programs that cut across the functional structure should have plans, budgets, and corresponding controls.

2. **Controls must be based on plans.**[63]
   The plan is the cornerstone of a control system. As stated in the definition of controlling by Koontz and O'Donnell, the controlling process involves establishing standards against which performance can be measured. These standards are embedded in the plans as objectives, specifications, deliverables, etc. The clearer the plans are, the more effective the controls will be.

3. **Controlling is a primary responsibility of every manager charged with executing plans.**[63]
   Planning and controlling go hand-in-hand. Question: Is PERT a planning tool or a control tool? The answer: It is both. Because of the dynamic nature of both functions, it is impossible to determine where planning stops and controlling starts. As a result of the feedback provided by the control system, an effective manager modifies the plan throughout the period of implementation. Thus, it is essential that each manager be responsible for both planning and controlling. The two functions may not be separated.

4. **The control itself should be exercised where the malfunction is likely to occur.**[23]
   Far too often the control is exercised one, two, or even three steps removed from where the malfunction occurs. This distal

approach creates two problems: it results in a significant delay in the feedback and it removes the responsibility for controlling from those who are most directly involved in the operation. People working where the malfunction is likely to occur should be the ones who exercise control. To this end, the employees need to receive immediate feedback on their performance, and they must be given the tools and authority to take corrective action.

5. **Controls must focus on key variables.**[1]

It is impossible for a manager or a team to attend to all variables associated with a given operation. The task at hand is to identify the key variables and then establish a control system that focuses on these variables. Salient characteristics of key variables include:

a. They are *important* in explaining the success or failure of the enterprise.

b. They are *volatile*: they can change quickly, often for reasons that are not controllable by the manager.

c. *Prompt action* is required when a significant change occurs.

d. The change is *not easy* to predict.

e. The variables can be *measured*, either directly or by a surrogate.

6. **Controls must be meaningful.** [23]

In the design of controls, it is important to recognize that what might be meaningful for one manager might not be for another. The lazy approach in establishing a control system is to provide the same control data to all managers throughout the organization. But this is irresponsible. Controls must be designed for different levels and different types of managers. To be truly effective, controls must be tailored to meet the unique needs of each manager.

7. **Controls must provide accurate and timely feedback.** [69]

Lawler points up the two main values of accurate and timely feedback: (1) it gives the individual the information that is needed to correct his or her behavior when it deviates from the standard or desired behavior; and (2) it provides the intrinsic motivation that will lead the person to perform at the standard or in an effective way.

8. **Feedforward control should be used to supplement feedback control.**[62]

Traditionally, managers have viewed feedback control as the essence of the control process. Outputs are compared with standards, and corrective action is taken whenever appropriate. But Koontz and Bradspies stress that sole reliance on feedback control — because of the delays in obtaining the needed information — may result in the system getting out of control.

To correct the deficiency found in sole reliance on feedback control, Koontz and Bradspies argue that managers should make use of feedforward control to supplement feedback control. The concept of feedforward control is shown in Figure 43. Here it is seen that information is obtained on both the input variables and the output variables, and corrective action is taken on both.

An illustration of feedforward control is found in the use of PERT as a tool for controlling a project. Throughout the duration of the project, an alert project manager will pay close attention to the critical path of the network — and will take necessary corrective action during the early stages of the project to prevent major scheduling problems from occurring later in the project.

Another example of feedforward control is found in the conduct of project review meetings. One project manager asks the task leaders to report only on what they accomplished during the *past* month. A second project manager, however, asks the task leaders to report on their plans for the *coming* month — and then makes suggestions for modifying these plans. The advantages of the second approach are obvious.

9. **Controlling requires action.**[62]

Some managers apparently assume that if they are measuring and evaluating they are therefore controlling. This is incorrect. Measuring and evaluating indeed are necessary for controlling, but they are not sufficient. The manager must act — take corrective action on the basis of the evaluation — to complete the control process.

10. **Controls must be economical.** [23]

If an enterprise had unlimited funds, it would be possible to

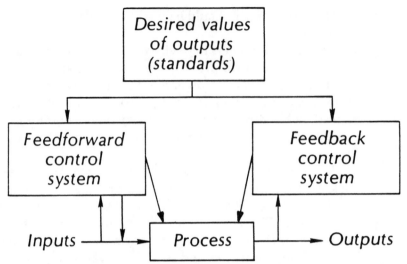

Harold Koontz and Robert Bradspies—"Managing Through Feedforward Control," *Business Horizons*, June, 1972, p. 29. Reprinted, by permission of the publisher.

Figure 43.   The concept of feedforward control

design a near-perfect control system. Obviously, this is not a realistic situation. The practical need is to establish an effective control system at a reasonable cost. Take, for example, a $100,000 project. How much of this amount might reasonably be used for purposes of carrying out the control function? As a rule of thumb, many managers suggest that 10 percent of the total project budget be used for managing the project. Inasmuch as controlling is only one part of the overall management function, we might estimate that about 3 percent of the project budget — or only $3,000 — could be used for the control function. This limited amount of money available for the control function means, of course, that the enterprise as a whole must establish a centralized management information system that is made available to all project managers.

THE MANAGEMENT INFORMATION SYSTEM

As every reader should know, a management information system is a vital tool for effective control. Accurate and timely information must be readily available to allow comparisons to be made between actual performance and planned performance. Normally, the individual unit has neither the time nor the resources to establish and maintain a management information system. Such a system must be established by the organization as a whole and made available to all of its members.

Bertram Colbert[14, p. 16] offers a succinct definition of a management information system:

> A management information system, simply, is an organized method of providing each manager with all the data and only those data which are needed for decision, when they are needed, and in a form which aids understanding and stimulates action.

Colbert goes on to list the characteristics of an effective management information system:[14, pp. 16-17]

- Considers the full effect of a decision in advance by supplying complete, accurate, and timely data for use in the decision making process.
- Provides a means for preparing and presenting information in a uniform manner.
- Identifies, structures, and quantifies significant past relationships and forecasts future relationships.
- Reports to each level of management only the degrees of detail needed.
- Presents data in a form which minimizes the need for analysis and interpretation.
- Provides flexibility and adaptability to change.

The key to the establishment of an effective management information system is to involve the users in the design process. Far too often, upper management has relegated the design task to information systems specialists without actively involving the organization's line managers. Not unexpectedly, when the system is put into operation, line managers from all quarters cry out that the system does not meet their particular needs. A reasonable solution to this problem is to establish a Management Information System Task Force comprised of both line managers and system specialists to identify information needs and then design a system tailored to meet these needs.

The area of management information systems offers exciting possibilities for the future. With rapidly advancing computer technology, it will be possible to design reasonably priced systems tailored to meet the needs of individual managers and teams throughout the organization. In the not-too-distant future, we should find large numbers of managers having ready access to computer terminals that can be used to call forth "all the data and only those data which are needed for decision, when it is needed, and in a form which aids understanding and stimulates action."

CONTROLLING QUALITY

In most enterprises, the control function is centered on three important variables: quality, schedule, and costs. Are we providing a high-quality product (or service)? Are we operating according to schedule? Are we operating within budget? For an enterprise to be successful in the long run, due attention must be given to all three questions. It is worthwhile to consider each.

Of the three control variables — quality, schedule, and costs — quality is by far the most difficult to assess. The reason lies in the difficulty of defining quality. Is quality found in the object itself or does it exist simply in the eyes of the beholder? This question has been debated amongst scholars since the time of Aristotle. There is no easy answer.

One can find readily numerous examples of disappointment in the quality of a finished product. An engineering group, for example, develops a product that the designers believe to be of high quality. Yet, upon receiving the product, the user is dissatisfied. The end product is not what the user had in mind. This is an all-too-common occurrence.

Take yet another example — one in which the user is satisfied with the quality of the end product but the designers are dissatisfied. The user believes the product is "right on target," but the designers believe that the product represents low-quality workmanship. Whatever the reason for the discrepancy in views, this situation does occasionally arise.

Thus, it seems clear that any definition of quality must involve assessments by both the designers and the users. In the view of the designers, was the product designed and constructed according to state-of-the-art knowledge? In the view of the user, does the product meet his or her needs? To proclaim that the product is of high quality, both questions must be answered in the affirmative.

The key to controlling quality is to agree upon clearly defined objectives prior to the initiation of a particular activity. These objectives, which should be crystal clear and verifiable, should be agreed upon by the designer and the user. Thus, if the agreement is to build a "Ford," then that is what is actually constructed. But if the agreement calls for a "Cadillac," then that is what is constructed. In either case, the end product can be judged to be high quality only if a clear agreement between the designer and the user has been reached prior to undertaking the activity — and the end product clearly satisfies this agreement.

In response to the question, "Where is quality — in the object or the perceiver?" we must answer, "It is in both." Here is an object that has been designed and constructed according to specifications. Here is the perceiver — with certain expectations — beholding this object. Quality is not found solely in either the object or the perceiver; rather, it is found in *the relation between the object and the perceiver.*

CONTROLLING SCHEDULE

It is generally agreed that controlling schedule is a more straightforward process than controlling quality. There should be clear agreement on the dates for the completion of a given activity or the delivery of a certain product, as well as the accomplishment of certain milestones along the way. Did we meet these dates or not? There should be little ambiguity in the answer.

The importance of controlling schedule varies considerably from one situation to another. It may be critically important in an environment in which a manufacturer is attempting to beat the competition in introducing a new product to the marketplace but it may be relatively unimportant in a research laboratory conducting fundamental research.

Assuming that the control of schedule is important, then the manager needs tools to aid in this process. PERT and CPM are effective tools for both planning and controlling. It is a fairly straightforward task to convert the information from a PERT chart or CPM chart to a simple Gantt chart, such as that shown in Figure 44. Seen here is a breakdown of tasks over time, with an indication of percentage of each task completed and percentage of each task that is scheduled but not completed. On the review date shown in this example, everything appears to be in good shape except Task A.

243

There may be no problem here if Task A is independent of the other tasks, but, if the completion of Task C is dependent upon the completion of Task A, there very well may be a schedule problem. If this is the case, the manager would be expected to take necessary corrective action.

It should be noted that some tasks do not lend themselves to reporting in terms of "percentage of work completed." In research

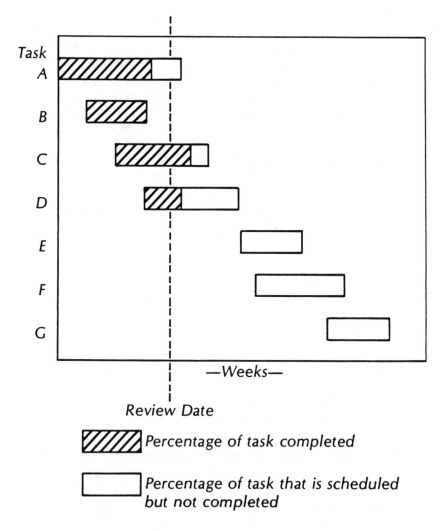

—Weeks—

Review Date

Percentage of task completed

Percentage of task that is scheduled but not completed

Figure 44.   A Gantt chart for control of schedule

and development, for instance, it is difficult to report with any degree of accuracy the percentage of work completed at any given time in the course of carrying out a project. In this case, it would be more appropriate to specify milestones to be achieved by certain dates for each task included in the project. The control function then focuses on these milestones.

CONTROLLING BUDGET

The controlling of costs also is a more straightforward process than the controlling of quality. Again, we are dealing with concrete facts and figures — as contrasted with subjective views. This is not to imply that control of costs is a simple matter but only simpler and more straightforward than the control of quality.

In the control of costs, Dennis Lock[73, p. 232] stresses the importance of three interrelated factors. His reference is to project management, but his point is relevant to any activity within an enterprise. He says:

> If a project is to be financially controlled with any degree of success, three factors must assume major significance in the considerations. These are budgets, the costs incurred, and the progress achieved in relation to those costs. A knowledge of budgets and costs by themselves will be of no use unless the corresponding progress can be gauged. All three basic factors must therefore be monitored during the active project life.

The requirements for effective cost control have been identified by Harold Schröder:[106, p. 27]

- Control must be exercised on a reasonable level of the project structure (or organizational structure).
- Actual cost information must be available quickly.
- The control system should identify costs not only when they arise but also when funds are committed.
- The recorded costs must contain the same elements as the planned costs to allow for meaningful comparisons.

To effectively control costs, it is important to monitor trends in expenditures. The cumulative expenditure chart presented in Figure 45 shows time on the horizontal axis and cumulative costs on the ver-

245

tical axis. This particular cumulative spending "curve" is a straight line, which reflects a planned constant spending rate for the entire activity. With the small circles representing the actual expenditures, it can be seen that there is reason for concern. A quick glance at this curve reveals that costs are accelerating and are likely to be above the expected curve by the next reporting date. Of course, if the work is proceeding ahead of schedule, there may be no reason for alarm. If the work is proceeding only according to plan, however, there is indeed reason for concern. Regardless of the specifics, the point to be emphasized is that it is important to study trend data for effective cost control.

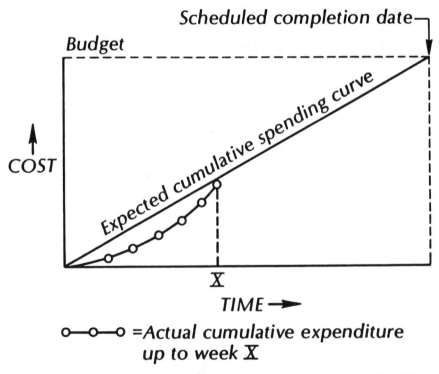

Dennis Lock—*Project Management*, Epping, Essex (England): Gower Press, 1977, Reprinted, by permission of the publisher.

Figure 45. A cumulative expenditure chart

QUALITY CONTROL CIRCLES

In no small number of organizations, the control function is viewed as the responsibility of middle and upper management. These managers establish objectives and standards for their particular areas and then compare actual performance against these objectives and standards. After analyzing deviations between the actual and the desired, the managers issue to their subordinates instructions for corrective action. This is a logical and systematic approach for carrying out the control function. It may be characterized as a Theory X approach to controlling.

As mentioned previously, there are at least two problems associated with a Theory X approach to controlling. The first is the long lag time between the occurrence of a deviation and the execution of the corrective action. Because the control function is located two or three steps removed from the locus of the malfunction, there may be a considerable delay in effecting the corrective action. The second problem is that the responsibility for controlling lies only with a relatively small number of people — namely, middle and upper managers. Consequently, people lower in the chain of command do not feel any real responsibility for the control function. They are simply carrying out orders issued from above.

A major thesis of Theory Z management is that the control function should be viewed as a responsibility of every member of the enterprise. Peter Drucker[23, pp. 268,269] states it well when he says:

> Responsibility requires self-control. That in turn requires continuous information on performance against standards. The information the worker needs must satisfy the requirements of effective information. It must be timely. It must be relevant. It must be operational. It must focus on his (or her) job. Above all, it must be his (or her) tool. Its purpose must be self-control rather than control of others, let alone manipulation.

As mentioned in Chapter I, the team is the basic unit of the Theory Z organization. These teams are found throughout the organization, and there are many overlapping teams. Each of the teams is given responsibility for developing its own plans (in the light of organizational objectives) and then making sure that the plans succeed. This is the essence of a Theory Z approach to the control function.

247

An excellent illustration of a Theory Z approach to carrying out the control function is found in the Quality Control Circle. As a practical means of applying the principles of participative management, the Japanese introduced the Quality Control Circle in 1962. Under the leadership of the Japanese Union of Scientists and Engineers (JUSE), the idea has grown to include eight million Japanese employees engaged in business, government, and education. According to the International Association of Quality Circles, numerous organizations in the U. S. are now employing the Quality Circle concept.

The essence of the Quality Circle concept is *participative problem solving*. Members of a work group, usually from eight to ten in number, meet on a regular basis to identify, analyze, and solve problems related to the work situation. The meetings are usually conducted for 60 minutes once a week under the direction of the unit supervisor. Inasmuch as the members of each QC team are meeting around a table, the concept of "circle" seemed appropriate as a designation.

A list of typical characteristics of Quality Circles is shown in Table 10. This is an instructive summary of goals, organization, selection of circle members, scope of problems analyzed by circles, training, meetings, and awards for circle activities. It also should be noted that, while the Quality Circle concept was originally intended for workers in a production department, the concept is applicable to any department within an enterprise.

The purpose of Quality Circles goes far beyond the improvement of quality. According to Diana Shott, Quality Circle Facilitator at the Genoa Plant of GTE Communication Systems, the goals of her company's Quality Circle program include:

- To improve company communications
- To promote job involvement
- To increase employee motivation and morale
- To inspire more effective teamwork
- To build an attitude of "problem prevention"
- To create a more effective problem solving capability
- To develop cost consciousness
- To provide opportunities for personal growth and recognition
- To reduce errors and enhance quality
- To increase productivity

Table 10. Typical Characteristics of Quality Circles

Goals

- To improve communication, particularly between line employees and management.
- To identify and solve problems.

Organization

- The circle consists of a leader and 8 to 10 employees from one area of work.
- The circle also has a coordinator and one or more facilitators who work closely with it.

Selection of Circle Members

- Participation of members is voluntary.
- Participation of leaders may or may not be voluntary.

Scope of Problems Analyzed by Circles

- The circle selects its own problems.
- Initially, the circle is encouraged to select problems from its immediate work area.
- Problems are not restricted to quality, but also include productivity, cost, safety, morale, housekeeping, environment, and other spheres.

Training

- Formal training in problem-solving techniques is usually a part of circle meetings.

Meetings

- Usually one hour per week.

Awards for Circle Activities

- Usually no monetary awards are given.
- The most effective reward is the satisfaction of the circle members from solving problems and observing the implementation of their own solutions.

249

The results of research on Quality Circles is impressive. In his booklet, *Quality Circles*,[42] Frank Gryna, Jr., lists some of the demonstrated benefits of Quality Circles. Over and above measurable savings, most of the benefits are in the area of attitudes and behavior:

- Circles enable the individual to improve personal capabilities.
- Circles increase the individual's self-respect.
- Circles help workers develop the potential to become the supervisors of the future.
- Circles increase the respect of the supervisor for the workers.
- Circles increase the workers' understanding of the difficulties faced by supervisors.
- Circles change some workers' negative attitudes.
- Circles reduce conflict stemming from the working environment.
- Circles help workers to understand better the reasons why many problems cannot be solved quickly.
- Circles involve workers more actively in their jobs.
- Circles instill in the workers a better understanding of the importance of product quality.

These are substantial benefits. Even if the monetary savings are only modest, the expected benefits in terms of attitudes and behavior certainly make the effort worthwhile.

The significant point to note about the Quality Circle movement is that it involves a genuine implementation of participative management. Workers are not merely reacting to plans drawn up by management, but rather, are working at the grass-roots level of identifying, analyzing, and solving problems. A function that was long considered to be the exclusive province of management is now being shared with the workers.

Here we can agree with Frank Gryna when he says:[42, p. 91]

> This research suggests that quality circles can make a major contribution to an enlightened industrial world. What is necessary first is the courage to admit that the long-standing roles of managers, production supervisors, and workers may need to be changed. We also need the wisdom to help those who have long been guided by another philosophy to understand and become comfortable with an expanded role for workers.

CONTROLLING YOUR TIME

Time is a precious asset for every manager. Many are the managers who work 60–70 hours each week and still complain that there is simply not enough time to accomplish everything that they would like to accomplish. Because of the importance of time management for the manager, it seems appropriate to devote the final section of this last chapter to the subject of "controlling your time."

Theory Z managers devote special attention to managing their time. These managers set stretch objectives for themselves and are usually successful in achieving the objectives. They are indeed productive! Yet they always seem to have time to spend with each of their employees, to assist a colleague in need, or to offer a warm welcome to an unexpected visitor. Considering the administrative demands of their jobs, how is it possible for these managers to have so much time available for the human demands? There is a simple answer: Theory Z managers know how to manage their time.

The classic text on the subject of time management is Alec Mackenzie's *The Time Trap*.[76a] Mackenzie did a thorough job of researching how managers in various quarters spend their time. His book is an excellent guide for identifying time wasters and for developing strategies for coping with them. The major time wasters identified by Mackenzie are listed in Table 11.

George Odiorne, an author well known for his books on management by objectives, believes that people get so enmeshed in activity that they lose sight of the purpose of their work. Some of his observations concerning this problem are listed in Table 12.

The key to moving out of the Activity Trap is to make management by objectives "a way of life." Annual objectives are converted into monthly objectives; monthly objectives are converted into weekly objectives; and weekly objectives are converted into daily objectives. The manager's primary attention is then placed on *results to be achieved* rather than on activities to be carried out. In the process of internalizing management by objectives, the manager becomes proactive in managing his or her own life. This is what time management is all about.

Long before the term "management by objectives" was introduced to the management world, a very famous American was using the concept to guide his daily life. In his *Autobiography*,[30a] Benjamin

Table 11.   Time Wasters for Managers

- *Unclear objectives*
- *Procrastination*
- *Lack of information*
- *Too much reading*
- *Interruptions*
- *Telephone*
- *Lack of delegation*
- *Lack of self-discipline*
- *Visitors*
- *Junk mail*
- *Poor filing system*
- *Lack of procedures for routine matters*
- *Socializing*
- *Unnecessary meetings*
- *Pet projects*
- *Attempting too much at once*
- *Span of control*
- *Can't say no*
- *Mistakes*
- *Disorganized secretaries*
- *Responsibility without authority*
- *Delegating tasks without authority*

Alec Mackenzie, *The Time Trap*, Adapted, by permission of the publisher.

Table 12. The Activity Trap

---

1. People get so enmeshed in activity they lose sight of the purpose of their work. This is called the Activity Trap.

2. People caught in the Activity Trap diminish in capability rather than grow.

3. The Activity Trap originates at the top of organizations and extends to the lowest levels.

4. Organizations that have become Activity Traps kill motivation of people working in them.

5. Most problems don't get solved in activity-centered organizations, and some problems get worse.

6. Activity-centered managers avoid reality by converting it into something else.

George Odiorne, *MBO II: A System Managerial Leadership for the 80s.* Belmont, California: Fearon-Pitman Publishers, Inc., 1979, Reprinted, by permission of the publisher.

Franklin describes his plan for a typical day. As indicated in Table 13, Franklin began his day at about 5:00 a.m. The ensuing hours were filled with meaningful activities — guided by a plan. He usually retired at about 10:00 p.m., which gave him some seven hours of sleep each night. The key to Franklin's daily plan was that *he set his objectives during the early hours of the morning and then reviewed his accomplishments during the evening hours.* Certainly, no person would deny that this printer/scientist/statesman was productive!

Going far beyond Ben Franklin's early use of time management, modern-day experts on the subject provide us with numerous guidelines. A sample of these guidelines is presented below:

1. **Objectives**: Plan your activities on the basis of clearly stated objectives — annual, weekly, daily.
2. **Priorities**: Maintain a current list of priorities of things to do.
3. **Concentration**: Work on only one thing at a time.
4. **Large tasks**: Divide large tasks into small "chunks" (each of which requires 15–30 minutes for completion) — and work on only one chunk at a time.

Table 13.   Ben Franklin's Daily Plan

The Morning *Question: What good shall* *I do this day?*	5 6 7	*Rise, wash, and address* <u>*Powerful Goodness!*</u> *Contrive* *day's business and take the* *resolution of the day; prosecute* *the present study, and breakfast.*
	{8–11}	*Work*
Noon	{12–1}	*Read or overlook my accounts,* *and dine.*
	{2–5}	*Work*
Evening *Question: What good* *have I done today?*	6 7 8 9	*Put things in their places.* *Supper. Music or diversion, or* *conversation. Examination of* *the day.*
Night	{10–4}	*Sleep*

The Autobiography of Benjamin Franklin, Benjamin Franklin, New York, Walter J. Black, Inc., 1941.

5. **Delegation**: Learn how to delegate and be willing to delegate.
6. **Secretary**: Train your secretary to be your personal assistant.
7. **Meetings**: Don't go to other people's meetings unless you are vitally concerned; learn how to be a leader of effective and efficient meetings.
8. **Readings**: Read only what you "need to know"; take a course in rapid reading.
9. **Phone calls**: Group your phone calls; learn how to conduct effective and efficient phone conversations.
10. **Socializing**: Schedule casual discussions for lunch period.

Many managers have reported that the conscientious application of these guidelines has helped them save anywhere from one to two hours each day. Suppose the savings is only one hour per day. In a year's time, this is no small amount. Think about what you might do with a "gift" of some 200 hours!

The experts in time management seem to be in fair agreement regarding what each manager should do in developing and implementing his or her own program in time management. A suggested strategy consists of the following five steps:

1. Systematically record how you plan your time (for a one-week period, in 15-minute intervals).
2. Identify your time wasters.
3. Develop a plan for improved time management.
4. Implement the plan.
5. Evaluate and revise as appropriate.

In carrying out this strategy, it is important that you be satisfied with small improvements. You should not expect miracles. Changing the habits that have been ingrained over many years will be no easy task.

Assuming that you are able to achieve long-term success in implementing your personal program in time management, you may expect to derive a number of substantial gains. The following are some of the expected benefits:

1. Less stress
2. Better physical health
3. Better mental health
4. A more well-balanced life
5. Greater long-term productivity

These are indeed substantial benefits. They give us a clue as to why the Theory Z manager is able to be a Theory Z manager.

SUMMING UP

Building on the ideas presented in this chapter, we can now outline a comprehensive strategy for controlling. The central theme of the proposed strategy is the uniting of scientific control techniques and active employee participation in the control process. Essentially, the strategy involves "giving" the control techniques to members of the organization so that they can make sure that their plans succeed.

The proposed strategy consists of the following 10 steps:

1. Upper management establishes a clearly defined organizational structure for the entire enterprise — including identification of responsibility centers and reporting relationships.
2. Upper management (in collaboration with the component managers) identifies key results areas for each component of the organizational structure in the light of the annual plan.

3. Members of each team (under the guidance of the team leader) develop a detailed component plan for the coming year in the light of the key results areas.

4. Members of line management work with information specialists to tailor the management information system to the needs of each component within the organization.

5. Members of each component continually compare actual performance with planned performance and decide upon corrective action.

6. Each component keeps higher-level management informed of performance, deviations, and plans for corrective action.

7. Teams take corrective action and follow up to assess results of corrective action.

8. Upper-level managers continually monitor performance of all components within their responsibility areas.

9. All managers use feedback information from the control process in the future development of their plans.

10. The management team continually evaluates the control system and makes improvements as appropriate.

This 10-step strategy is a uniting of management by objectives and participative management. It incorporates the rationale and techniques of management by objectives, and, throughout the process, it actively involves the organization's members. This is Theory Z management at its best.

Theory Z management views the team as the basic unit of the organization. Each team needs a detailed plan to help it move from where it is to where it wants to be. The successful execution of the plan is dependent upon an effective control system. The task of upper management is to make certain that each team has the control tools it needs.

The benefits of effective control are clear. Each team in the organization needs to "stay on course" in directing its efforts toward organizational objectives. And to stay on course requires that the team members know whether or not they are on course. The control system provides the answer.

Exercise X

Managing Your Time

The purpose of this exercise is to help you develop a plan for managing your own time. Three tasks are included in the exercise.

(1) In Exercise XA (below), estimate in minutes how you spend your time in a "typical" workday. Use the blank spaces at the bottom of the list for adding any activities not included.

(2) In Exercise XB (page 258), list your major time wasters. (Refer to Table 11.)

(3) In Exercise XC (page 259), list several goals that will help you overcome your time wasters.

(4) And finally: Convert your plan into action!

Exercise XA

How do you spend a "typical" day?

Activity	Minutes
Planning......................................	_____
Consulting....................................	_____
Attending Meetings.........................	_____
Phone Calls..................................	_____
Reading.......................................	_____
Writing..	_____
Monitoring and Controlling..............	_____
Socializing....................................	_____
....	_____
....	_____

257

Exercise XB

What are your major time wasters?

Exercise XC

What are your plans for improved time management?

Epilogue

As we draw to the close of the text, it is appropriate to summarize the principal ideas presented in the ten chapters. There are a number of salient points worthy of special mention.

The purpose of the book has been to present basics of management within an articulated theoretical framework. No new theory has been presented. Rather, the Theory Z model represents a synthesis of facts, principles, and theories that have been generated during the past quarter-century.

It is important that each manager have a useful model of management. Such a model would contain values, goals, facts, principles, and strategies. Without a model, each managerial decision to be made may appear to be a traumatic event, but, with a useful model to provide guidance, decisions can be made on a more rational basis. The intent of this book has been to provide the reader with a practical management model — one that can aid in decision making and can help the individual become a more effective manager.

Research and practical experience have shown that the Theory Z model is an effective approach to management. While this model may not work in all situations, it can indeed work in many situations — especially if the manager fully grasps the salient features of the model, acquires the skills necessary for implementing the model, and then conscientiously applies these skills on a daily basis.

For purpose of review, the Theory Z model contains the following salient features:

1. The Theory Z manager has a *philosophy of management* that builds on the strengths of both scientific management and human relations management.
2. As an *effective human being*, the Theory Z manager is a person of both reason and compassion.
3. As an *effective leader*, the Theory Z manager demonstrates an equal concern for production and people.
4. The Theory Z manager makes effective use of *participative management*.

261

5. The Theory Z manager views *management by objectives* as an effective strategy that applies to all of the functions of management.
6. Theory Z *planning* involves "giving" the systems approach to planning to all members of the management team so that they can be involved actively in the planning process.
7. Theory Z *organizing* focuses on both stability and flexibility.
8. Theory Z *staffing and staff development* endeavors to meet the needs of both the organization and the individual employee.
9. Theory Z *motivating* demonstrates a concern for both organizational goals and employee goals and is able to achieve a synergistic relation between the two.
10. Theory Z *controlling* involves "giving" scientific control techniques to all members of the organization so that they can control their own performance.

These salient features describe a management model that is compelling — compelling from the standpoint of both empirical research and common sense. But this question arises: If the model is so compelling, why isn't it used on a wider scale? There are several barriers. One barrier is the great stress placed on the achievement of short-term goals, which often precludes the effective use of the Theory Z model. A second barrier is the traditional reliance on the Theory X model, with the view that Theory X and effective management are one and the same. Still a third barrier is the high degree of skill needed to be an effective Theory Z manager, which is considerably higher than that required to be an effective Theory X manager. Then, finally, we find the age-old problem of resistance to change. These are telling barriers, but they are not insurmountable.

If these barriers can be overcome, then an organization or a unit within the organization might expect to derive a number of benefits. The implementation of Theory Z should yield the following gains:

- More effective use of human resources
- Greater job satisfaction and higher employee morale
- Less absenteeism and lower voluntary turnover
- Higher productivity.

These gains would be no small achievement. In fact, their accomplishment is what management is all about. This, then, is the challenge for each manager: *Become a better Theory Z manager so that you become a better manager.*

Dear Reader:

We have now come to the end of our story about Theory Z management. I hope that it will be viewed by many as a beginning. If so, I would like to leave you with this thought:

Scientific management without human relations management is sterile;

Human relations management without scientific management is blind;

But the uniting of scientific management and human relations management in the form of Theory Z management can transform mediocrity into excellence.

My best to you,

Bill Hitt

Bibliography

1. Anthony, Robert, and John Deardon. *Management Control Systems.* Homewood, Illinois: Richard D. Irwin, Inc., 1980.

1a. Argyris, Chris. *Integrating the Individual and the Organization.* New York: John Wiley & Sons, 1964.

2. Barnard, Chester. *The Functions of the Executive.* Cambridge, Massachusetts: Harvard University Press, 1958.

3. Beckhard, Richard. "The Confrontation Meeting." *Harvard Business Review*, March-April, 1967, pp. 149-55.

4. Bennis, Warren. "Changing Organizations." In *Planning of Change*, edited by Bennis, Benne, and Chin, pp. 568-579.

5. Bennis, Warren, Kenneth Benne, and Robert Chin (eds.). *The Planning of Change.* New York: Holt, Rinehart & Winston, 1976.

6. Blake, Robert, and Jane Mouton. *The New Managerial Grid.* Houston, Texas: Gulf Publishing Company, 1978.

6a. Blanchard, Kenneth, and Spencer Johnson. *The One Minute Manager.* New York: William Morrow and Company, 1982.

7. Buber, Martin. *A Believing Humanism: My Testament, 1902–1965.* New York: Simon and Schuster, 1967.

8. Buber, Martin. *Between Man and Man.* Boston: Becon Press, 1955.

9. Buber, Martin. *Pointing The Way.* New York: Harper & Row, Publishers, 1963.

10. Buber, Martin. *Ten Rungs: Hasidic Sayings.* New York: Schocken Books, 1962.

11. Chaddock, Paul. "Selection and Development of the Training Staff." In *Training and Development Handbook*, edited by Robert Craig, Chapter 3.

12. Christensen, C. Roland, et al. *Business Policy: Texts and Cases.* Homewood, Illinois: Richard D. Irwin, 1978.

13. Churchman, C. West. *The Systems Approach.* New York: Dell Publishing Company, 1968.
14. Colbert, Bertram. "The Management Information System." *Management Services,* September-October, 1967, pp. 15-24.
15. Cooper, C. L., and J. Marshall. "Occupational Sources and Stress." *Journal of Occupational Psychology,* 49, 1976.
16. Craig, Robert (ed.). *Training and Development Handbook: A Guide to Human Resources Development.* New York: McGraw-Hill Book Company, 1976.
17. Csikszentmihalyi, Mihaly. "Play and Intrinsic Reward." *Journal of Humanistic Psychology,* Vol. 15, No. 3, Summer, 1975, pp. 41-63.
18. Dale, Ernest. *Management: Theory and Practice.* New York: McGraw-Hill Book Company, 1973.
19. Davis, Sheldon. "An Organic Problem-Solving Method to Organizational Change," The Journal of Applied Behavioral Science, Vol. 3, No. 1, 1967, pp. 3-21.
20. Davis, Stanley, and Paul Lawrence. *Matrix.* Reading, Massachusetts: Addison-Wesley Publishing Company, 1977.
21. Dewey, John. *How We Think.* Boston: D. C. Heath and Company, 1933.
22. Doyle, Michael, and David Straus. *How To Make Meetings Work.* Chicago: Playboy Press, 1976.
23. Drucker, Peter. *Management: Tasks • Responsibilities • Practices.* New York: Harper & Row, Publishers, 1973.
24. Drucker, Peter. *Managing for Results.* New York: Harper & Row, Publishers, 1964.
24a. Dyer, William. *Contemporary Issues in Management and Organization Development.* Reading, Massachusetts: Addison-Wesley Publishing Company, 1983.
25. Dyer, William. *Team Building: Issues and Alternatives.* Reading, Massachusetts: Addison-Wesley Publishing Company, 1977.
26. Edgerton, Henry, and James Brown. "Perspectives on Planning." In *Planning and the Chief Executive,* The Conference Board, 1972, pp. 1-11.
27. Emerson, Ralph Waldo. *Emerson's Essays.* New York: Thomas Y. Crowell Company, 1926.
28. Eysenck, H. J. "Reason with Compassion." In *The Humanist Alternative,* edited by Paul Kurtz. London: Pemberton Publishing Company, Ltd., 1973.

28a. Fayol, Henri. *General and Industrial Administration*. London: Sir Isaac Pitman & Sons, Ltd., 1949.

29. Fear, Richard. *The Evaluation Interview*. New York: McGraw-Hill Book Company, 1973.

30. Ford, Robert. *Motivation Through The Work Itself*. New York: American Management Association. 1969.

30a. Franklin, Benjamin. *The Autobiography of Benjamin Franklin*. New York: Walter J. Black, Inc., 1941.

31. French, John, and Robert Caplan. "Organizational Stress and Individual Strain." In *The Failure of Success*, edited by Alfred Marrow, pp. 30-66.

32. French, Wendell, and Robert Hollman: "Management by Objectives: The Team Approach." *California Management Review*, Spring 1975, pp. 13-22.

33. Fromm, Erich. *The Art of Loving*. New York: Harper & Row, Publishers, 1956.

34. Fromm, Erich. *The Revolution of Hope: Toward a Humanized Technology*. New York: Harper & Row, Publishers, 1970.

35. Galbraith, Jay. *Designing Complex Organizations*. Reading, Massachusetts: Addison-Wesley Publishing Company, 1973.

36. Gardner, John. *No Easy Victories*. New York: Harper & Row, Publishers, 1968.

37. Gardner, John. *Self-Renewal: The Individual and the Innovative Society*. New York: Harper & Row, Publishers, 1965.

38. Gellerman, Saul. *Management by Motivation*. New York: American Management Association, 1968.

39. Gerstner, Louis. "Can Strategic Planning Pay Off?" *Business Horizons*, Vol. 15, No. 6, December, 1972, pp. 5-16.

40. Gibran, Kahlil. *The Prophet*. New York: Alfred A. Knopf, Inc., 1923.

41. Goetz, Billy. *Managerial Planning and Control: A Managerial Approach to Industrial Accounting*. New York: McGraw-Hill Book Company, 1949.

42. Gryna, Frank. *Quality Circles: A Team Approach to Problem Solving*. New York: American Management Association (AMACOM), 1981.

43. Hamilton, Edith, and Huntington Cairns (eds.). *The Collected Dialogues of Plato*. New York: Bollinger Foundation, 1961.

43a. Hamilton, H. Ronald. "A Comparative Assessment of Your Planning System." Columbus, Ohio: Battelle, Memorial Institute, 1977.

44. Harrison, Robert. "When Power Conflicts Trigger Team Spirit." *European Business*, Spring 1972, pp. 57-65.

45. Hatvany, Nina, and Vladimar Pucik. "Japanese Management Practices and Productivity." *Organizational Dynamics*. Vol. 9, No. 4, Spring 1981.

46. Hemphill, John, and Alvin Coons. "Development of the Leader Description Questionnaire." In *Leader Behavior: Its Description and Measurement*, edited by Ralph Stogdill and Alvin Coons. Columbus, Ohio: Bureau of Business Research, Ohio State University, 1957.

47. Hinrichs, John. *The Motivation Crisis*. New York: American Management Association (AMACOM), 1974.

48. Hodnett, Edward. *The Art of Problem Solving*. New York: Harper & Row, Publishers, 1955.

49. Jaspers, Karl. *Philosophy* (II) Chicago: The University of Chicago Press, 1969.

50. Jaspers, Karl. *Reason and Anti-Reason in Our Time*. New Haven: Yale University Press, 1952.

51. Jaspers, Karl. *Way to Wisdom*. New Haven: Yale University Press, 1954.

52. Kant, Immanuel. *Groundwork of the Metaphysic of Morals*. New York: Harper & Row, Publishers, 1964.

53. Katz, Daniel, and Robert Kahn. *The Social Psychology of Organizations*. New York: John Wiley & Sons, 1978.

54. Kellogg, Marion. *Career Management*. New York: American Management Association, 1972.

55. Kepner, Charles, and Benjamin Tregoe. *The Rational Manager: A Systematic Approach to Problem Solving and Decision Making*. New York: McGraw-Hill Book Company, 1965.

56. Kierkegaard, Sören. *Purity of Heart Is To Will One Thing*. New York: Harper & Row, Publishers, 1948.

57. Kierkegaard, Sören. *Works of Love*. New York: Harper & Row, Publishers, 1964.

58. Knight, Margaret. *Humanist Anthology: From Confucius to Bertrand Russell*. London: Pemberton Publishing Company, Ltd., 1961.

59. Koontz, Harold. *Appraising Managers as Managers*. New York: McGraw-Hill Book Company, 1971.

60. Koontz, Harold. "Making Managerial Appraisal Effective," *California Management Review*, Vol. 15, No. 2, Winter 1972, pp. 46-55.

61. Koontz, Harold. "Shortcomings and Pitfalls in Managing by Objectives." *Management by Objectives.* January 1972, pp. 6-12.
62. Koontz, Harold, and Robert Bradspies. "Managing Through Feedforward Control." *Business Horizons,* June 1972, pp. 25-36.
63. Koontz, Harold, and Cyril O'Donnell. *Management: A Book of Readings.* New York: McGraw-Hill Book Company, 1976.
64. Koontz, Harold, and Cyril O'Donnell. *Management: A System of Contingency Analysis of Managerial Functions.* New York: McGraw-Hill Book Company, 1976.
65. Koontz, Harold, Cyril O'Donnell, and Heinz Weihrich. *Management.* New York: McGraw-Hill Book Company, 1980.
66. Kurtz, Paul. *The Fullness of Life.* New York: Horizons Press, 1974.
67. Kurtz, Paul (ed.). *The Humanist Alternative: Some Definitions of Humanism.* London: Pemberton Publishing Company, Ltd., 1973.
68. Landen, Delmar, and Howard Carlson. "New Strategies for Motivating Employees." In *The Failure of Success,* edited by Alfred Marrow, pp. 177-187.
69. Lawler, Edward. "Control Systems in Organizations." In *Handbook of Industrial and Organizational Psychology,* edited by Marvin Dunnette. Chicago: Rand McNally College Publishing Company, 1976.
70. Levinson, Harry. "Management by Whose Objectives?" *Harvard Business Review,* July-August 1970, pp. 125-34.
71. Likert, Rensis. *The Human Organization: Its Management and Value.* New York: McGraw-Hill Book Company, 1967.
71a. Likert, Rensis, and M. Scott Fisher. "MBGO: Putting Some Team Spirit into MBO." *Personnel,* January-February, 1977.
72. Lippitt, Gordon. "Developing Life Plans: A New Concept and Design for Training and Development." *Training and Development Journal,* May 1970, pp. 2-7.
73. Lock, Dennis. *Project Management.* Epping, Essex (England): Gower Press, 1977.
74. Locke, Edwin, Karyll Shaw, Lise Saari, and Gary Latham. "Goal Setting and Task Performance." In *Handbook of Industrial and Organizational Psychology,* edited by Marvin Dunnette. Chicago: Rand McNally College Publishing Company, 1976.

75. Lopez, Felix. *Personnel Interviewing: Theory and Practice.* New York: McGraw-Hill Book Company, 1975.

76. Lowry, Richard (ed.). *The Journals of A. H. Maslow.* Monterey, California: Brooks/Cole Publishing Company, 1979.

76a. Mackenzie, Alec. *The Time Trap.* New York: The American Management Association, 1974.

77. Maier, Norman. *The Appraisal Interview: Three Basic Approaches.* La Jolla, California: University Associates, 1976.

78. Maier, Norman. *Problem-Solving Discussions and Conferences: Leadership Methods and Skills.* New York: McGraw-Hill Book Company, 1963.

79. Marrow, Alfred (ed.). *The Failure of Success.* New York: American Management Association (AMACOM), 1972.

80. Marrow, Alfred, David Bowers, and Stanley Seashore. *Management by Participation.* New York: Harper & Row, Publishers, 1967.

81. Martin, Charles. *Project Management: How To Make It Work.* New York: American Management Association, 1976.

82. Maslow, Abraham. *Eupsychian Management: A Journal.* Homewood, Illinois: Richard D. Irwin, Inc., 1965.

83. Maslow, Abraham. *The Farther Reaches of Human Nature.* New York: The Viking Press, 1971.

84. Maslow, Abraham. *Motivation and Personality.* New York: Harper & Row, Publishers, 1970.

85. Maslow, Abraham. *Toward a Psychology of Being.* New York: VanNostrand Reinhold Company, 1968.

86. May, Rollo. *Psychology and the Human Dilemma.* New York: VanNostrand Reinhold Company, 1967.

87. McConkey, Dale. *MBO for Nonprofit Organizations.* New York: American Management Association, 1975.

88. McGregor, Douglas. *The Human Side of Enterprise.* New York: McGraw-Hill Book Company, 1960.

89. McMahan, John, and Joseph Yeager. "Manpower and Career Planning." In *Training and Development Handbook*, edited by Robert Craig, Chapter II.

90. Mead, Margaret. "The Future as the Basis for Establishing a Shared Culture." *Daedalus,* Vol. 94, No. 1.

91. Morgan, Henry, and John Cogger. *The Interviewer's Manual.* New York: The Psychological Corporation, 1972.

92. Morrisey, George. *Management by Objectives and Results in*

the Public Sector. Reading, Massachusetts: Addison-Wesley Publishing Company, 1976.

93. Moustakes, Clark. *Loneliness and Love.* Englewood Cliffs, New Jersey: Prentice-Hall, Inc., 1972.

94. Moustakes, Clark (ed.). *The Self: Explorations in Personal Growth.* New York: Harper & Row, Publishers, 1956.

95. Odiorne, George. *MBO II: A System of Managerial Leadership for the 80s.* Belmont, California: Fearon Pitman Publishers, Inc., 1979.

96. Ouchi, William. *Theory Z: How American Business Can Meet the Japanese Challenge.* Reading, Massachusetts: Addison-Wesley Publishing Company, 1981.

97. Owens, James. "Participation — Prove It Works." *Training in Business and Industry*, Vol. 10, No. 2, February 1973, pp. 56-59.

98. Pascale, Richard, and Anthony Athos. *The Art of Japanese Management: Applications for American Executives.* New York: Simon and Schuster, 1981.

98a. Peters, Thomas, and Robert Waterman, Jr. *In Search of Excellence: Lessons from America's Best-Run Companies.* New York: Harper & Row, Publishers, Inc., 1982.

99. Porter, Lyman, and Edward Lawler. "What Job Attitudes Tell About Motivation." *Harvard Business Review*, January-February, 1968.

100. Riesman, David. *The Lonely Crowd.* New Haven: Yale University Press, 1961.

101. Rogers, Carl. *On Becoming a Person.* Boston: Houghton Mifflin Company, 1961.

102. Saitow, Arnold. "CSPC: Reporting Project Progress to the Top." *Harvard Business Review*, January-February, 1969.

103. Schein, Edgar. *Process Consultation: Its Role in Organization Development.* Reading, Massachusetts: Addison-Wesley Publishing Company, 1969.

104. Schmuck, Richard. "Developing Collaborative Decision Making: The Importance of Trusting, Strong, and Skilled Leaders." *Educational Technology*, October 1972, pp. 43-47.

105. Schmuck, Richard. *The Second Handbook of Organization Development in Schools.* Palo Alto, California: Mayfield Publishing Company, 1977.

106. Schröder, Harold. "Making Project Management Work." *Management Review*, December 1970, pp. 24-28.

271

107. Schuler, Randall. "Definition and Conceptualization of Stress in Organizations.," *Organizational Behavior and Human Performance*. December, 1979.

108. Schumacher, E. F. *Small is Beautiful: Economics as if People Mattered.* New York: Harper & Row, Publishers, 1973.

109. Schutz, William. *Joy: Expanding Human Awareness.* New York: Grove Press, Inc., 1967.

110. Shepard, Herbert. "Rules of Thumb for Change Agents." *Organization Development Practitioner*, November 1975, pp. 1-5.

111. Sherwin, Douglas. "The Meaning of Control." *Dun's Review and Modern Industry*, January, 1956.

112. Shonk, James. *Working in Teams.* New York: American Management Association (AMACOM), 1982.

113. Stein, Barry, and Rosabeth Kanter. "Building the Parallel Organization: Creating Mechanisms for Permanent Quality of Work Life." *The Journal of Applied Behavioral Science*, Vol. 16, No. 3, 1980, pp. 371-88.

114. Tannenbaum, Robert, and Sheldon Davis. "Values, Man, and Organizations." *Industrial Management Review*, Winter 1969, pp. 67-83.

115. Tannenbaum, Robert, and Warren Schmidt. "How To Choose a Leadership Pattern." *Harvard Business Review*, May-June 1973, pp. 162–180.

116. Tillich, Paul. *The Eternal Now.* New York: Charles Scribner's Sons, 1956.

117. Truell, George. "Where Have All The Achievers Gone?" In *Motivation: Key to Good Management*, edited by Thomasine Rendero. New York: American Management Association, 1974.

118. Urwick, Lyndall. *The Golden Book of Management.* New York: Arno Press, 1979.

119. Walker, James. *Human Resource Planning.* New York: McGraw-Hill Book Company, 1980.

120. Walton, Richard. *Interpersonal Peacemaking: Confrontation and Third-Party Consultation.* Reading, Massachusetts: Addison-Wesley Publishing Company, 1969.

121. Watson, Charles. "Getting Management Training To Pay Off." *Business Horizons*, Vol. 17, No. 1, 1974, pp. 51-58.

122. Weber, Max. "Bureaucracy." In *From Max Weber: Essays in Sociology*, edited by H. H. Gerth and C. Wright Mills. New York: Oxford University Press. 1958, pp. 196-244.

123. Weber, Max. *The Theory of Social and Economic Organization*. New York: The Free Press of Glencoe, 1964.

123a. Webster, Richard. "Interview Cycles." Copyrighted by Management Development Institutes, April, 1982.

124. Weihrich, Heinz. "A Hierarchy and Network of Aims." *Management Review*, January 1982, pp. 47-54.

125. Wheelis, Allen. *The Quest for Identity*. New York: W. W. Norton & Company, 1958.

126. Whyte, William. *The Organization Man*. New York: Simon and Schuster, 1956.

127. Woodworth, Robert, and Harold Schlosberg. *Experimental Psychology*. New York: Henry Holt and Company, 1954.

128. Yutang, Lin (ed.). *The Wisdom of Confucius*. New York: Random House, Inc. (The Modern Library), 1938.

129. Zand, Dale. "Collateral Organization: A New Change Strategy." *The Journal of Applied Behavioral Science. Vol. 10, No. 1, 1974, pp. 63-89.*

Appendix

Evaluating Your Organization's Management System

*An Exercise in the Use of a Theory Z Management Model:
An Assessment Inventory*

Evaluate the management system of your present organization, by completing the Assessment Inventory that begins on the next page.

After completing the Inventory, list what you consider to be the 5 major strengths of your organization's present management system:

1.

2.

3.

4.

5.

Then list the 5 major areas in which your organization's management system needs improvement:

1.

2.

3.

4.

5.

A Theory Z Management Model:
An Assessment Inventory

INSTRUCTIONS

The purpose of this inventory is to make an assessment of the management system in your organization. Included in the inventory are 100 items that have been drawn from the vast literature on management. In essence, we are presenting here a model of a Theory Z management system as viewed by the experts in the field of management.

You are to respond to each item with a number from 1 to 5 according to the following scale: 5 = Excellent, 4 = Good, 3 = Satisfactory, 2 = Poor, 1 = Missing. Please be as honest as possible in responding to each item.

After you have completed all 100 items, please calculate the category scores. First, add the item scores for each category and record in the space at the bottom of each page. Next, divide each of these category scores by 10 and record the resulting scores (to one decimal place) in the spaces below:

1. Philosophy of Management .... _____
2. The Manager as an Effective Human Being ...... _____
3. Leadership Styles .... _____
4. Participative Management .... _____
5. Management by Objectives .... _____
6. Planning .... _____
7. Organizing .... _____
8. Staffing and Staff Development .... _____
9. Motivating .... _____
10. Controlling .... _____

1. Philosophy of Management

1.1 Our organization has a written philosophy of management that serves as the foundation stone for the entire enterprise. _____

1.2 Our philosophy of management includes a clear statement of organizational values. _____

1.3 Our philosophy of management includes a clear statement of organizational goals. _____

1.4 Our philosophy of management includes a clear statement of strategies. _____

1.5 Our philosophy of management (including values, goals, and strategies) is internally consistent. _____

1.6 Our philosophy of management demonstrates an awareness of the larger environment of which the organization is a part. _____

1.7 Our philosophy of management is operational — it works. _____

1.8 Our philosophy of management is followed by each member of the management team. _____

1.9 Our philosophy of management has been communicated to all employees within the organization. _____

1.10 Our philosophy of management is self-renewing: it is revised as appropriate to be responsive to changing needs and conditions. _____

Sum of Scores = _____

2. The Manager As An Effective Human Being

2.1 My manager has a unified philosophy of life that he/she lives by on a daily basis. _____

2.2 My manager is a person of integrity. _____

2.3 My manager is an open-minded person. _____

2.4 My manager is an independent thinker. _____

2.5 My manager is a responsible person. _____

2.6 My manager is an effective communicator. _____

2.7 My manager is a rational and logical decision maker. _____

2.8 My manager is an effective problem solver. _____

2.9 My manager shows an active concern for the welfare of other persons. _____

2.10 My manager is enthusiastic about the job. _____

Sum of Scores = _____

3. Leadership Styles

3.1 The leaders in our organization have a clear vision of the desired state of the organization. _____

3.2 The leaders in our organization are able to influence others so that they will strive willingly toward the achievement of organizational goals. _____

3.3 The leaders in our organization are able to focus on both the short-term and the long-term needs of the organization. _____

3.4 The leaders in our organization are proactive — they make things happen. _____

3.5 The leaders in our organization surround themselves with excellent people. _____

3.6 The leaders in our organization make effective use of management by objectives. _____

3.7 The leaders in our organization actively promote participative management. _____

3.8 The leaders in our organization are able to be tough and do battle when the situation calls for it. _____

3.9 The leaders in our organization use joint problem solving as the primary means of resolving conflicts. _____

3.10 The leaders in our organization serve as excellent role models for other persons. _____

Sum of Scores = _____

4. Participative Management

4.1 Employees and managers throughout the organization feel a genuine responsibility for the achievement of organizational goals. _____

4.2 Honest and open communication prevails throughout our organization. _____

4.3 The people in our organization trust each other. _____

4.4 A high degree of cooperation prevails throughout our organization. _____

4.5 The people in our organization strive for win-win solutions to conflicts rather than win-lose solutions. _____

4.6 There is a great deal of group participation in goal setting in our organization. _____

4.7 Our organization makes effective use of group problem solving. _____

4.8 Our employees actively participate in those decisions that influence their work. _____

4.9 Managers and employees throughout the organization participate actively in reviewing and controlling their own work. _____

4.10 Much of our success as an organization can be attributed to effective teamwork. _____

Sum of Scores = _____

5. Management By Objectives

5.1 Our organization has a comprehensive management by objectives program that is strongly supported by upper management. _____

5.2 Our managers view management by objectives as a system of management that applies to all of the functions of management. _____

5.3 Our managers have received training in the principles and methods of management by objectives. _____

5.4 Our management by objectives program is implemented in a uniform manner throughout the organization. _____

5.5 An important part of our management by objectives program is the establishment of unit objectives prior to developing individual performance objectives. _____

5.6 Emphasis is placed on vertical and horizontal integration of objectives throughout the organization. _____

5.7 Performance objectives are developed jointly be-

279

tween the individual employee and the immediate
supervisor. _____

5.8 Our objectives are reviewed periodically throughout
the year. _____

5.9 Our managers are willing to change objectives during the year whenever the situation warrants. _____

5.10 Our managers view management by objectives as
an effective management tool. _____

Sum of Scores = _____

6. Planning

6.1 Our managers view the planning function as the
foundation and guide for all of the other management functions. _____

6.2 Those persons who are responsible for executing the
plans are actively involved in developing the plans. _____

6.3 Written plans are prepared for the total organization, including all line units and all support units. _____

6.4 The organization carefully prepares guidelines and
procedures for use by all units to assure consistency
in planning. _____

6.5 A well developed procedural methodology is used
to constantly review the business environment and
analyze the possible impacts. _____

6.6 Alternative and contingency plans are developed
for key issues. _____

6.7 All plans are integrated and coordinated with
operating budgets. _____

6.8 Our plans are well-documented, including planning
assumptions, objectives, strategies, and budget
allocations. _____

6.9 Strategic plans and tactical plans are well
integrated. _____

6.10 Our plans are reviewed periodically throughout the
year. _____

Sum of Scores = _____

7. Organizing

7.1 Our organizational structure is designed to facilitate effective and efficient decision making. _____

7.2 The key activities that must be carried out to achieve the enterprise objectives have been clearly defined. _____

7.3 The activities that must be carried out have been grouped on a logical basis. _____

7.4 The responsibilities of each member of the organization have been clearly defined. _____

7.5 Authority is delegated as far down in the organization as practicable. _____

7.6 Responsibility and authority are congruent for all management positions. _____

7.7 The number of persons reporting to each manager is reasonable. _____

7.8 Our organizational structure is designed to provide stability. _____

7.9 Our organizational structure is designed to provide flexibility. _____

7.10 Our organizational structure is evaluated and revised on the basis of its contribution to enterprise objectives. _____

Sum of Scores = _____

8. Staffing and Staff Development

8.1 Our organization's staffing and staff development program is guided by a clear statement of organizational mission and goals. _____

8.2 We have a Human Resources plan that is an integral part of the organization's operational plan. _____

8.3 Our recruiting and selection program is effective in getting the right people for the right jobs at the right time. _____

8.4 Our organization has an effective orientation program for new employees. _____

281

8.5 Our organization provides effective formal training for its employees. _____

8.6 Our managers view "coaching" (on-the-job-
training) as one of their most important
responsibilities. _____

8.7 Our managers view personnel assignment and
utilization as an effective means for developing
staff. _____

8.8 Our organization has an effective career planning
program for its employees. _____

8.9 Our organization has an effective performance appraisal program that is directed toward the improvement of job performance. _____

8.10 The various components of our staffing and staff
development program are systematically evaluated
and revised as appropriate. _____

Sum of Scores = _____

9. Motivating

9.1 Our organization promotes good physical health for
its employees. _____

9.2 Our employees tend to be free from excessive job
stress. _____

9.3 Our employees have a clear understanding of their
job responsibilities. _____

9.4 Our organization provides job security based on
performance. _____

9.5 Our employees are treated as persons (rather than
as "numbers" or "things"). _____

9.6 Our employees feel that they are part of a team. _____

9.7 Our employees feel that their jobs are important. _____

9.8 Our employees get recognition for good
performance. _____

9.9 Our organization provides considerable opportunity
to its employees for growth and development. _____

9.10 Our organization provides career planning assistance for its employees. _____

Sum of Scores = _____

10. Controlling

10.1 The control function is viewed as a major responsibility of every member of the organization. _____

10.2 Our organization focuses more on self-control than the control of others. _____

10.3 Control is normally exercised where the malfunctions are likely to occur. _____

10.4 Our control system is tailored to our organizational structure. _____

10.5 Our controls are tailored to well documented plans. _____

10.6 Our controls focus on *key variables* — those that are important in explaining the success or failure of the enterprise. _____

10.7 Our control system provides accurate and timely feedback. _____

10.8 The information provided by our control system is readily understood by all users of the information. _____

10.9 The information provided by our control system is a useful guide for corrective action. _____

10.10 Our control system is economical — it is cost/effective. _____

Sum of Scores = _____

Author Index

Subject Index